# Genealogical Abstracts
# from the
# *Wauwatosa News*
## 1899–1904
## (Wisconsin)

Elizabeth Doherty Herzfeld, CGRS

HERITAGE BOOKS
2016

# HERITAGE BOOKS

*AN IMPRINT OF HERITAGE BOOKS, INC.*

## Books, CDs, and more—Worldwide

For our listing of thousands of titles see our website
at
www.HeritageBooks.com

Published 2016 by
HERITAGE BOOKS, INC.
Publishing Division
5810 Ruatan Street
Berwyn Heights, Md. 20740

Heritage Books by the author:

*Burials at Wauwatosa Cemetery, Milwaukee County, Wisconsin*
*Genealogical Abstracts from the* Wauwatosa News, *1899–1904 (Wisconsin)*
*Old Cemetery Burials of Milwaukee County, Wisconsin: Volumes I and II*
CD: *Wisconsin: Volume 1*

International Standard Book Numbers
Paperbound: 978-0-7884-1199-1
Clothbound: 978-0-7884-6325-9

# TABLE OF CONTENTS

Foreword                              v

Introduction                          vii

Wauwatosa News Abstracts              1

Index                                 173

# FOREWORD

This book of Wauwatosa News abstracts is presented with the
hope of simplifying efforts of future researchers seeking information
about early Wauwatosa residents

Readers will reconize in the names of contemporary parks and
streets, the names of many early Wauwatosa residents.

Coincidentally this book was published in 1999, during the 100th
year anniversary of the Wauwatosa News.

Because of the old type and the condition of the newspapers, there
was some difficulty in deciphering names and some other information.

# INTRODUCTION

The following information was taken from *The Wauwatosa Story*, published by the Sesquicentenial Committee, 1985:

Wauwatosa was named after Chief Wau-wau-tae-sie of the Pottawatomies. The land was sold to the U.S. Government by an 1833 Treaty. The First permanent settlement was made by Charles Hart followed in 1835 by 17 settlers.

The original boundaries of Wauwatosa were Greenfield Ave. on the south and Hampton Ave. on the north; 27th St. formed the eastern boundary and 124th St. the western. Wauwatosa has aptly dubbed itself the City of Homes, and does indeed have many lovely old and new homes.

Early Town of Wauwatosa settlers in 1840 were: Benediah Barber, Hiram W. Blanchard, John Bowen, S.C. Brantt, Benson Brazee, A.O.T. Breed, Clark Brookins, Silas Brown, Bigelow Case, John Crawford, Robert Curran, George B. Dousman, C.F. Ellsworth, John Foley, Albert Fowler, E.G. Fowler, Daniel Fowler, Elias Gilbert, Ephriam Gilbert, H.Payson Gilbert, Hezekiah Gilbert, Richard Gilbert, Sr., Richard Gilbert, Jr., L.L. Gridley, Charles Hart, Oliver Hart, Thomas B. Hart, Frank Hawley, L.T. Howard, Henry H. Hoyt, Thomas D. Hoyt, Levi Hubbel, Charles James, Nathaniel Leland, William R. Longstreet, Harrison Ludington, Hosea L. Maynard, David Morgan, Frank Morgan, Timothy Mower, Alexander Munroe, William Nobles, Alfred Orendorf, Tobias Osborn, R. Painter, L.B. Potter, J.C. Putney, Thomas J. Rice, Thomas M. Riddle, Hiram J. Ross, Squire Sackett, Alvin Swan, Emery Swan, Nathaniel Swan, Seth Swan, E.D. Underwood, William O. Underwood, Gideon Wales, Jonathan Warren, Joseph Warren, L.A. Warren, Lyman Wheeler, Sanford Wheeler, and Benjamin F. Wheelock.

Other early residents were: Elizabeth Boyden, Rev. Luther Clapp, Rev. Crawford, Dr. Andrew Clark, Jr., Harriet Denning, Mr. Fingado, Mr. Fisher, Dr. L.C. Halsted, Richard Hoppin, Emerson D. Hoyt (Wauwatosa's first mayor), Lowell Damon (Wauwatosa's first postmaster whose 1847 home still stands) W.R. Manning, Rev. S. Merrill, Henry Rose, Mr. Spears, Mr. Stickney, Rev. William Talford, Deacon Joseph A. Warren and wife, J.D. Warren, Nathan Wesson, and F.H. Westover. Hannah Hoyt and John Bowen were married 12 Dec 1837 by a circuit riding minister. Harriet Denny was the wife of E.D. Underwood.

Wauwatosa Civil War Volunteers, 1861-1865: John Alwynse, Charles Baltes, Ernst Barfoot, James Barnes, Edward Barber, John D. Barrett (killed), Paul Barrett, Frederick Barnekow, Christion Bessenger, Albert Blanchard, Charles Brown, Norton Brunning, Randal Brunning, William Bates, Morris Conley, Benjamin Cooke, Truman Curtis, Charles Cupple, Aaron Catlin, Charles Chase, Herbert Damon, Martin Dailey, Alfred Denny, William Farris, Berkley Farrell, Charles Fingado, James Foley, David Fexter, Elbert Fowler, Charles Fowler, Judson Hart, Lewis Hartman, Levi Halsted, Frank Hawley, Dexter Hill, William Holston, Elam Hopeman, David Horning, William Howard, Charles Hubbell, Samuel Hubbell, Daniel Hutchinson, Robert Jacks, Moses Jerome, Newton Johnson, Peter Keefe, William Kleinman, Justus Koon, Samuel Koon, Phineas Leland, Moses Lyons, Lowell Maynard, William Moore, Augustus Mower, Charles Mower, George Mower, John Munroe, Philip Muth, Fanning Nangle, John Noyes, John Pelton, Henry Potter, Daniel Reilly, Thomas Reilly, Elgar Rose, Edwin Sackett, Benjamin Siegert, George D. Underwood, John Warren, Charles D. Watson, Frank Wesson, John Wesson, Warren Wesson, William Wesson, and Rollin Wheeler.

Wauwatosa News is a weekly paper, now called Wauwatosa News-Times, that initially came out on Saturday. It was first published in 1885, but after a few issues were published, it folded.

It has been continuously published since March 11, 1899, when Charles R. Perry and Lysander R. Gridley formed the Wauwatosa Printing Company to publish the Wauwatosa News. Gridley served as editor, Perry contributed an occasional article. In 1907 John R. Benoy purchased the News and took over management followed by his son Cornelius Benoy until 1941. The only known copy of the first paper was found at the Historical Society after other surviving early editions were microfilmed. Therefore abstracts from that paper, along with the missing issues do not appear in this book.

**Some items appearing in the Wauwatosa News Diamond Jubilee Issue dated October 30, 1974:**

One memoir mentioned that around 1892 William Worm challenged the legal existence of the village. Charles G. Perry and Lyman G. Wheeler, area legal experts, came to the villages rescue (page 16).

In another memoir, James Gregg Raschka describes how his great grandmother, Mrs. Gregg, had been left land in Wauwatosa by her father, Jacob Carter. She and her husband Luther B. Gregg built the first hotel in Wauwatosa on that land. It was called the Irvington and it opened in 1898. (page 18)

"The Little Red Store" was built in 1854. The article said that it replaced a shanty put up by Jonathon Warren in 1837, in which the Presbyterian minister preached sermons as early as 1838. "The Little Red Store" was built by Dr. Levi Halstead in 1854 and was used as a dwelling until Haltead lived until he left to fight in the Civil War. Dr. Halstead succeeded the settlement's first doctor, Dr. Andrew Clark. T.M. Riddle purchased the building for a grocery store and the duties of a railroad depot; an express office and post office were added later. The post office was moved from Nathan Wesson's home and Riddle was made postmaster in 1861. Riddle died in 1869 and his son, Thomas Riddle, took over the store. He sold the store to Lysander Gridley in 1873. By 1915, the building was owned by D.C. Jacobus of the Wauwatosa Fuel and Supply Co. (page 18)

J.S. Stickney and Charles Stickney, of the Pickle Company family, and H.B. Hunter, donated a lot worth $3000 for the first library in 1895. (page 41)

**Captions under some of the pictures that appeared in the diamond jubilee issue.**

Members of Miss Chamberlin's first grade class in 1906 were: Harold Garvens, Everett Lund, Anna Hebner, Harriet Godfrey, George Bartel, Meta Arvelt, Regina S. (her last name seems to be missing from the caption below the picture), Cathryn Morton, Myrtle Baltes, Howard Morion, Eric Roepke, Mildred Henke, Florence Scott, Alma W. James Sporleder, Erving Luetzou, Millard Smith, and Susie Bachman (page 38)

First graders from Wauwatosa Grade School, 1911 or 1912, Lois Becker, Margaret Godfrey, Kenneth Findley, Tom Scott, Leona Bridges, and Lucille Wienhold. (not all the children in the picture are named in the caption) (page 38)

Miss Greenwood's 1918 kindergarten class: John Thomas, Anne Spalding, Jeannette Davies, Judson Titsworth, Margo Miller, Fora Williams, Lois Johnstone, Jean Johnson, Alice Titsworth, Lulu Williams, and Janet Jackson (page 41)

There also appears a picture of Archie Johnson in his Light Guard uniform taken around 1900. (page 41)

# WAUWATOSA NEWS

## April 1, 1899

Thomas Wright is dangerously ill.

Miss Lois Rogers visits Chicago.

Miss Nettie Crane visits Chicago.

Miss Corinne Mitchell went to Chicago.

Chas. Seymour came to town.

James Godfrey is home from Madison vacation.

Prof. A.P. Hollis was in Madison.

Miss Lula Shaw was in Madison.

Rev. C.W. Damon will preach at Palmyra.

Eugene Wright returned from Port Washington.

Mrs. E.P. Woodmansee returned from Menasha.

Miss May Carlton, of Madison, is visiting friends here.

D.A. Lewis, of Baraboo, is visiting his mother.

Miss Louise Landolt is ill with tonsilitis.

Miss Fern Hurlbut is home from an extended visit to Iowa.

Prof. E.C. Cornelius vacationed at Monroe, Wis.

Miss Josie Klein, of Milwaukee, visited Mrs. Horning.

Ralph Kneeland is home from school at Appleton, Wis.

J.F. Woodmansee is home on vacation from Madison.

Mrs. J.M. Leighton, of Waukesha, is visiting friends here.

Miss Sutherland is home from school out east.

Mrs. C.F. Eckel, of Port Washington, visiting Mrs. W.H. Wright, her sister.

Miss Mary Earls will to spend the summer in Delavan and Park Ridge, Ill.

Jas. D. Godfrey is home from Madison with his roommate, Mr. Kelly.

H.G. Glasier will move his family to the Brockway house, W. Main St.

Miss Laurine Wright returned to school in Oshkosh.

Simon Burgmeyer, of Dayton, Ohio, is visiting his uncle, F. Yanke.

Rev. Benson and Mrs. Benson returned from Kenosha.

Billy Sanderson will be home from Delafield to help at the Minstral Show.

Captain Henry Leisk is up and about after confinement with sciatic reumatism.

Miss Franee Sanderson is home from school in Kenosha.

Pastor Rader, St. John's Lutheran church, held Confirmation.

E.L. Kenyon, steward of the county hospital for the insane, is recovering from illness.

Edgar W. Coleman and wife returned from Florida.

H.B. Hunter and family have returned to their residence on E. Milwaukee Ave.

Richard Dewey, Jr. purchased a ranch in Colorado where he will enter the cattle business.

St Martha's Guild, of Trinity Episcopal church, to meet at the residence of J.M. Hess on W. Main St.

A number of Wauwatosa young women attended an "at home" at the home of Miss Jessie Currie in Milwaukee.

Dr. M.J. White, of Milwaukee County Asylum for Insane, was called east because of his mother's serious illness.

Mrs. J.T. Greenwood and children are staying with Mr. C.K. Rogers while her sister, Lois is in Chicago.

The former residence of Sidney Squires, deceased, on State St. is being improved.

Mr. and Mrs. Robert Stocks, of Ottowa, Wis., are visiting their daughter, Mrs. Oscar Helgesen.

R.S. Walker is pastor of the Baptist church.

James Shaw is home from the University of Wisconsin to take part in the Iowa-Wisconsin debate at the Davidson, in Milwaukee.

Mrs. George W. Ringrose and daughters, Miss Florence Ringrose, of Wauwatosa, and Mrs. Charles A. Davis and Mrs. L.M. Turner, of Milwaukee, were visiting in Pewaukee.

School Teachers: Miss Smith went to her home in Racine, Miss Walker to her home in Milton, and Miss Doty to her home in Dane Co., for school vacation

Mr. T.E. Zimmermann is overseeing the drilling a well for Charles Bohler in Elm Grove and W.H. Hoyt, of Burleigh St. in Wauwatosa, Mr. P. Bauer of Milwaukee is the contractor.

Mr. W.A. Clapp attended a Congregational church council in Milwaukee to act on the severance of pastorial relations between Rev. S.S. Matthews and Hanover St. Congregrational church in Milwaukee.

Assemblyman Fred Hartung, Side supervisors, H.F. Seefeld and August M. Siegfried, Town clerk H.P. Bradley and Treasurer M.H. Adams attended a town board meeting.

Wm. Hawley, of Wauwatosa, was badly injured in an accident at E. P. Allis Co's machine shop in Milwaukee. His left foot was caught in the cog wheels of a large machine and his thigh and calf were badly lacerated. He was taken to the Emergency hospital where he is resting easily and it is thought that he will not lose his limb.

**Complete List of Municipal Candidates**

First Ward Alderman: Norman L. Kneeland, Wm. von Baubach, Frank E. Loveland, R.M. Brown, and Charles B. Perry

Second ward Alderman: Charles A. Breed, Christoph Dropp, Theodore E. Zimmermann, H.A. Bardenwerper, and Ferdinand Bark

Third ward-Alderman: Fred H. Bark, J.D. Warren, G.A. Kurtz, and L.R. Gridley

Fourth ward-Alderman: D.P. Jones, Samuel J. Decker, Max Rosenthal, F.J. Schmidt, and H.A. Propp

The following nominations were made at the Republican city convention: Mayor, Emerson D. Hoyt; Theasurer, Frank E. Loveland; Assessor, Alonzo F. Kellogg; Justices of the Peace, Edward R. Morley and H.W. Glasier; First ward, Charles B. Perry; Second ward, John F. Dittmar; Third ward, L.R. Gridley; Fourth ward, Max Rosenthal; at large, G.A. Kurtz. After the convention adjourned, members of the city committee elected Charles B. Perry, chairman; G.A. Kurtz, secretary; and John F. Dittmar, treasurer

The Citizens' organization nominated: C.G. Porter and W.J. Potter First ward alderman; H.W. Bardenwerper and J.L. Hooley, Second ward alderman; Fred W. Braun and Frank Rogers, Third ward alderman.

**Short Sketches of Candidates**

Emerson D. Hoyt, Republican candidate for mayor, well known resident of Wauwatosa, active in community affairs and well equiped to fill any public office. He was born in Wauwatosa, which has always been his home. He has been the Mayor of Wauwatosa since the village became a city in 1897.

Frank E. Loveland, Republican candidate for city treasurer, also nominated by the Citizens' organization. He is well known to Wauwatosa citizens as a courteous and obliging official. He was born in Wauwatosa and except for a few years spent in Vermount has always made it his home. He is employed in the office of the Milwaukee Pickle Co. in this city.

A.F. Kellogg, Republican candidate for assessor, has been a resident of Wauwatosa for fourteen years. Before this time he lived on a farm in an adjoining town for many years. He is an active citizen and the present assessor, whose judgement of property values is good.

E.B. Morley, Republican candidate for justice of the peace, was elected to this office in 1898 to fill a vacancy and judged numerous cases fairly and impartially. He has been a resident of Wauwatosa for some time and before that he lived in Rhinelander, Wis. He also conducts a real estate, loan and insurance business.

H.W. Glasier, Republican candidate for justice of the peace, is a genial gentleman currently engaged in the school supply business. He formely worked for Chicago, Milwaukee and St. Paul railway.

T.M. Hammond, Citizen candidate for Mayor, has recently become a resident of this part of Wisconsin. He was born in Rock Co., Wis. about 34 years ago. He was in teaching and university work for several years and is currently interested in the Sunday school supply business. He lives with his father-in-law, Mr. Merrick.

John M. Dunlop, Citizen candidate for assessor, has been a resident of Wauwatosa for several years. He is engaged in the floral busines and his green-houses are located at the corner of Church and W. Milwaukee Sts. He has stated that he has no desire or time to attend to the duties of an assessor.

Daniel T. Pilgrim, Citizen candidate for justice of the peace, has lived in Wauwatosa for about fifteen years, before that time he farmed in the neighboring town of Granville. His children, Mrs. George Wells, Jr., Mrs. H.G. Schoonmaker, and D.T. Pilgrim, Jr. live in this city.

N.L. Kneeland, Republican candidate for alderman, owns and works a farm in the eastern part of Wauwatosa. He is at present an alderman, having been appointed to fill a vacancy caused by the resignation of W.J. Underwood.

William von Baumbach, Republican candidate for alderman, has been a resident of Wauwatosa for many years. He raises fruit on land he owns near North Ave. He has been a member of the village board since Wauwatosa first became a village and has proven himself to be one of the most useful and conservative officials.

Charles A. Breed, Republican candidate for alderman, has been in this position since the first city election in 1897. He was born in Wauwatosa and has lived in Milwaukee Co. since then except for a few years in California.

Christoph Kropp, Republican candidate for alderman, has resided in Wauwatosa for eight years. He was formerly engaged in the wagon and carriage business in Milwaukee. This is his first try for an official position.

John Hamme, Republican candidate for alderman, is at present a clerk in Kurth Brothers' store. This is his first campaign for office.

Fred H. Bark, Republican candidate for alderman, is involved in the upholstery business in this city. He is well known and a present member of the common council. He was appointed to fill a vacancy caused by the resignation of F.W. Kalfahs

Samuel J. Decker, Republican candidate for alderman, he resides on Grand Ave. and is an enterprising, well-informed citizen and would make a good working member of the council, looking carefully to the interests of the entire city.

David P. Jones, Republican candidate for alderman, has lived in Wauwatosa for several years. He works for Thomas Greenwood and this is his first campaign for offical position.

H.W. Bardenwerper, of Wauwatosa, is an independent candidate for alderman.

C.A. Porter, Citizens' candidate for alderman, has resided at the corner of E. Center St and 5th Ave. for several years. He is the court reporter in Judge Sutherland's court and has taken an active interest in political matters.

W.J. Potter, Citizens' candidate for alderman, resides at 2nd Ave and E. Milwaukee Ave. He has conducted a bicycle manufactory, repair shop and sales store for the past few years. This is his first campaign for office in Wauwatosa.

### Sketches of Town Candidates

H.P. Bradley, Republican candidate for town clerk, has been a resident of Wauwatosa for the past fifteen years. He has been in town clerk's office for five years and is a careful, competent and courteous man. He is picked out as a sure winner.

A.L. Story, Republican candidate for treasurer, was born in Wauwatosa over forty years ago and has always lived in the town. He and his brother from Milwaukee, are associated under the firm name of Story Brothers in the stone quarrying business. He has long been active as a republican in political circles. He is respected and will make a capable official. This is his first try for public office.

W.E. Fisher, Republican candidate for assessor, is the son of ex-Senator, Charles Fisher, with whom he resides on North Ave. He is competent to fill the office.

F.C. Charles Voigt, Republican candidate for assessor, is a well-to-do resident of over twelve years in Wauwatosa. He is a road superintendent and knows property values in the town. He would be a competent and painstaking official.

W.H. Taff, Republican candidate for justice of the peace, resides in the portion of Wauwatosa known as Silver City where he held the office of justice of the peace for several years.

George Jeffrey, Republican candidate for justice of the peace, is one of the pioneer residents. He presently holds the office, but tries few cases. He prefers to act as peacmaker between litigants and many of them have departed his court with their difficulties settled and no justice costs to pay.

R.J. Matthias, Republican candidate for justice of the peace, is a property holder in Wauwatosa. He formerly lived in central Wisconsin where he was justice of the peace for twelve years.

D.L. Hunter, Republican candidate for constable, was a popular deputy sheriff for the past four years. He resides in the Silver City section of the city and is active in Republican circles. He would make a well qualified and ready official.

H.W. Gransee, Republican candidate for re-election as constable, he resides on 39th St. near Grand Ave. in Wauwatosa.

Robert Behling, Republican candidate for constable, lives on 56st St. near Grand Ave. He was formerly in the milk business and is the son-in-law of Charles Duenkel, a prominent resident of Wauwatosa.

F.A. Conrad, Democratic candidate for town clerk, is a resident of the Silver City section of the town. He was formerly the proprietor of Conrad's Grove saloon and dancing pavillion, but during the last three years has not been actively engaged in any business.

P.J. Deuster, Democratic candidate for treasurer, resides on Blue Mound Rd. near the Soldiers' Home. He is presently employed as a saloon keeper.

M.F. Adams, Democratic candidate for assessor, is a son of M.H. Adams, the Republican treasurer of Wauwatosa. He is about 24 years of age and has assisted his father in collecting taxes. He is married and lives at the corner of 36st and State.

Max Foley, Democratic candidate for assessor, is a son of the late Michael Foley. He is unmarried, about 22 years old and lives on the farm belonging to the estate.

A.E. Stroud, Democratic candidate for justice of the peace, is about 60 years old and has frequently been a candidate in the county and city of Milwaukee. He held the position as justice in this town several years ago. He lives on Vliet St.

William McClintock, Democratic candidate for justice, has been a justice of the peace in this town for several years. His office is at 36st and State St. in the old E.D. Holton mansion and is at present the chairman of the Democratic town committee.

Matthew Riley, Esq., Democratic candidate for justice of the peace, is a farmer who was a justice eight years ago in this town. He has frequently been a candidate since that time, but without success.

Fred Behling, Democratic candidate for constable, is currently a town constable. He was appointed to fill a vacancy. He is a ready, obliging and careful official and generally can be found at Justice McClintock's court ready for immediate delivery.

Michael Schlehlein, Democratic candidate for constable, is the son-in-law of P.J. Deuster, Democratic candidate for treasurer. For a short time he conducted his father-in-law's saloon. He is now erecting a building on Blue Mound Rd. where a saloon will be located.

Daniel Frazier, Democratic candidate for constable, is one of the old soldier boys that keeps their eyes on the National Home. His present residence and business office is at Rudolph Ferdinand's saloon on Blue Mound Rd.

## Death Notice

Elizabeth Boyden, former resident of Wauwatosa, died Monday at Waukesha. Miss Boyden was born in New Salem, Mass. in 1811 and as a child removed with her family to New York state She came to the Wisconsin Territory in 1837 with T.B. Hart and his wife, Miss Boyden's sister. They settled in Wauwatosa and were amoung the early settlers of Milwaukee County. She resided with her sister until her death in 1895? when she went to Waukesha to live with her nephew, J.G. Hart. Miss Boyden was the first public school teacher in Wauwatosa, the school was held in an addition to T.B. Hart's modest home. She is survived by a niece, Mrs. E.L. Blodgett and nephew, T.W. Hart, both of this city.

Rev. Horatio Gates, rector of Trinity church published "The Parish Messenger", in it is a memorial to the recently deceased son, Blanchard Ross Ordway, child of Mr. and Mrs. Frank Ordway, of Church St.

## APRIL 8, 1899

Miss Nettie Crane retruned from Chicago.

H.N. Andrews reports his printing business is doing well.

J.M. Nash went to Sheboygan on business.

Miss Isabel Stickney is home from Ypsilanti, Michigan.

Mrs. B.B. Farries and children returned to Chicago.

Mrs. W.K. Wilson and family moved to Milwaukee.

Prof. E.C. Cornelius returned from vacation.

H.S. Tipple went to Madison on business.

J.O. Martin and family returned to the city for the summer.

F.W. Schneck's family returned from Texas.

J.H. Pitcher, of Eagle, was in town greeting friends.

F.R. Crabtree and family returned from a stay in Chicago.

Alice Phillips, daughter of G.G. Phillips, is ill with scarlet fever.

Miss Florence Seymore of Chicago was visiting friends here.

Mrs. R.J. Matthias, of Vliet St. in Wauwatosa, is ill with inflamatory rheumatism.

Miss Allee Sanderson, of Milwaukee, was visiting friends here.

Mrs. J. Hamme, of Waukesha, is visiting her son, John Hamme, of Garfield Ave.

Michael Kallis is excavating the ground for the new Wendel home on Church St.

Miss Mabel Bjorquist is ill with scarlet fever at her home at 3rd and E. Milwaukee Ave.

Dr. G.D. Hathaway, health commissioner of Wauwatosa, has ordered the city schools closed until April 17, 1899.

Mrs. Lyman G. Wheeler will host the next meeting of the Women's Club at her home on Wauwatosa Ave.

Mr. Clarence Gunn moved his family to their new residence on 56st and Grand Ave.

Mr. Abbott, of Madison, visited J.F. Woodmansee at his home on Greenfield Ave. in this city.

Mr. J.F. Woodmansee returned to his classes in Madison after voting

Prof. A.P. Hollis returned from two days in Madison to direct the Minstrel show.

Assemblyman Hartung went to Madison to attend the evening session of the assembly.

Milwaukee people who attended the W.H.S.(Wauwatosa High School) minstral show were: Mrs. W.G. Marling, Miss Florence Eddy, Miss Marling, Miss Willets, Mr. Willets and Mr. Wadsworth as guests of Mrs. F.A. Pavy.

If elected, R.J. Matthias hopes to have his justice office at the location of Justice McClintock's office when the term commences.

James E. Leonard bought out his partner, Joseph Luke, in the firm of Luke and Leonard and will conduct the meat market and business at the present location.

Mr. and Mrs. E.S. Turner, Mrs. Lizzie Gilson, Mrs. C.F. Eckel and her son, Stanley Eckel, of Port Washington; Mrs. Geo. Hawes and R.L. Gove, of Waukesha, attended the funeral of Thos. Wright.

William Sanderson was unable to come home to help with the minstral show due to the fact that his school, St. John's, was in session the entire week.

"Hobson's March" music by E.A. Nash, of Darlington, Wis., was dedicated by its composer to Co. D. First Wisconsin volunteer infantry.

Newly elected town officers are expected to appear before H.P. Bradley to qualify in their official capacities.

A ball is to be given at Peter Gerggin's hall, a hay loader is to be given away.

Bachman Brothers, of this city, are constructing a house for Joseph Johnson on Fourth Ave. opposite the residence of Mr. Cheney

The South Milwaukee Journal is published by L.J. Russell and L.A. Miner, it is Republican in politics

Miss Cornelia Wheeler read a paper on "The Thirty Year War and it's Effects on Germany and America" at the Wauwatosa Women's Club. Marion Jean Craig will be reading from Cyrano de Bergerac at the next meeting.

Prof. F.A. Lydston, of Church St., is having an exhibition of his work at Wheeler's photograph studio in this city.

Dr. S.S. Leonard, chairman of the county board of Milwaukee, is doing well after he was thrown from his buggy near John F. Dittmar's residence.

Rev. Horatio Gates, of Trinity Episcopal church, told his parishioners Easter Sunday that he had received a large sum of money to be used to reduce the indebtedness of their church.

The results of the city election are as follows: Mayor, E.D. Hoyt; Treasurer, F.E. Loveland; Assessor, A.F. Kellog; Justices of the Peace, E.B. Morley and H.W. Glasier; Aldermen-First ward, N.L. Kneeland and Wm. von Baumbach; Aldermen-Second ward, Chas. A. Breed and C. Kropp; Aldermen-Third ward, Fred H. Bark and Frank Rogers, who is the brother of Alderman L.C. Rogers and the son of C.K. Rogers; Aldermen-Fourth ward, D.P. Jones and S.J. Decker

The results of the Town of Wauwatosa election are as follows: Town Clerk, H.P. Bradley; Treasurer, A.L. Story; Assessors, W.E. Fisher and F.C. Voigt; Justices of the Peace, George Jeffrey, R.J. Matthias and W.H. Taff; Constables, D.L. Hunter, H.W. Gransee, and R. Behling

Participants in the W.H.S. minstral show were: Ralph Hayward, David Swan, Arthur Thomas, Ed Pavy, Harold Bogers, J. Hurlburt, Charles Moore, Percy Myers, Len Gridley, W. Garvens, W. Smith, F.J. Harriman, Miss Helen Stickney, Jessie Wood, Laura Loveland, Hettie Conley, Nellie Warner, Winnefred Phillips, Alice Smith, Elsie Conley, and Alice Potter. Miss Mabel Thomas acted as accompanist.

Attendants at the regular common council meeting: Alderman Baumbach, Lefeber, Kneeland, Rogers, Breed, Picker and Bark; Mayor Hoyt in the chair.

A fire in the home of W.A. Godfrey on E. Milwaukee Ave. is thought to have been started by children playing with matches. With the help of neighbors most of the personal belonging were removed from the dwelling. The fire was confined mostly to the roof and attic, however other areas of the house sustained water damage.

Program of the Easter service at Trinity Episcopal church: Processional "In the Light of God", Henry B. Koney; Kyrie, W.A.C. Cruickshank; Hymm, C.S.G. Livey; Sermon, Rev. Horatio Gates; Offertory solo, Edward Hurding Blair, Recessional, Lewis? H. Eaton.

## Marriage

Mr. Fred Sporleder, son of August Sporleder, and Miss Schmelling, of Wauwatosa, were married April 2, 1899 at the home of the bride's parents on Lisbon Rd. Pastor Tuder, of St. John's Lutheran, presided.

Gail Mirian Randolph, of Troy Center, Wis., married Dr. W.A. Perkins, of Milwaukee, at the home of the bride on April 5, 1899. Dr. Perkins formerly had his dental business in Wauwatosa.

## Death

Emma Uhl, daughter of Leonard Uhl, of Lisbon Ave., town of Wauwatosa was buried from St. John's Lutheran Church on Apr. 4, 1899, with burial at Wauwatosa Cemetery. The attendance was very large with nearly 50 carriages in the procession.

Thomas Gore Wright, aged 16 years, died Tuesday at the home of his parents Mr. and Mrs. W.H. Wright. He was born in Milwaukee in March, 1883 and had been suffering from lung trouble for about two years. Funeral services were held at his parents' home on First Ave., this city, by Rev. R.S. Walker, burial at Wauwatosa cemetery.

Mrs. Kurt Albertine died Friday, she was 33 years old and leaves a husband and three children. Mr. L. Nickel, of Garfield Ave. in Wauwatosa, is a brother.

Mr. and Mrs. E.B. Pares' infant child died Monday.

### April 15, 1899

E.H. Schwaiger, of Milwaukee, was in Wauwatosa.

Mr. and Mrs. W.G. McNair, of Milwaukee, were visiting friends here.

D.P. Jones, alderman elect, filed his oath of office.

The ladies of St. Martha's Guild of the Episcopal church met with Mrs. Hunter.

Mrs. John Hamme is recovering rapidly from a long illness.

Steward Kenyon is again able to attend his duties at the county insane asylum after a recent illness.

H.W. Glasier and family have moved from E. Center St. to W. Main St. next to the L. Brockway's home.

St. Agnes Guild, of Trinity Episcopal church, met at Miss Murphy's home.

Mr. E.G. Chatfield, of Milwaukee, was here visiting friends, he is the nephew of L.R. Gridley.

Mrs. Cadwell and Miss Ethel Cadwell, her daughter, are planning to remove to Colorado Springs, CO soon..

Mrs. John Koerner and her little son are visiting her parents in Janesville, Wis.

D.T. Pilgrim needed to use dynamite to break the frost while excavating the basement of the new Pabst block.

A.J. Gamm, jeweler, has moved his family from 7th Ave. to the house of Charles Worm on Western Ave.

W.A. Godfrey's home on Milwaukee Ave. is being repaired after a recent fire.

Mrs. C.G. Porter is improving slowly after a painful accident near the residence of Louis Merrick on 2nd Ave.

D.L. Hunter has decided not to qualify as constable.

R.A. Dix moved his family from Garfield Ave to a house on county property on the continuation of W. Main St.

Wm.R. Woodmansee is now a solicitor for advertising and job printing on this paper.

F.W. Lambrecht has resigned his job as perscription clerk at Gregg's Pharmacy and he and his family will move to Berlin in Green Lake County, Wis.

Mrs. A.H. Wheeler, our local photographer, has returned from visiting friends and relatives in Medina and elsewhere in New York state

D.T. Pilgrim's son, D.T. Pilgrim,Jr., is moving fill from the excavation of the Pabst block at N. Main and State Sts. to his father's property on Church St.

Mr. S.P. Croft and Mr. H.G. Schoonmaker, with their workman, have gone to Iowa where they have a railway grading contract on the Northwestern railway.

Rev. J.P. Dysart, superintendent of the Children's Home society is looking for a good home for a 17 year old girl for the summer. She will do light housework for small wages.

T.J. Ferguson has leased land on Ludington Ave. belonging to M.W. Strong to establish an ornamental tree nursery. John Dunlop, popular Wauwatosa florist will be in charge.

G. Steinhagen, is platting a tract of land for Mr. Angermeyer near the Gettleman Brewing Company for house lots.

Some travelers are astonished and not very pleased when they first behold the room equipments at the city hotel run by Marshal Marquardt.

Frank E. Swann sold twenty-five steers at $4.02 1/2 per hundred weight and J.S. Stickney sold seventy at between $4 and $4.50 per hundred weight bringing a good profit.

Wm. Hawley is resting easily at his father's residence after his accident at the Allis machine shop. "Billy" is expected to be up and about in a couple months.

Mrs. Emily Carl will close her restaurant, The Wauwatosa Exchange, to embark in other business. The stock and fixtures are being offered for sale.

M.H. Adams, former town treasurer, turned over about $10,000 to the new treasurer, A.L. Story.

The following citizens have moved: C.W. Heaford will occupy the Summers house on Windsor Ave.; F.A. Lydston is moving to G.W. Ringrose's house on E. Milwaukee Ave.; A. Gregg will move to the Lydston house on Church St.; A.P. Hamilton will occupy the Howard house on First Ave.; and J. Nash has leased the Colby house on Warren Ave.

Fred H. Bark is very busily engaged in his carpet cleaning and relaying business and is prepared to put new touches on furniture that needs repair.

Ferdinand Bark was seen holding the reins of his furniture tally-ho drawn by a pair of spanking browns. In the carriage were Mrs. Hess, Mrs. Hadley, Mrs. Tisdale, Mrs. Murphy, Mrs. Shaw, Mrs. Knowles, L.C. Rogers, and E.A. Schmitz. They were going to a surprise party given by Mrs. Ira Lillibridge one half mile south of the city. Other people present were Mrs. M.J. White, Mrs. H. Gates, Mrs. G.P. Dousman, and Mrs. C.T. Fisher. The Hon.Chas. Fisher chaperoned the party.

**Death**

Mrs. Ellen Kelly died Tuesday at the age of 83 years. She was living on Watertown Plank Rd., and was a resident of Wauwatosa for about fifty years. She had one daughter, Mrs. Ellen McGrath, who lived with her mother, and sons, Garret Kelly, Bryan Kelly, and John Kelly, of Milwaukee and James Kelly, of Minneapolis, who survive her. Funeral was at Holy Cross Church with burial at Calvary cemetery.

### April 22, 1899

Mrs. George Lingelbach is ill.

Dr. J.M. White was in Madison.

W.M. Harvey and family moved to the city.

Miss Lillian von Baumbach is in Chicago visiting.

Miss Katherine Farnham is in Chicago visiting.

Thos. Rice is seriously ill at home.

J.P. Regan made a flying trip to Chicago.

Chas. Godfrey was in St. Louis on business.

Mrs. John Taylor is ill with the grippe.

Will Sanderson returned to St. John's school.

Frank Buck was in Wauwatosa.

D.W. Jackson and family, of Alice St., have moved to town.

Mrs. Stringham, of Sparta, is visiting Mrs. C.S. Farnham.

J.W. Foreman, of PortageCity, Wis., called on Henry Watner.

J.D. Warren is putting a new foundation under his house.

Miss Isabelle Stickney has returned to school in Ypsilanti, Mich.

E.S. Turner, of Pt. Washington, was in the city visiting.

Miss Grace Menish spent time with friends in Milwaukee.

S.D. Hoyt has returned to his electrical duties in Fond du Lac.

Mrs. Seymour, of Chicago, a former residence of Wauwatosa, was visiting friends here.

Chas. McKay, of the Chronic Insane Asylum, has moved here with his family.

The new prescription clerk at Gregg's Pharmacy is H.M. Steusloff, of Waukesha.

St. Martha's Guild met with Mrs. T.C. Murphy, of Wauwatosa Ave.

H.W. Glasier was in Ripon, Wis. on business

Mrs. Hadley and Mrs. Tisdale visited Mrs. Louis Rogers, of Douglas Heights.

Dr. E.A. Schinitz is moving into the McIntosh house in Douglas Heights.

Chas. Mathison has been promoted to steward of the county hospital.

Miss Marguerita Wallace, of Milwaukee, was visiting Miss F. Menish

John Dittmar will build a house north of his blacksmith shop.

Mrs. J.M. Nash and her daughter, Hattie Nash, will be visiting in St. Paul and Minneapolis.

Miss Strong and Miss Dewey, of Queechy, Vt., are visiting Mrs. Frank Loveland

Wm. Haertel, of Milwaukee, will manage the local laundry.

N.H. Noble, of N. Greenfield, Wis., was in town on business.

J.P. Dysart, of Ripon, superintendent of the Children's Home Society, was in town.

W.M. Harden, secretary of Wauwatosa Milling Co., is going to Waterford for a visit.

Miss Ella Pierce, of Milwaukee, is visiting Miss Lillibridge and other friends.

Bessie Horning, daughter of Mrs. Mary Horning of W. Main St., has scarlet fever.

C.T. Chandler's dental office is located above Koerner's drug store.

Prof. A.P. Hollis will lead a men's class at the Congregational Sunday school.

J.S. Davis, D.D., of Lawrence Univ., in Appleton will preach at the Methodist church.

Mrs. Buckingham, of Ludington, Mich., sister of L.G. Wheeler, of Wauwatosa, is visiting relatives here.

Mr. C. Stewart, of Concord, Mass., grandfather of Mrs. H.F. Bradley, celebrated his 93rd birthday Wednesday.

Rev. Sutherland will preach at the Congregational Church on "How a Good Man was Rewarded."

T.T. Zimmermann's work horse dropped dead while in harness, there was no apparent cause for the sudden death.

August Krehl's hand was burned when he was carrying a glass of gasoline that caught fire.

M.F. Adams, son of ex-town treasurer Adams, went to Iowa to work on the railway grading contract of Mr. Croft and Mr. Schoonmaker.

Mrs. A. Koenig and sons, Walter Koenig and Fred Koenig, leave for a tour of the old country.

John J. Robinson is available to do painting, paper hanging, and decorating.

Miss Helen Barnes, state secretary of the YWCA for Ohio and Michigan, spoke at the Congregational church.

F.B. Morley sold his busines in Wauwatosa to H. Watner. He expects to go to Janesville to work for a firm there.

Mr. and Mrs. W.H. Englehart were given a surprise party to celebrate both their birthdays.

Prof. Turneaure, of the University of Wisconsin, and three members of the senior civil engineering class were in the city to test the strength and vibration of the Milwaukee railroad bridge, this is a regular part of the class.

W.H. Taff, Justice of the Peace, is established in the rooms formerly occupied by Justice Rausch.

Mr. and Mrs. H.H. Benson were given a birthday supper at the Congregational Church for the joint celebration of their birthdays, she was 80 years old yesterday and he is 83 today.

St. Agnes Guild, of Trinity Episcopal, met at Miss Blanche Landolt's home. They will meet with Miss Louise Landolt April 27, Miss Alice McLean May 1, and Miss Lillie von Baumbach, May 8.

Dr. J.D. Cutler has successfully performed a skin graft on Will Hawley, who was recently injured at E. P. Allis shops in Milwaukee.

The newly appointed trustees of the Milwaukee County Home for Dependent Children met at the office of T.J. Fleming where they elected Adolph Speigel president and T.J. Flemming, secretary. Supervisor Stewart will remain in charge.

Present at the annual banquet of the Methodist Social union were: Rev. E.S. McChesney, W. Esslinger, Mrs. Lucy Ryder-Myers, Atty. J.E. Wildish, Pres. C.A. Little, of the Evanston theological institute, Miss Bessie Greenwood, and Rev. W.D. Cole.

### Marriage

W.H. Landolt and family will attend his son, Edward Landolt's wedding to Miss Louise Minton of Chicago.

20

**Death**

T.D. Crawford, of the Chicago Board of Trade, died Sunday at the Milwaukee Sanitarium in this city, after a week's illness.

Mrs. Elizabeth Luetzow, wife of Albert Luetzow, died Thursday April 20, 1899,after a lingering illness.

### April 29, 1899

Mrs. J.O. Myers was in Waukesha Wednesday.

W.R. Cundall was in Chicago

Postmaster Landolt and family are in Chicago

Walter Wood was sick this week

D.M. Jones returned from Chicago

J.T. Van Vechten and daughter are visiting in Troy Center

Mrs. Charles Farnham is recovering from her recent illness

W.J. Fisk, of Green Bay, was here to visit his brother, Dr. Fisk.

W.A. Gilbert has returned from his trip to the Dakotas.

David Barnes and wife returned from Colorado Springs, Col.

Mrs. M. Horning, of W. Main St., has tonsilitis.

Rev. R.S. Walker and his wife went to Edison, Nebraska.

Maj. P. O'Connell, of the National Home, (this is the veterans' hospital) is in Denver, Col.

Rev. Cyrus Damon has moved into his home on W. Main St.

Miss Clara Snyder, of Chicago, is visiting at the F.W. Schneck home.

W.I. Gildas and family will live in the former residence of Mrs. Wilson.

Miss Myrtle Nettleton returned from Chicago where she spent the winter.

Morry Hess will be the driver of Leonard's meat market wagon.

E.W. Cook will occcupy the Clapp residence on Wauwatosa Ave.

Chas. Godfrey was in northern Wisconsin on business.

Mrs. S.K. Curtis and W.J. Underwood of Minneapolis were in the city.

Mrs. de Nevlen has returned to Fond du Lac, Wis. after visiting Mrs. Dr. Fisk.

John Layton and wife, of South Bend, Ind., visited Mrs. A.B. Mower.

C. Fingado has painted his shop which adds much to it's appearance.

Mrs. D.A. Lewis and daughter, of Baraboo, visited Mrs. S.S. Lewis.

Miss Katherine Gaffney, formerly of the sanitarium, was in the city to visit friends.

Postmaster M. O'Regan, of the National Home, was in this city on business.

Mrs. V. Jacobus and daughter, of Oregon, Wis., are visiting C.C. Jacobus.

Lorraine Tragard broke her arm when she fell from her tricycle.

Albert Taylor, telegraph operator, worked in Tom Regan's place at the local depot. Tom has been ill.

Ray Fisk has gone to Oconomowoc Lake to open their cottage for the season.

Garry Jacobus returned to Chicago after a visit to his brother, Charles Jacobus.

Gilbert Brockway and Archie Schneider are going to California to engage in fruit farming.

Miss Perkins was called to Oshkosh, Wis. by the serious illness of her mother.

Mr. and Mrs. L.V. Gridley and Mrs. Chatfield and daughter, Mary Chatfield, of Milwaukee, were guests of Mr. and Mrs. L.L. Gridley.

The young son of H. Rudolph, of Lisbon Ave., broke his collar bone in an accident.

John Dunlop, manager of the new nursery, has it well under way.

J.E. Leonard has moved to the Fricke house on Western Ave.

Joe Roehl will occupy the Barnes house on Wisconsin St.

Rev. John Schneider preached on the "Model Wife" at the Methodist church Sunday and will speak on "A Model Husband." next.

Rev. Horatio Gates will speak at the last meeting of the School and Home Alliance.

S.T. de Ranitz, of 183 Ogden Ave., Milwaukee, is the agent for a new farmer's gate the opens and shuts without a driver leaving his vehicle.

Mr. Louis Manuegold, of Wauwatosa, took out a building permit to build a home for his family near 29th and Highland Blvd.

The editorial staff of the Parish Message are: Rev. Horatio Gates, Mr. E.Harding Blair, Mrs. W.J. Potter, and Miss McLean. The paper contains a picture of a former member of the vested choir, B. Herbert Hicks, who now resides with his parents in Brooklyn, NY.

Information on the where abouts of the gardening equipment belonging to J.O. Myers that was borrowed by an industrious party one dark night would be appreciated.

G. Steinhagen, civil engineer, is engaged in surveying for a grading project at the Veterans' home in Waupaca.

Dwight B. Lewis has become a salesman for the Petley Shirt Co. of Milwaukee, Dwight is a hustler and should be good at the job.

The Prof. Lydston drawing of paintings at the Wheeler studio was attended by many persons from Milwaukee and other neighboring cities.

N.J. Swan, Jr.'s bicycle was taken while parked on State St. near the post office. Nat offers a reward for its return.

Postmaster Landolt has decided to locate the postoffice in the new Pabst block.

Director Gruenwald called a meeting concerning a new school

building, William Davelaar was elected chairman and Clerk Coughlin stated the purpose of the meeting.

A petition was presented to request the board to appoint Mr. W.H. McClintock as justice to fill the vacancy caused by the resignation of Phillip G. Dick.

## Sporting News

Fetterly, of the Michigan State League, pitched for Wauwatosa in the All Stars vs. Academy. Perey, for the Milwaukee team, twirled a good game, but Wauwatosa was out to win. Bert Gridley was struck on the ear by a foul tip while umpiring which required stitches. Other players for the All Stars were "Kid" Tipple, "Pokey" Wright, Lud Rhinehart, Lumb, Winding, S. Wright, (the Wrights were brothers) Dickerson, Rogers, umpires: Gridley and Murphy, scorer: R. Tipple. Players for the Academy were: Vernett, Perey, Benton, Gold, Merrill, Smith, Riedeburg, and Roberts.

## Birth

A baby boy has arrived at the John Woodside home on State St.

Deputy Sheriff Ferdinand is the proud father of a baby girl born last Apr. 23, 1899..

## May 6, 1899

Miss Manon was at Cedar Creek.

Albert Farries drove to Mukwonago.

St. Martha's Guild met with Mrs. F.J. Ordway.

St. Agnes' Guild met at Miss Maud Curtis's residence.

Miss Alice McLean has returned from two weeks in Chicago.

Miss Lillian Doherty, of Racine, is visiting friends in the city.

Mrs. W.H. Landolt and daughters, Loleta Landolt and Esther Landolt, returned from Chicago.

Miss Monty, Miss Higging, and Miss Emery, of the county asylum, were in Chicago.

Eugene Wright expects to spend the summer in Port Washington.

Mr. Theodore M. Hammond returned from a trip through the east.

Joseph McNab, of Chicago, formerly of this city, is visiting friends here.

George Koerner will be at Koerner's Pharmacy during the absence of John Koerner.

Mrs. L. Brockway entertained the Woman's Foreign Missionary society of the M. E. church.

C.A. Carver, frieght agent, was looking for business for the Wabash railroad.

Rev. C.H. Holden, of Detroit, former pastor of the Baptist church was visiting Dr. Bevier.

Gilbert Brockway and Archie Schneider left for California.

Mr. E.B. Butterworth, of Wauwatosa Ave., has started his duties with the Western Railway Weighers association.

Miss Margaret Delpsch, Sadie Philips, Walter Garvens and Perey Myers are the new editors of the School Column.

Mr. Frank Mayer, Jr. of Ludington Ave., shot the first wild goose in Wauwatosa this season.

Rev. Schneider, of the Methodist church, will give a sermon on "The Modern Theatre".

H.F. Zarse, of Hanover St., in Milwaukee will act as manager of Kurth Bros. grocery here. He will and his family reside here.

H.P. Bradley, town clerk, moved two doors down on Wells St from his former home.

Rev. and Mrs. D.W. Hulbert and their son Judson Hulbert, William Farries, Mr. J.F. Cushing, Dwight Watson, and Mr. M.E. Watson attended the dedication of the Wayland academy gymnasium in Beaver Dam.

Augustus Gregg, son of Landlord Gregg, of the Irvington Hotel, and Ruby Louise Breed, daughter of Alderman Breed, both of this city, received one of the first marriage licenses issued by the county clerk in Milwaukee under the new license law.

Mr. Bair and Mr. Briggs, both of Milwaukee, provided the music for the Home and School Alliance's last meeting.

A.B. Myers and the gas well company, of Milwaukee, that he is connected with will start boring for gas soon.

During a recent thunder storm, one cow was killed and another was knocked senseless when lightning struck the pump house which stands near the barn. Jake Johnson, superintendant, of the Daniel Wells farm, reported there was some damage to the building, but little damage from fire.

P.G. Dick and W.H. McClintock resigned the office of Justice of the Peace.

F. Schultz, M.E. Sanderson, H.W. Gransee, P.G. Dick, N. Grant, Chris Sarnow, and George Winding presented a petition asking that C.J. Cox fill the vacancy caused by the resignation of P.G. Dick.

An application was presented to request that Fred Behling be appointed as constable to fill a vacancy.

Peter Bruskowitz presented a verbal complaint concerning the stoppage of a water course on N. Fond du Lac Rd.

Otto Luehring was appointed constable to fill a vacancy.

The certificate of election of Dr. J.S. Cutler and Wm.R. Netherent was read. Lyman G. Wheeler was nominated for president of the school board and Mr. Netherent as vice president. Commissioners Netherent and Schneck along with the president were appointed to the budget committee.

Dr. W.C. Wendel will occupy the Seymour house on Church St.

E.C. Nettleton, the grocer, moved into Dr. Wendel's home on Church St.

Mr. Lowther, who acted as assistant water works engineer, was in the city.

Mrs. C.C. Jacobus and her son are visiting friends and relatives in Chilton, Wis.

Byron Farries, of Chicago, son of Supervisor Farries, was in town.

Albert Taylor, of Creston, Ind., formerly of Wauwatosa, is visiting friends here.

Jacob Cervaart died last Monday, he was and old resident of the town of Greenfield, he will be buried at Wauwatosa cemetery.

Paul Warren has won third prize for his landscape photograph of a Wauwatosa scene in the Harper's Young People's Round Table contest.

Miss Ida Crowl, of Beaver Dam is visiting Miss May Foiler, Miss Carrie Warren and Mrs. Edith Taylor, of this city, who were her classmates at Fox Lake young ladies college.

**Death**

Miss Jeanette Espenet, a graduate of Wauwatosa High School, died May 3, 1899 at St. Mary's hospital, Milwaukee.

Anton T. Falbe, of Homewood, was buried at Wauwatosa cemetery May 1, 1899.. J.H. Stover, of Milwaukee, delivered the funeral address. Mr. Falbe leaves four sons and two daughters.

Richard Brown, aged 55, died May 5, 1899 of pneumonia at his home on Alice and Vine Sts. He was born in Selby, England and has lived in this city about ten years. He was a bookkeeper at Godfrey's commission house in Milwaukee. Mr. Brown leaves a wife, mother and sister, who all reside in Wauwatosa. Rev. John Schneider will officiate, he will be buried at Wauwatosa cemetery. The Masonic and I. O. F. lodges of which he was a member will attend the body.

William Stein who lives on Howard Rd. suffered a double loss Apr. 30, 1899, lightning struck his barn causing a fire that killed part of his live stock and his wife, a long time sufferer of consumption passed away the same day.

## May 13, 1899

W.G. Cutler, of Chicago, is visiting his son, Dr. J.S. Cutler.

Wm. Sanderson is expected home to spend Sunday.

Miss Florence Seymour, of Chicago, is visiting friends here.

E.H. Schwaiger, of Milwaukee, was in the city.

Harry Hughes paid a flying visit to friends here

Mrs. L. Hurlbut and daughter returned from a trip to Maryland.

Mrs. Capt. Leisk is leaving for a five weeks sail with the captain.

Franee Sanderson was home from school in Kenosha.

Mrs. W.H. Wright is visiting her daughter, Miss Laurine Wright, in Oshkosh.

Mrs. W.E. White has returned from a visit to Milwaukee.

Mrs. R.W. Vaughn, of Chicago, is visiting her parents, Mr. and Mrs. Wm. Farries.

Miss Margaret Wallace, of Milwaukee spent Sunday with the Misses Menesh.

Mrs. Chamberlain and daughter, Eva Chamberlain, visited Mrs. Woodmansee.

Miss Lillian von Baumbach has returned from a visit in Chicago.

Mrs. Holston, of Milwaukee, was the guest of Smith McCormack.

Mrs. J.K. Douglas, of Troy Center, spent a week with her father, J.T. Van Vechten.

R.J. Matthias moved his family to the former residence of H.P. Bradley on Wells St.

Two new scarlet fever cases reported at the homes of C.B. Perry and R. Duff.

Miss Margeret Koerner held a luncheon for her Sunday School class and a few friends.

H.D. Colby had great luck on his fishing trip to northern Wisconsin.

Mrs. Thos. Reynolds, of Jacksonport, Wis., is visiting her brother, Jas. E. Foley and other relatives in the area.

Mrs. Clarence Whitney, of Rice Lake, has joined her husband who is one of the NEWs force of printers.

Miss Clara Siegler, of Norfolk, Nebraska, is visiting her brother, Mr. F. Siegler, teacher at the Lutheran school in this city.

Miss Mary James royally entertained a party of young folks.

Mrs. Farries and Mrs. Servis, of Boseman, Mont., have been visiting Mrs. G.C. Murphy.

A grand May ball will be held at Chas. Ziekuhr's hall on Watertown Plank Rd.

Alex Rogers entertained some Milwaukee friends at his home on Wauwatosa Ave.

Miss Carrie Warren broke her arm when she slipped on a stone while tying her horse.

Mrs. Horning, of Kenyon Ave., burnt her hands and face severely with gasoline at her home.

Deputy Sheriff Ferdinand has moved his family into the former home of Sidney Squires, now owned by Jacob Fehl.

Jesse Boorse, former electrician at the county alms house, has a new position in Chicago as inspector with the Chicago Telephone Co.

Mr. L.J. Mueller supervised the repairs on the water tank in compliance with his contract.

Miss M.J. Comstock, superintendent of the Deaconess home in Milwaukee, will speak at the M. E. church.

Mrs. E.L. Blodgett is making improvements on her residence on W. Main St.

Mr. J.D. Bartel will be in the city to put a stone basement and foundation under the home he owns on W. Main St. occupied by W.H. Lamb,

John Koerner, druggist, went to Janesville to visit Mrs. Koerner's relatives and to look over the field in the interest of his remedy "Cutano."

Rev. Sutherland will speak on the tramp problem in Germany, Mrs. J.O. Myers will lead the discussion of the Applied Christianity class.

Phillip G. Dick, Justice of the Peace, surrendered his docket to Town Clerk Bradley. The outfit made a good sized wagon load.

City Health Officer Hathaway will fumigate the public schools against scarlet fever with a solution called Formaline.

Mr. Kemper directed a concert by the All Saints' Cathedral Choral-Union for the benefit of the Trinity church.

Mr. and Mrs. G.P. Dousman entertained wardens and vestrymen of Trinity Episcopal church. Those present were: Rector H. Gates and wife, Choir-master Bair, Warden W.H. Landolt, Vestrymen: Mr. White, Mr. Potter, Mr. Horle, Mr. Wood, Mr. Curtis, and Mr. Helgesen.

Prof. A.P. Hollis, of W.H.S., had his article on Dr. Sheldon, who was the principal of the Oswego, NY Normal before his death, printed in *The Educational Gazett*. This article was given as an address by Mr. Hollis before the alumni of the Oswego normal.

Mr. Thomas Diamond, former resident of Wauwatosa, was in town. He now has a small fruit farm at his home in Brookfield.

Mrs. E.D. Holton, of Grand Ave., Milwaukee, will give a reception in honor of Miss M.E. Brehm, national organizer of the W.C.T.U., who will speak on temperance, at the First Baptist church.

The town board meeting was attended by Chairman Hartung, Supervisors, Seefeld and Seigfried, Town Clerk, H.P. Bradley, and Treasurer, A.L. Story

Chairman Hartung, Members Seefeld, Seigfried and Dr. E.C. Grosskopf attended the town board of health meeting where it was reported that there were eighteen cases of diptheria, five new cases of scarlet fever and one case of tuberculosis, there were two deaths from diptheria.

Oscar Hurlbut returned from the east and will hold down the first corner for the Crescents who play at Menominee Falls today. The following players and "rooters" will leave at noon: Lumb, Wheeler,

Tipple, Sheriff, Keek?, Gettelman, Hook, George Rogers, "Squib" Wright, H. Meyer, Murphy, Winding, Wood, Hayes and Davelaar.

**School Column**

Misses Jessie Currie and Franee Sanderson visited the high school.

Miss Mabel Bjorquist is expected to return to school after a long absence.

Mr. and Mrs. Cornelius will entertain the teachers at their home.

Miss Hetty Conley was kept home with a severe case of tonsilitis.

Miss Winifred E. Jones read a paper at city hall before the primary teachers on "Literature for Young Children."

**Marriage**

Miss Ruby Breed married Augustus Gregg at the home of Mr. and Mrs. Charles A. Breed, parents of the bride, May 10, 1899. Rev. J.W. Sutherland, of the Congregational church, presided. The bride and groom will spend their honeymoon in northern Ohio. They will then reside in the Lydston house on Church St., Wauwatosa. Guests were: G.W. Carter, L.E. Carter, E.B. Carter, F.D. Preston, A.S. Gregg, Wm. F. Wesson, E.E. Gaudern, W. Davis, R. Wilder, Chas. Van Alstine, Alfred Dawson, L.M. Turner, J.H. Dellicker, C.W. Heatford, W.K. Gaylord, C.S. Carter and family, S. Gregg and family, L.B. Gregg and family, R.C. Sherwin and family, G.H. Fowler and family, H.H. Goodrich and family, Wm. Hart and family, Z. Douglas and family, C.S. Westover and family, Miss L. Merritt, Miss Florence Breed, Miss Ida Bowen, Miss Butler, Miss Norton, Mrs. E. Gregg, Mrs. A.O.T. Breed, Mrs. J.D. Sherman, Mrs. G. Wells, Mrs. L.C. Williams, Mrs. C.G. Breed, Mrs. W.V. Goodrich, Mrs. Butler, Mrs. S.F. Griggs, Mr. Wm. Turner, Mr. G.A. Breed, George Carter, Bert Carter, Dr. H.S. Sercombe.

**Death**

Mrs. Conrad Frey, died May 8, 1899 at her home. The funeral was held Thursday afternoon from St. John's Lutheran church, Rev. Wm. Rader officiated, burial was at Wauwatosa cemetery.

The funeral of Richard Brown was held at his late residence at Park and Vine Sts. Rev. John Schneider, of the Methodist church, presided. The music was furnished by Miss Hart, Miss Pilgrim, Mr. F.W. Schneck, and J.T. Greenwood. The burial was at Forest Home where the body was committed to the grave with Masonic services, conducted by Mr. Tompkins. Mr. Brown had been the treasurer of the Masonic Lodge in this city since its organization.

**Our Neighbors**

Robert Behling and family, of Milwaukee, have moved.

Mr. Sylvester, of Milwaukee, will move into his summer cottage soon.

F. Shrubbe will give a party for his Milwaukee friends.

Otto Garvens went to Hales Corners to buy agricultural implements.

Mr. and Mrs. R.W. Rogers, of Chicago, are visiting Mr. Rogers parents Mr. and Mrs. J.P. Rogers.

**Advertisement**

R.F. Wiesenthal has pasture for horses available on Greenfield Ave.

## May 20, 1899

Miss Miriam Hoyt returned from a Madison visit.

John Koerner and family returned from Janesville.

Brevit Waite, of Baraboo, was here visiting the H.S. Tipple family.

Albert Taylor has returned from the telegraph office in Green Bay.

Mrs. C.C. Jacobus and her little son retruned from their visit to Chilton, Wis.

B.F. Wilson, of Star Lake, Wis., a former resident of Wauwatosa, was here visiting friends.

Chas. Cuno, of Oconomowoc, was in town, he was the former superintendent of the electric plant.

E.D. Hoyt and Chas. Stickney returned from a fishing trip in northern Wis.

John Dunlop has been planting shade trees on Wauwatosa Ave.

Geo. C. McCarthy has started a new shoe shop in the Gridley building.

Chas. Zickuhr will give another dance at his place on Watertown Plank Rd.

A Dance party at F. Schrubbe's was attended by about sixty couples, the T.P.A. had thirty-five present.

Discussion of the tramp problem with Prof. Hollis will be continued tomorrow.

J.L. Morton had his foot stepped on by a horse and as a result is limping.

Wm. Regan is off duty from the depot for a week's vacation, in his place is Thos. Regan, Albert Taylor will work the key at night.

$1000 was paid to Mrs. Brown by the Independent Order of Foresters which was the life insurance carried by the late Richard Brown.

The shoe store of C.S. Raesser was damaged by fire. Mr. Raesser was the former superintendent of the home for dependent children here.

Participants in the program at the Missionary Tea at the Congregational church were Mrs. Moorehouse, Miss McDermott, Mrs. Cook, Mrs. Watner, J.O. Myers, and Miss Helen Myers. About seventy persons attended.

At the town board meeting a communication from Phillip G. Dick asking to withdraw his resignation as justice of the peace was read. F.W. Vollrath, who has a butcher shop on 30th and National Ave. requested a license to hold a monthly cattle fair.

Miss E.D. Santley, of Madison, is visiting Prof. A.P. Hollis.

Rev. R.S. Walker returned from Edison, Neb., he reports his wife's health is improving.

Rev. Schneider will speak on card playing at the Methodist church.

N.J. Swann, Jr. severly sprained his ankle by falling from a horse.

Dan Hutchinson, of Sheboygan Falls, a former resident, is visiting here.

Mr. and Mrs. O.S. Badger returned to their old home in Coventry, VT. accompanied by Mrs. H.D. Colby, who will remain about a month.

A birthday party was given for Mrs. C.S. Dreutzer last Tuesday.

August Kringel will be the new superintendent of the home for dependent children.

The following ladies were entertained at a dinner given by Mrs. W.R. Cundall: the misses Lou Harriman, Edith Glasier, Ethel Cadwell, Jessie Cundall, Hattie Chamberlin, Mary Belle Kellogg, Mary Myers, and Helen Lewis.

Mrs. W.D. Mellvaine, of Oak Park, Ill., and Mr. and Mrs. E.W. Fowler, of Chicago, have been visiting here. Mrs. Mellvaine and Mrs. Fowler are the sisters of J.D. Warren, Luther Warren and Mrs. J.W. Wheeler.

**Marriage**

Richard Geske, of Milwaukee, and Miss Mary Blohm, daughter of John Blohm, foreman of Chas. Stickney's farm, will be married May 20, 1899, at the home of the brides parents by Rev. Wm. Henkel. They will reside in Milwaukee.

Paul Grebel, of Milwaukee, and Miss Martha Scheibe, daughter of Gustav Scheibe, were married May 17, 1899, at Frieden's Lutheran church by Rev. Wm. Henkel. They will have an "at Home" at their residence on Green Bay Ave., Milwaukee on Tuesday.

**Death**

The three year old son of R.E. Sullivan was killed by a C.&N.W. train Thursday while playing on the tracks two blocks from his home. Mr Sullivan is a N. Greenfield saloon keeper.

## School Column

Mrs. E.C. Evans, of Wauwatosa, has made several visits to the high school this week.

Misses Allee Hart, Margaret Hart, and N. Sutherland paid a visit to the high school.

An Article by George Schneck will be published next week.

Miss Genske is the fourth grade teacher.

Athletic records were set by Harold Rogers for the high jump and shot put, David Swan, and George Schneck for the vault.

## Our Neighbors

County Superintendent Stiles visited district 10.

Dr. Wm. Lewis, of Milwaukee, visited friends here.

E.F. Van Vechten and family, of Milwaukee, visited J.P. Rogers.

H.S. Temple and family, Miss Temple and C.H. Jacobs, all of Milwaukee, visited W.S. Taylor.

Mr. and Mrs. R.W. Rogers, the guests of J.P. Rogers, will reside in Woodworth, Wis.

## June 3, 1899

J.T. Greenwood is ill with appendicitis.

Miss Mabel Lewis has returned from school in Prentice.

Rev. and Mrs. Benson have returned from a visit to their daughter in Beloit, Wis.

Mrs. Ira Kennedy, of Sixth Ave., is visiting relatives in Menasha, Wis.

Dr. and Mrs. Fisk are spending the day in their cottage at Oconomowoc lake.

L. Brockway is in Fargo, ND, he will return next week.

Miss von Baumbach, of Milwaukee, visited Miss Lillian von Baumbach.

C.H. Tesch, of Milwaukee, was in town.

Miss Agnes Roddis has had a relapse of typhoid fever and is dangerously ill.

Messrs Fred Morton, Chas. Godfrey, Dr. H.G. Morton, and E.M. Lewis spent time at Lake Beulah.

H.W. Glasier was in La Crosse on railroad business.

Wm. Haertel, manager of the laundry, will move to rooms above the laundry.

Mrs. Lingelbach moved to the city yesterday.

Mrs. A.A. Rork, of Appleton, Wis., was here visiting friends. She was one of the city's early settlers and a resident for many years.

W.J. Armour, former newspaper printer and ex-soldier, paid a visit to the news office.

Edward Radzinski, a teamster for Burnham's brick yard, was kicked by a horse, his arm was severly lacerated.

Mayor Hoyt appointed Matt Goebel and Jacob Gunderman weed commissioners for the coming year.

A horse belonging to Chas. Flugado was kicked by another horse and had it's leg broken, it was necessary to kill him.

Adam Currie and his family will travel to Scotland, his native land, and other European countries.

Dr. E.C. Grosskopf will be in Columbus, Ohio to attend an American Medical association meeting

Henry Kurth, of Kurth Bros. grocers, moved to Milwaukee. Mr. Zarse, who will take Henry's place at the store will move into the house vacated by Mr. Kurth.

In the parade on Memorial day, the horse that George Stafford was riding, danced and pranced to the music all the way to and from the cemetery in perfect time to the music, to the admiration of all.

A son of Gustave Lentz, cut his leg badly while playing on the grounds of the Lutheran school and required stitches.

E.C. Nettleton plans to visit southwestern Missouri to look after his mining interests. He owns land situated in the heart of very rich lead and zinc deposits. B.J. Thomas will manage the grocery while he is gone.

The following officers were elected at the Royalclub, a young ladies social organization: President, Gertrude Cook; vice-president, Calla Canright; treasurer, Florence Waklie; secretary, Fay Rogers; committee on program, Florence Ringrose, and Margaret Derbin.

Rev. John Schneider, of Wauwatosa, delivered an excellent address at the Memorial Day exercises in West Bend.

Mrs. J.L. Morton and Mrs. Frederick L. Morton gave an "at home" assisted by Mrs. F.W. Wood, of Milwaukee, Mrs. Thos. Greenwood, Mrs. J.T. Greenwood, Mrs. Jas. Lefeber, Mrs. D.G. Hathaway, Miss Amanda Lefeber, and Miss Sylvia Lefeber.

**Deaths**

Frank J. Digman died May 27, 1899 from paralysis. He was the father of Hubert Digman of this city. Mr Digman was 68 years of age, and a resident of Wausau. His funeral was in Wausau, he leaves eight children, Mrs. Digman died about nine years ago.

Stephen H. Seamans died at his home on Kavanaugh place May 30, 1899, after a long illness. Mr. Seamans was an old and well known resident of this city, about 64 years of age. He leaves a wife and five children, Emily Seamans, Julia Seamans, Emogene Seamans, Arthur Seamans, and Howard Seamans. He was born in Albion, NY and came to Wauwatosa in the early sixties, he was engaged in business in Milwaukee. Rev. Gates and Rev. Wright conducted the services with burial at Forest Home cemetery.

Mr. and Mrs. Wm. Zimmerman, of Wauwatosa buried their only child in Butler.

**Our Neighbors**

C.J. Rogers has been visiting his father, J.P. Rogers.

C.W. Loomis and A.B. Garvens visited friends in Saylesville.

Howard Taylor and wife, of Milwaukee, visited W.G. Taylor.

W.A. Briggs and wife, of Milwaukee, visited Mrs. W.G. Taylor, the sister of Mr. Briggs.

Guy Curtis had his foot crushed in an accident in the Bay View rolling mills.

Mr. and Mrs. Thomas Smith, of Chicago, have been visiting J.B. Johnson.

Henry W. Feerick, Butler's postmaster is recovering from a broken leg.

### June 10, 1899

Jacob Schmidt is a clerk at Lefeber Bros.

Mrs. Cyrus Pedrick is on a visit to Ripon, Wis.

John Greenwood is better after a week's illness.

Mrs. Wm. von Baumbach is on a visit to Waupun, Wis.

Prof. A.P. Hollis was in Janesville.

C.C. Jacobus took a trip to Oregon, Wis.

Chas. Godfrey was in Michigan on business.

St. Martha's guild met with Mrs. Hunter.

Miss Agnes Roddis's health is improving.

L. Brockway is home from his western trip.

Miss Kate Lehman, of Neosho, is visiting Miss Van Vechten.

Miss Maud Barnes has returned from school in Hillsboro, Wis.

Mrs. Dr. Barnett, of Ripon, Wis., is visiting Mrs. W.R. Cundall.

St. Agnes guild met at the home of Miss Kershaw.

Mrs. Caroline Mower celebrated her 84th birthday Friday.

Rev. W. Bergholz, of Kewaunee, Wis., was the guest of F. Siegler.

Mr. and Mrs. J.S. Stickney and Miss Ann Smith are at their Lake Keesus cottage.

Miss Marie Elwell, of Milwaukee, visited Miss Helen Godfrey.

Joe Keeler and Barney Blum are going fishing at Lake Okauchee.

E.V. Tanner, of St. Gallen, Switzerland, was the guest of his cousin, Mrs. J.W. Hess.

Miss Bertha Hess has been on a visit to Chicago and Waukegan.

John Wagner is now occupying his new shoe shop.

S.D. Hoyt, of the Fond du Lac Electric Co, was here to visit his father.

Mrs. R. Cadwell is in Waukesha before she leaves for her Cleveland and Colorado Springs trip.

Miss Mary Earls left for Clarmont, New Hampshire after visiting her sisters in Delavan Wis. and Park Ridge, Ill.

Mr. and Mrs. John Muller, of New York City, are visiting G.A. Kurtz and family. Mrs. Muller is Mr. Kurtz's sister.

Miss Margaret Wallace, of Milwaukee, and Duncan Menish, of Ohio, were guests at Mr. and Mrs. Frederick Wahl's wedding.

Constable H.W. Gransee arrested a suspicious character who proved to be an escaped inmate from the Waukesha reform school, who had been missing for about one year.

C.H. Tesch, of Milwaukee, will present his plan to lay sewer pipe to the town board.

Lawerance Horning, of Kenyon St., this city, was taken severely ill with cramps while at work at National Straw works in Milwaukee. He is back at work.

A base ball club was organized by the Misses Beth Godfrey, Madeline Haney, Laura Stewart, Florence Adams, Loleta Landolt, and Myrtice Cochrane.

The regular meeting of the water commission was attended by Commissioners Currie, Hoyt, Breed, Stickney and Luetzow.

Prof. A.P. Hollis has resigned to take a higher paying position as principal and superintendant of the Broadhead schools.

A musical entertainment was given by the band and Boys Brigade during which Mabel Potter recited "Brought Back", Bandmaster Goodwin favored the audience with a cornet solo; Hattie Swan and George Schneck preformed a piano duet. Four of the Boys' Brigade, C.K. Moore, David Swan, Ralph Hayward, and Robt. Ferris rendered a musical selection. The Misses Nina Scholl and Alice Brown, of Granville, were imported to play a piano duet.

Miss Alice Smith recited "The Whistling Regiment". Otto Zillmer recited "Fitzjames and Roderick Dhu", and Ned Keats and Dave Swan played a violin duet. Mr. Paul Warren concluded the program with a band selection.

The following person were appointed highway superintendents at the Town Board Meeting: John Kerber and Joseph Cheany. Among the citizens of the town who were present were County Treasurer Henry F. Schultz and Deputy County Treasurer E.A. Sims.

Wauwatosa High School Lyceum reception was held by President Wm. Woodmansee. A piano solo was played by Geo. Schneck, address by Prof. E.C. Cornelius, vocal solo by Miss Smith and speaches by President Woodmansee, Miss Potter, S.J. Swan, Arthur Thomas, Miss Walker, and David Swan.

**Marriage**

Miss Grace Menish, of Wauwatosa, and Frederick B. Wahl, of Milwaukee, were married at the home of the brides's parents on W. Main St. Rev. McNary, of Grace Episcopal church, Milwaukee, officiated. John Dummer was best man and Miss Florence Menish, sister of the bride, was bridesmaid. They will tour the state on their honeymoon and be at home to friends after July 1st at 101 Garfield Ave., Milwaukee.

**School Column**

Mr. Parker, state inspector of high schools, visited our school.

Miss Dolly Gregg, of Elm Grove, visited the sixth grade.

Mr. Stiles, county superentendent, paid a call.

Katherine Duff, of the third grade, is back at school after a bout with scarlet fever.

Charlotte Williams is back in her seat and has decided to abandon the study of poison ivy.

Miss Agnes Roddis is still exceedingly weak, but physician and friends are hopeful.

A Mr. Peterson, who represents a book company, heard some of our classes recite.

Prof. Cornelius gave an address at the last meeting of the Lyceum.

**Our Neighbors**

Otto Garvens went to Hale's Corners on business.

Miss Bessie White, of Kenosha, is visiting Mrs. J.B. Johnson.

Mrs. Mary Garvens and Mrs. Elizabeth Curtis visited friends in Greenfield.

J.B. Johnson, Miss Johnson, and Master Archie Johnson are at Lake Beulah.

**Butler Briefs**

Allen Cogswell, of Chicago, is visiting Mrs. Bevier, his aunt.

Mrs. Fred Rother and daughter, Miss Mabel Springsted, left for a trip through the west.

### June 17, 1899

H.S. Tipple, of Alice St., is quite ill.

Miss Louise Landolt is in Chicago visiting.

Miss Bertha Hess has returned from Chicago.

Rev. and Mrs. H.H. Benson have returned from Beloit, Wis.

John M. Wheeler is up after 10 days of illness.

Mrs. Kate Turney, of Toledo, Ohio, is visiting Mrs. C.H. Shaw.

Adam Currie and family left for a three months trip abroad.

Mrs. G.W. Murphy visited in Milwaukee.

August Krehl has severed his connection with Koerner's Pharmacy.

A.S. Gregg has moved into the W.G. Taylor house on Kavanaugh Pl.

Jerry Keeler, who works at the depot, is in Waukesha.

Mrs. A.H. Hudson, of Grand Rapids, Mich., is visiting the W.H. Lumb family.

T.H. Scott, of Chicago, visited his sister, Mrs. J.H. Waldie.

The Misses Franey Sanderson and Edith Gates returned from Kemper Hall.

G.W. Blackburn, of Waukesha, was in the city on real estate business.

A.P. Hollis, went to Brodhead Friday and will spend Sunday at his home in Madison.

George W. Ringrose, H.P. Bradley, and T.M. Hammond were at Beaver Lake.

Bert Gridley will be the assistant manager at the opera house in Appleton.

Dr. John, former pastor of the M. E. church here, is visiting friends.

Miss Corinne Mitchell, of the local laundry, will make a trip to Chicago.

D.T. Pilgrim, Jr. will excavate foundations for two residences on Pabst Ave.

Mrs. L.V. Tupper has returned from a visit in Chicago, her son, Claude Tupper, is in New Orleans, La.

Miss Edna Hooley returned from Madison to spend her vacation here at home.

George Koerner has returned from his Janesville vacation.

Dr. E.C. Grosskopf has returned from the American Medical association meeting in Columbus, Ohio.

Alderman Fred Bark and family were in Dillman to visit Mrs. Bark's parents, August Sieglow and wife.

Arba Rice and Demerit Hoyt, who are with the electric company of Fond du Lac, Wis., were here visiting their homes.

Mrs. A.W. Dillingham, of Sheboygan, was here visiting her daughter, Mrs. H.P. Bradley, of Wells St.

Mr. and Mrs. Hunter went to the graduation of their daughter, Joyce Hunter, at Milwaukee Downer college.

W.R. Cundall went to New York and Boston on business, his wife will spend his absence at the home of her mother, Mrs. S.S. Lewis.

Miss Frances Darling, of Oakfield, Wis., who graduated from W.H.S in '89, was here visiting friends.

G.P. Dousman directed the raising and graveling of Schiller Ave.

Mr. and Mrs. Art Young, of New York City, are visiting Miss North, Mr. Young is a famous cartoonist and author.

R. Tennant, Jr., son of Mr. and Mrs. R. Tennant, was visiting his parents and attended the grand lodge of Masons in Milwaukee.

J.H. Johnson, of Wauwatosa, will build a store building on his lot next to the laundry.

J.D. Gilbert has been quite ill with poison ivy that he contracted while gathering ferns to decorate the Congregational church.

E. Blodgett, of Sixth Ave., will be in Covington, Ky. supervising the placement of machinery from the works of E. P. Allis & Co., his employers.

County Treasurer, H.L. Schultz held up the members of the town board at his residence.

Dr. S.S. Leonard cut his fingers to the bone while operating on a horse because of the animals struggles.

Town Clerk Bradley returned from his fishing trip to Beaver Lake.

Justice Glasier has received complaints of small boys swimming in the mill pond without bathing suits.

John Raymer, post graduate teacher at U. of W. Madison, is an applicant for the position of assistant principal of W.H.S., made vacant by the resignation of Mr. Hollis.

Will Sanderson, of this city, and a Chicago student, will split the $50 prize for highest average in studies at St. John's military academy. Will was also awarded the Wenner medal for proficiency in Spanish.

Max Rosenthal shot two of three dogs that attacked his livestock.

A pleasant reception was given by the superintendent of the Congregational Sunday school, J.D. Gilbert and his wife.

President Charles Kendall Adams will give the address at the comencement exercises at the University of Wisconsin, Madison.

## Town Board Meeting

C.H. Tesch, representing the Park Hill land company, appeared before the town board and filed a written spplication for permission to lay sewers and water pipes in the Merrill Park district.

John F. Frawley appeared on behalf of Mrs. Ellis to object to the change of grade of the roadway fronting her property on Park Hill Ave.

Otto Sasse was instructed to obtain a list of properties where sidewalks are out of repair.

Engineer Reinertsen attended to explain the elevations of some streets in the Merrill Park district.

## Marriage

Mrs. Nancy J. Goodrich, of Brookfield, and Simon C. Groot, of Rock Elm, Wis., were married June 11, 1899, at the Methodist parsonage in Wauwatosa, Rev. John Schneider, presided.

## Death

Mrs. Christine Duenkel died Friday, 10:30 PM, June 9, 1899 at her son, Henry Duenkel's home on State St. She was 85 years and 10 months. Mrs. Duenkel came to Milwaukee from Germany in 1846 and has resided here since. She leaves four sons, Henry Duenkel and Charles Duenkel of this city; William Duenkel of Barton; and Herman Duenkel of Waukesha. The funeral services were held Monday and burial was in Waukesha.

## Children's Day program

The salutation at the Children's Day program at the Congregational church was given by Mary Clapp, the address by Harold Rogers; recitations by Helen Myers, Lena Loveland, Glen Gilbert, Spencer Pease, Eleanor Swan, Ada Pares, George Cornelius, and Paul Godfrey; Offering by: Rachel Gilbert, Mary Gilbert, Marion Godfrey, and Marion Rogers.

## School Column

This column is edited by Chas. Loomis, Miss Olive Horning, Miss Mabel Potter, and Miss Laura Loveland.

Miss Lillie Kirschner visited the high school.

Prof. Powell of Oakwood, Wis., visited our school.

Miss Hattie Prentice paid a visit.

Miss Walker is the German teacher.

Mr. Turner, a freshman at Carroll College, visited some of our freshman classes.

Mr. Cornelius has been training the seniors for their comencement orations.

Myron R. Churchill, who is in newspaper work in Marinette, Wis., visited Miss Smith.

Miss Edna Hooley, class of '98, is home from the university for the summer.

Harold Rogers gave a speech on athletics.

Miss Ruth Ellis is back after a week's visit to her brother in Chicago.

Maude Curtis gave an interesting talk on the founding of the Soldiers Home.

Ralph Hayward and Charles Fisher wish to buy a large number of hairribbons.

Chas. Moore had his first piano lesson this week.

One of the teachers has taken to calling Miss Sadie Phillips, Miss Stickney.

Former teachers: Mr. Turner, of Burlington schools, Miss Speigelberg, of South Side high school, and Mr. Goodall, of Milwaukee, have been in the city.

Miss Agnes Roddis is much improved.

The following teachers are leaving our school: Miss Genske to Oshkosh, Miss Doty to Whitewater, Mr. Hollis to Brodhead, and Miss McKowan to Horicon.

**Death**

The mother of Mattie Neary, of the class of '99?, passed away June 12, 1899.

The rest of 1899 newspapers, all of 1900 and 1901 and the first part of 1902 are missing.

### March 8, 1902

Mrs. N.L. Kneeland is back from a visit in Chicago.

Miss Joyce Hunter was home from Madison.

Miss Nellie Wells, of Greenfield Ave., is quite ill.

Mr. John Dunlop entertained friends Thursday.

St. Martha's Guild met with Mrs. W.J. Potter.

Mrs. C. Robertson, of 5th Ave., entertained last night.

Mr. and Mrs. C.G. Severance entertained at cards.

Mr. G.H. Prest returned from a visit to Canada.

The Ladies' Whist club met with Miss Isabel Stickney.

Mr. Irving Piper, of Eagle, was the guest of Thos. Helgesen.

Mrs. W.H. Wright gave a lunch for the German Club.

W.M. Harden and Allen Breed left for Encampment, Wyoming.

Miss H. Rice is well and back to work at the postoffice.

Mr. Stephen Croft's best horse died.

The Douglas Heights Kensington club met with Mrs. Wilcox.

Mrs. Cook is visiting her daughter Miss Gertrude Cook at Pillsbury Academy in Minnesota.

The Twentieth Century Topic club will meet with Mrs. Frank Durbin.

Mr. and Mrs. Bissell, of Montello, Wis., are visiting Mrs. L.S. Pease, of Wauwatosa Ave.

Mr. and Mrs. Frank Chadbourne, of Fond du Lac, are visiting Mrs. D.G. Hawley, of Church St.

Mrs. Theresa Schubel is recovering from injuries received in a street car accident.

Miss Bertha Hacker, of Hartford, Wis., spent two weeks with Mrs. D.F. Philipp, of 7th Ave.

Robert Walker, of Chicago, and A.E. Kerr, of Waukesha, spent time with Franklyn Harriman, of Wauwatosa Ave.

Henry Hemsing, C.H. Norton and Chas. Chase were in Chicago for an automobile exhibition.

Mr. and Mrs. J.R. Douglas, of Troy Center, and Will Lehmann, of Neosho, were guests of J.T. Van Vechton.

The Young Woman's Auxillary, of the Congregational church, met with Miss Myrtle Nettleton.

Mr. Hemsing, Sr., of 3rd Ave., is somewhat improved from a stroke of Paralysis.

Rev. and Mrs. R.M. Vaughn, of Janesville, are visiting Mrs. Vaughn's parents, Mr. and Mrs. Wm. Farries, of 1st Ave.

Mr. J.F. Dittmar is finishing the second floor of his building on Wisconsin St. for dwelling purposes.

Mrs. W.A. Clapp lost a pair of eye-glasses.

Mrs. Wm Sparling and Miss Alle? Goodhue (paper damaged), of Trempealeau, are visiting Mr. and Mrs. Nettleton, of Milwaukee Ave.

W.C. Bradley will conduct a meeting of the Waukesha County Farmers' Institute on agriculture.

The common council meeting was attended by Mayor Hoyt, Aldermen Lefeber, Hamme, Jones, Thomas, Breed, and Baumbach.

A story about the underground railroad helping slaves escape mentions the names of Rev. E.D. Underwood, Mr. J.M. Warren, Warner Mower and Mr. Stickney. In March, 1854, Sherman Booth, of Milwaukee, was imprisoned for seven years for aiding in the escape of Joseph Glover, a fugitive slave.

Augustus Mower was the first from Wauwatosa to enlist for the Civil War.

Lyman G. Wheeler will run for Circuit Judge on the Republican ticket. He has his law office in Milwaukee and is hoping to succeed Judge Warren D. Tarrant. He has never held office before and is not a politician. He is the son of Lyman Wheeler who settled in Milwaukee county in 1836. Mr. Wheeler was born May 4, 1863 on a farm (the rest of the paper is missing).

**Death**

Mrs. Helen Grace Tragard, wife of Rudolph Tragard, died March 1, 1902, at her home on Kenyon St., after a lingering illness. Mrs. Tragard was born in Cooksville, Wis., she was a member of the Congregational church of Wauwatosa and the Wauwatosa Woman's club. She leaves her husband and two children, Loraine Armin Tragard, aged 6 and Kenneth Tragard, aged 4 and a large circle of friends. The funeral took place from her residence, Rev. A.R. Thain presided.

**East Elm Grove**

Wm. Zahn is visiting his grandfather, Mr. H. Garvens.

Mrs. Clara Curtis entertained a few friends at tea.

W.G. Taylor has rented the J.A. Warren farm.

Mr. Chas. Swett and family, of Dartford, Wis., will live on the Warren farm.

**October 18, 1902**

This paper is in very poor condition.

Mrs. G.C. Murphy has returned from Fond du Lac.

Mrs. Ben Lamb is recovering from her recent illness.

Mr. W.J. Underwood was in town for a few days.

Mrs. Arthur Weber was here visiting friends.

Demerit Hoyt was home for a few days.

Miss Lillie McLean visited Miss Maud Curtis.

Mr. and Mrs. Will Godfrey entertained at cinch.

Mrs. Wm. Godfrey went to Chicago to visit her sister.

Mrs. J.J. Green, of New Ulm, Minn. is visiting her sister Mrs. C.G. Dreutzer.

Mrs. Edward Bussewitz has returned from a visit to relatives in Chicago.

Claud Cairncross has been appointed subsititute mail carrier for the city of Wauwatosa.

Mrs. C.G. Dreutzer, of E. Milwaukee Ave., will entertain.

Richard Sporleder has been appointed day operator at Milton Junction.

Miss Margaret Durbin entertained thirty friends.

Miss Louise Landolt is unable to work at the post office due to illness.

Miss Myrtle Farnham who was injured by falling from a chair is able to get around.

Mr. and Mrs. Chas. Davis, of Milwaukee, will spend the winter with Mr. and Mrs. Ringrose.

Miss Hoyt, of N. Main St., gave an informal for Miss Juliet Harris, of Reedsburg, Wis.

Mrs. Eugene Sutton? and her daughter, Bernice Sutton?, of South St. Paul, Minn. are visiting Jacob Burke?, of E. Center St.

Capt. W.H. Landolt attended the annual Veteran's Assoc. in Oconomowoc.

Mr. E.W. Chubb, of Kavanaugh Pl., is going hunting in South Dakota.

Street Commissioner Warren is putting in stone crossings to assist pedestrians.

Rev. M.A. Packer, of Eau Claire, and Rev. Granger Smith, of Evansville, were visiting at the Baptist parsonage.

Misses Florence Everett and Daisy Everett began teaching in Granville last week.

Miss Florence Adams became ill while visiting in Oconomowoc and is unable to return to her home in this city.

Miss Myrtle Nettleton, of E. Milwaukee Ave., entertained at cinch in honor of her guest, Miss Woocester, of Trempeleau, Wis.

Miss Alice Hart was given a shower by Misses Gertrude Doud, Aldine Foley, and Hattie Moan.

Dr. W.F. Beutler is the superintendent of the asylum for chronic insane.

Mrs. Chas.T. Fisher, of North Ave., is in Kirksville, Mo. to attend her daughter, Miss Nellie Fisher, who is ill.

Mr. J.D. Cole has returned from the G.A.R. (Grand Army of the Republic) National Encampment where he represented Wauwatosa.

Mrs. D.T. Pilgrim, Jr., of E. Center St., was surprised by friends Saturday.

G.J. Davelaar, L.G. Wheeler, Fred Hartung, and Barney Eaton were the speakers at a Republican rally held at Neumiller's hall on Lisbon Rd.

Fred Ludington's white horse hit it's head on a tree while running around the pasture and when it fell it broke it's back. The horse was used as a saddle horse by Miss Alice Ludington.

The Twentieth Century Topic Club met at Mrs. I.C. Lillibridge's home on Blue Mound Rd., musical solos were played by Miss Kelly, of Milwaukee.

An annonymous letter saying a committee has been formed including T.J. Ferguson, Joseph Schwaiger, J.E. Thomas, F.M. Heiden, Charles Leutzow, L.R. Gridley, and Fred H. Bark to find out who has been dumping trash in the Menomonee River. There was a sarcastic reply printed directly after this letter regarding annonymous letters.

### January 10, 1903

Miss M. Kroesing paid a visit to Milwaukee

Miss Gertruce Crane, of Fifth Ave., entertained at tea.

Rev. C.T. Everett is holding a special meeting in Millard, Wis.

Mrs. C.V. Burnside has returned from Evanston, Ill.

Arthur Brockway was appointed night operator at Elm Grove.

Mrs. E.M. Guile and family moved to Milwaukee.

Mr. C.R. Davis was in Racine on business.

Mrs. Chas. Butler, of Oak Park, Ill., visited with Mrs. L. Rhodes.

John Greenwood will host a meeting of the Evening Cinch Club.

Norman Quin, of Beloit, is a guest of Mrs. Jessie Wood, Wisconsin St.

Mrs. L.S. Pease will visit relatives in Montello, Wis.

Mr. and Mrs. G.W. Sanford, of Second Ave., returned from a visit in Chicago.

Mrs. Spooner, of Green Bay, is visiting Mrs. Geo. Hunt, her daughter.

Mrs. E.C. Stevens, of Oakland, Cal., is visiting her son, Fred La Mont, of W. Milwaukee Ave.

Rev. A.C. Payne and family, of Berlin, Wis., will rent and occupy the Hemsing house on Third Ave.

Edgar A. Goldthorp, of Morgan Bros., lumber mfgs. in Oshkosh, is here to visit his parents, Rev. and Mrs. Goldthorp.

Miss Florence Ringrose entertained the freshmen of W.H.S. with lunch after a sleigh ride.

Mrs. F.W. Schneck, Mrs. Joseph Lefeber, and Mrs. W.B. Rice entertained the ladies of the M. E. Church.

Mrs. Theresa Potter entertained at the home of her daughter, Mrs. J.H. Cushing, Wauwatosa Ave., to celebrate her 83rd birthday. Her children, C.T. Fisher, Mrs. Chas. Stickney, Mrs. H.P. Gilbert and husbands plus twelve of her grand children were present.

H.D. Hallett, consulting electrical engineer, of Aurora, Ill., has filed plans for a proposed Electric Light plant.

D.E. Cameron, of Milwaukee, installed the new officers, Claude A. Tupper, regent; B.F. Hemsing, vice-regent; H.A. Propp, orator; W.H. Landolt, secretary; Henry Watner, collector; H.P. Morse, treasurer; Allen Williams, chaplain; H.W. Bardenwerper, guide; and J.D. Gilbert, warden, of the Wauwatosa Council, No. 1553, Royal Arcanum.

The new directors for Wauwatosa Town Insurance Co. are A.W. Smith, secretary; Wm. Farries, treasurer; Jas.H. Dean, John Seivers, and H.L. Moore, president.

Mrs. John Greenwood gave a talk on the history of Holland, Mrs. L. Brockway spoke of the eventful year of 1902 and Miss Hoyt presented the home life of German women. Mrs. E.W. Chubb, of Kavanaugh Pl., will be in charge of the next meeting, which will be a social event.

Miss Ida Winters will lead the B. Y. P. U. at the Baptist Church.

**Birth**

Mr. and Mrs. George Hunt, Second Ave., have a son born Jan. 3, 1903.

A girl was born Jan. 5, 1903 to the family of K.N. Putnam, of Wauwatosa Ave.

**Marriages**

May Curtis and Eugene Butters, of Waldo, Sheboygan Co., Wis., were married at the home of Mrs. E.M. Curtis, of Blue Mound Rd., by Rev. Perry W. Lonfellow. They will live on the Butters homestead in Waldo.

Miss Alice Hart and Demerit Hoyt will be wed Oct. 22, 1903, at the home of the bride's parents, Mr. and Mrs. W.A. Hart, of Warren Ave.

Mr. and Mrs. Charles Stickney, of E. Milwaukee Ave., will have the wedding of their daughter, Miss Isabelle Stickney and Dr. F.Gregory Connell, of Leadville, at their residence, Oct. 21, 1903.

Miss Mary Flaven and Henry Walker, formerly of this city, were married Jan. 7, 1903, at St. Thomas church, Milwaukee. Rev.Father Blackwell presided. The couple will live on Chestnut St. in Milwaukee.

Miss Mable Grace Farries and George Moore Watson were married Jan. 8, 1903, at the home of John Farries by Rev. P.W. Longfellow assisted by Rev. D.W. Hulburt. They will live in the Willis Watson residence on Fond du Lac Ave.

**Death**

Luther A. Warren died Jan. 6, 1903. He was the son of Jonathan M. Warren and Lavinia Damon. Mr. Warren was born in Grafton, Mass., March 31, 1834. In August 1838, his parents moved to Wauwatosa where they raised a large family of whom, Mrs. John M. Wheeler, of Wauwatosa, Mrs. Wm. Mellvaine, of Oak Park, Ill., Mrs. E.W. Fowler, of Chicago, and Mr. J.D. Warren, of Wauwatosa still survive.

The family first lived in a log house on the river, but in 1842 moved to a log house on the site of the present homestead on Wauwatosa Ave. His parents were among the original members of the Congregational church in the city.

As a young man Mr. Warren taught in the public school during winters and farmed the rest of the year. In 1859, he moved to the Underwood (now Robbins) farm, he then moved to Milwaukee in 1865, where he remained for twenty seven years. He was associated with Northwestern National Fire Insurance Co. In Milwaukee he was a member of Grand Ave. Congregational church, where he was church treasurer and leader of the choir for many years.

Mr. Warren married Miss Anna L. Hoppin, Jan. 11, 1859, at Columbus Wis. She and her daughters, Mrs. C.G. Wade, Mrs. Wm.R. Netherent, and Mrs. H.W. Nickerson, who all reside here, survive him along with fifteen grandchildren. Mr. Warren has resided at the Warren homestead for the past ten years.

The funeral was held at this homestead, Dr. Thain officiated with interment at Wauwatosa cemetery.

**Letters at the postoffice that have not been picked up.**

Mrs. Francis Cronk, Mrs. E. Evenstein, Mrs. W. Schmidt, Muriel Danielson, Mrs. E.N. Fergeson, A.B. Cunelly, and W.E. Poppleton

**Common Council**

Mayor Hoyt, Aldermen Breed, Baumbach, Gunn, Hamme, Lefeber, Martin, and Menninger attended the meeting.

## February 14, 1903

Capt. and Mrs. H. Leisk are spending a few days in Chicago.

Miss Mae Rood attended the Junior Prom in Madison.

Mr. C.H. Ruggles returned from his trip out east.

Geo. Carter, of Ripon, is visiting his sister, Mrs.L.B. Gregg.

Miss Winifred Jones is spending a few days in Racine with her parents.

Mrs. E.H. Schwaiger, returned from a visit to La Crosse, Wis.

Lester Pavey has accepted a position in Fond du Lac.

Mrs. C.A. Curtis has found a pocket book on N. Main St.

Mr. Young, of Salt Lake City, Utah, is visiting Dr. J.S. Cutler.

Miss Mary Sage, of Delavan, is visiting her sister Miss Jeanette Sage.

Miss Sanborn, of New Hampshire, is the guest of Miss Charlotte Rogers, of Blue Mound Rd.

Miss Ada Pares was surprised by friends.

Miss Helen Rice will give a St. Valentine party for her playments(sic).

Rev. J.O. Ward has resigned from Trinity Church.

Mr. and Mrs. Wm. Maxon, of Cedar Lake, Wis., are visiting her sister, Mrs. Joseph Cutler.

Miss Lizzie Matzahn returned to her home in Vernon, Minn. after visiting Mrs. Fred. Picker, of State St.

Rev. W.E. Hopkins, who was a Missionary in India, will talk about his work at the Baptist Church.

Mrs. L.C. Rogers and her mother, Mrs. C. Taylor, will hold a cinch party at Mrs. Rogers home on Kavanaugh Pl.

Mr. and Mrs. Neil Menish, of W. Main St., were surprised by friends.

The recovery of Mr. L.L. Gridley, a veteran pioneer, from a serious illness is doubtful.

The Women's Missionary Society of the Methodist Church met for tea at J.B. De Swarte's home.

Rev. D.W. Hulburt has been appointed Field Secretary for the Baptist state school in Beaver Dam, Wis.

Two cows belonging to Daniel Doherty died from eating shredded corn stalks from which the binding twine had not been removed.

Miss Gillyn, of Grand Ave., Milwaukee, formerly from Chicago, will be in the city to give beauty treatments.

Mrs. Dutcher, Miss Grace Young, and Mrs. Roddis, of Milwaukee, will speak at a meeting of the American Outdoor Art Association.

Mrs. P.W. Longfellow entertaind the Baptist choir in honor of her cousin, Miss Elnora B. Pleasants, of Minot, N.D., who spent the winter in Chicago studying music. Those present were: Mr. and Mrs. A.W. Smith, Mr. and Mrs. Dr. Taylor, Mr. and Mrs. G.E. Smith, the Misses Amanda Lefeber, Janet Smith, and Anabel Farries.

Peter J. Somers, of Granville, and C.B. Perry, of Wauwatosa, represented their cities at a meeting pertaining to the building of a bridge over the Menomonee River.

Rev. Goldthorp will speak at the Methodist church morning and evening service. Mrs. Joseph Lefeber is the leader

**Marriage**

Albert R. Gridley, son of Mr. and Mrs. L.R. Gridley, of Greenfield Ave., married Miss Mary E. Thorburn February 12, 1903, at the home of her father, Adam Thorburn, of Pearl St., Janesville, Wis. They will live in Janesville.

Mrs. Josephine Fisher and Ewald Wendt were married at the home of the bride's aunt, Mrs. Louisa Rhodes, February 11, 1903. They will live in Horicon, Wis. where Mr. Wendt is engaged in business.

Miss Jessie V. Currie, formerly of Wauwatosa, married Thomas Eggleson, February 11, 1903, at the home of the bride's parents,

Mr. and Mrs. William Currie, of Marshall St., Milwaukee, Rev. E.E. Richardson, presided.

Miss Daisy Ruth Danielson, of Calumet, Mich., and James Dudley Godfrey, of this city, will marry soon.

### Death

Mrs. Sarah A. Galloway, wife of John M. Galloway, of Milwaukee, died at her home on Sycamore St., February 8, 1903, at the age of 58 years. She was a daughter of the late William Hemsing, of Wauwatosa, and is survived by her husband and two sons, B. Frank Hemsing, of this city, is a brother. The funeral took place from her home with Rev. Perry, of the Washington Ave. M. E. church, officiating. Interment was at Wauwatosa Cemetery.

### February 28, 1903

Jesse F. Cory has moved to Milwaukee.

Mr. W.H. Goodall is in Indiana on business.

Mrs. J.A. Kershaw has been in South Milwaukee on a visit.

Edward Pares gave a birthday party.

Mrs. Adam Currie will entertain the reading circle.

Mrs. J.S. Cutler and her daughter were in West Bend, Wis.

Captain and Mrs. H. Leisk entertained at dinner.

Mr. and Mrs. H.N. Andrews entertained informally.

Assistant Postmaster Lewis has been laid up with the Grippe.

Mr. and Mrs. C.G. Dreutzer spent some time in Chicago.

Mrs. E.A. Schmitz will entertain at cinch at the Irvington.

Mrs. Adam Currie will host the Kaffee Klatsch club.

Mr. A.C. Hanson entertained friends at the Irvington.

Miss Isabel R. Walker returned from a visit in Milton, Wis.

Miss Myrtle Nettleton gave a lunch for Hattie Nash.

Mrs. Oscar Helgesen is in Eagle, Wis., because of the serious illness of her mother.

Town Treasurer Story will receive taxes at the town clerk's office.

The Kensington Club will meet at Mrs. W.C. Wendel's home on Church St.

Mmes Frederick Ludington and Harry Ludington will entertain the cinch club.

Bishop McCabe gave a lecture at Summerfield Methodist church.

Frank Taylor, has been visiting his parents here, he returned to his home in Jamestown, North Dakota.

Mrs. Adams and Mrs. Tisdale were the winners at the Married Ladies' Cinch club held at C.G. Dreutzer's home.

Henry Engelhart has purchased the J.R. Thomas barbering business.

Mrs. Walter Rice and Miss Mary Hart will entertain the M.E. Church people.

Miss Mary Wales, who is spending the winter with her sister in Waukesha, was in the city on business.

Misses Laurine Wright and Inez Wright, of Murray Ave., Milwaukee, will entertain in honor of Miss Hattie Nash.

Col. M.T. Moore, brother of Wm. Moore and H.L. Moore, of North Ave., is reported seriously ill at his home in La Crosse.

Ray Stevens, of Milwaukee, gave an interesting chalk talk at the high school.

Mrs. Breed, mother of Ald. Chas. Breed and Mrs. G.H. Fowler is seriously ill at the home of her daughter, Mrs. Wm. Wesson, in Milwaukee.

Rev. Klein, of Brookfield, conducted the service at the newly organized branch of the Reform Evangelical German church.

Mr. and Mrs. J.W. Kutzner have been visiting her father, H. Watner, they returned to their home in Melrose, Minn.

Mr. and Mrs. Robert Chafe are moving to Clifton, Ark. where Mr. Chafe will join his brother and brother-in-law in the lumber business.

Mrs. C. Hughes, a hairdresser from Milwaukee, will be giving beauty treatments Saturday.

A reception will be given for Mrs. James D. Godfrey at the home of Mrs. E.R. Godfrey, Sr., by Mrs. Edwin R. Godfrey, Sr., Mrs. Edwin R. Godfrey, Jr., Mrs. William A. Godfrey, Mrs. Charles H. Godfrey, and Mrs. Harry G. Morton.

Mr. W.H. Clark, Grand Chief Templar of Wisconsin, for the Independent Order of Good Templars, will give a lecture on his trip to England, Holland and Sweden at the Baptist church.

Miss Gillyn, of Milwaukee, formerly of Chicago, will be here to do beauty treatments on Wednesdays.

Mr. O.L. Gridley, of North Ave., who has been ill, had his ice house filled by member of the Country Cousins club, the ladies arrived in the afternoon to serve dinner.

A Farmers' Institute will be held in Brown Deer, Wis., conducted by R.J. Coe, of Ft. Atkinson, Wis., assisted by W.F. Stiles, of Lake Mills; C.P. Goodrich, of Ft. Atkinson; A.F. Postel, of Menomonee Falls; C.E. Matteson, of Pewaukee; and N.E. France, of Platteville.

Miss Ellen C. Sabin, President of Milwaukee Downer College, will speak at the Woman's Club.

Isabel Everett will lead the B. Y. P. U. at the Baptist church.

**Birth**

A son was born to Mr. and Mrs. H. Bryne, February 25, 1903.

Mr. and Mrs. Sam. Kissinger are the parents of a 12 pound girl.

**Marriage**

Miss Hattie Glendene, daughter of Mr. and Mrs. John M. Nash will be wed to Eugene Turner Wright, March 11, 1903, at the home of her parents on Warren Ave.

## June 6, 1903

Miss Alice Kershaw is ill with tonsilitis.

Miss Beth Godfrey is visiting friends in Edgewood, Ill.

Miss Mary Myers was in Chicago.

A.L. Carlton returned from a business trip in California.

Miss Margaret Youngclaus visited friends here.

Mrs. W.A. Godfrey is visiting her sister, Mrs. Morse Ives, in Chicago.

Mr. J.G. Davelaar spent the week at Lake Keesus.

Percy Myers spent several days in Appleton, Wis.

Miss Lou Harriman is spending the week in Buffalo and the east.

Mrs. J.W. Sercomb, of Chicago, is visiting W.B. Rice on Second Ave.

Sterling Wood is in North Dakota on business for the Milwaukee Road.

Mr. H.W. Glasier was in Richland Center, Wis.

Mrs. L. Brockway and her father, Mr. Ryan, are visiting in Madison, Wis.

Pearl Chatfield, of Waupun, visited Mrs. A.M. Chatfield, of Greenfield Ave.

The T. C. T. club will meet with Mrs. C.S. Clark, of Wauwatosa Ave.

Miss Mary E. Hulburt left to visit friends in Madison and Evansville.

Miss Bessie Smith, of Platteville, spent time with her mother, Mrs. Ella Smith.

Miss Lou Landoldt (sic) will give a shower for Miss Rood.

Mr. H.C. Freshour, of Bridgeport, Conn., was here to visit his niece, Miss Henrietta Akin.

Mrs. Walter Beggs and her son, Charles Beggs, of Milwaukee, visited Mrs. W.B. Rice, of Second Ave.

The Woman's club will hold its annual picnic at the home of Mrs. F.A. Sabins, of Whitefish Bay.

Mrs. L.C. Tisdale entertained at her home on Kavanaugh St.

Miss Frane Sanderson is leaving to attend commencement exercises at St. Mary's school in Knoxville, Ill.

Mrs. Harold Nickerson will teach Domestic Science at the summer vacation school in Milwaukee.

Mrs. Lyman, of Eau Claire, is visiting Miss McPheeters at the home of G.C. Rogers on Blue Mound Rd.

Miss Rice and Miss Dodd will hold a show for Miss Rood.

Miss Margaret Wallace returned home after a visit with Miss Flora Menish, of W. Main St.

Miss Maude Curtis went to Beloit to visit Miss Gertrude Simmons at Emerson Hall (I believe this is a college residence).

Misses Gertrude Rosenthal and Florence Ringrose gave a lawn party at Florence's home on Fifth Ave.

Miss Maude Barnes returned from school at Westby, Wis. to spend the summer with her aunt, Mrs. Wilkinson on Chestnut St.

Mr. L.G. Wheeler is doing as well as can be expected from a fever that he is thought to have contracted on his recent trip to Arkansas.

The W. H. S. Junior class gave a party at the Edward Pares's home on Third Ave.

Messrs. F.W. Schneck and G.W. Barrett were chosen as lay delegates to the annual Methodist conference.

H.W. Bardenwerper, P.W. Longfellow, and D.W. Hulburt, of Wauwatosa, will address the Milwaukee Baptist association in Kenosha.

An appeal of the Hercules Powder Co. will be heard by Justice Matthias.

Mr. Beggs has cut off commission tickets. L.C. Wheeler writes letter regarding this matter.

The Wauwatosa Minute Men elected Fred Ericsson as a new member at their meeting. Lieut. Dreher was placed in charge of the artillery squad.

President John I. Beggs, of the Milwaukee Electric Railway & Light Co., made a statement for the Milwaukee Sentinel explaining his position on the franchise and commutation question.

J.O. Myers says he did not authorize the use of his name to call a special meeting of the Advancement Club.

Louis Button will lead the B. Y. P. U. at the Baptist church.

**Letters uncalled for at the post office.**

Miss Mabel Hotchkiss, E.J. Loew, Julia Lyons, John Kluth, David Lyons, and Christina Trausfeldt

**Common Council**

Attendants: Mayor Hoyt, Alderman Breed, Baumbach, Gunn, Jones, Menninger, Kennedy, Hamme and Lefeber.

The mayor presented the name of Fred Prudisch, Jr. to replace F.E. Woller who resigned as school commissioner from the Fourth ward. He was confirmed.

**Marriage**

Miss Anna May Allen, daughter of Mr. and Mrs. James Allen, married William L. Cox, of Milwaukee, June 3, 1903, at the home of her parents on N. Main St. Elder Edwin Hyde, of Milwaukee, assisted by Rev. C.E. Goldthorpe, officiated. The maid of honor was Miss Elsie Hempsing, the best man was Frank Cox, brother of the groom, Miss Hinn played the wedding march. Misses Mildred Brockway, Mable Lefeber, and Florence Lefeber assisted at the luncheon. The couple will honeymoon in the Wisconsin Dells and will be home to their friends on Fortieth St., July 1.

**Death**

Dr. Fiske Holbrook Day died in Lansing, Mich. on May 30, 1903. Dr. Day was a pioneer physician and resident of Wauwatosa. In 1892 he retired after 40 years as a practicing physcian and moved to Lansing.

Dr. Day was born in Richmond, NY, March 11, 1826. He graduated from Jefferson Medical college in Philadelphia in 1849, and located in Wauwatosa in 1851. Mrs. Day died in 1889. The doctor is survived by four daughters, Mrs. B.F. Davis, of Lansing,

Mich., Mrs. W.L. Culver, of Oakland, Cal., Mrs. John J. Bush, of Lansing, and Mrs. J.L. Buckbee, of Rockford, Ill.

The funeral services were conducted by Rev. F.S. Gray, of the Episcopal Church, with interment at Wauwatosa Cemetery. Mrs. Davis, Mrs. Bush and Mrs. Buckbee, with their husbands, were present.

**Ads**

The Adam Forepaugh and Sells Brothers circus will appear in Milwaukee.

J.R. Johnson, of Wells farm on Watertown Plank Rd., has seed potatos.

Fishing Tackle and Target Rifles are in stock at H.P. Hemsing Co.

J.L. Morton, of Wauwatosa Ave., has carpeting and a refrigerator for sale.

W.E. Fisher has seed corn for sale at Meadow Brook Farm.

L.R. Gridley has a house for sale on Motor Ave. also a 12 room furnished house for rent for the summer season.

### July 4, 1903

Miss Elsie Moore is visiting in Lowell, Wis.

Miss Lill von Baumbach is home from Boston.

Mr. and Mrs. C.T. Everett are visiting in Chicago.

Mrs. E.M. Guile and daughter went to Powers, Mich.

Miss Alice Smith is visiting friends in West Allis.

Mr. and Mrs. John P. Gregg were here this week.

Mr. and Mrs. P.C. Clansen were in Okauchee.

Mr. H.W. Glasier is going to Cleveland, O on business.

Miss Isabel Everett is visiting relatives in Chicago.

Rev. and Mrs. Thain and daughter were in Oak Park, Ill.

Ned Hayes and Burley Allen were in Edgerton, Wis., camping.

Mr. and Mrs. Chas. Dalke are visiting friends in Chicago.

Mrs. W.A. Hart is visiting her daughter, Mrs. S.D. Hoyt in Fond du Lac

Mr. and Mrs. G.E. Smith will have a picnic for friends on their lawn.

Ralph Ellis, a senior at Madison, will spend his vacation out east and is presently in Buffalo..

The F.W. Schneckaal family are at their summer home on Lake Okauchee, Wis.

Misses Loleta Landolt and Madeline Haney are in Chicago.

Mr. E.C. Cornelius and family will spend the summer in Monroe, Wis.

Matt. Ehrlicher, of Memphis, Tenn., formerly of Wauwatosa, is here visiting friends.

Miss Lolita Goodhue, of Whitewater is the guest of Miss Hazel Harriman.

Mr. and Mrs. D.B. Lewis, of Indianapolis, are visiting Mrs. S.S. Lewis

Mr. and Mrs. Chas. Earls, of Chicago, are visiting Mr. and Mrs. F. Picker.

Mr. J.L. Morton and son, Fred Morton, are going to visit relatives in Masschusetts.

Mr. and Mrs. W.R. Cundall left for a trip in the east.

Mrs. J.H. Tuttle, of Decatur, Mich., will spend the summer with her daughter, Mrs. A. Landolt.

A.C. Hanson is convalescing at his parent's home at Pine Lake.

Dr. and Mrs. Moses White and son, Reg. White, are taking a trip to the Pacific coast.

Miss Mary Myers left on a trip to Denver, Colo.

Mrs. J.E. Phillips, of Western Ave., entertained for Mrs. H.L. Pelton, of Milwaukee.

The Country Cousins Club will picnic at the former homestead of G.H. Rogers, on North Ave.

Mr. A. Thierfeldt and family, of Milwaukee, are visiting F.H. Bark, of Garfield Ave.

Miss Frances Wagner is almost recovered under the care of the specialist Dr. H. Nolte, of Milwaukee.

Rev. C.H. Holden, of Chicago, former pastor of the Baptist church here, and family visited C.S. Clark.

Mrs. J.L. Hooley and daughter, Edna Hooley, will spend a month in New York and Boston.

Prof. and Mrs. Merica will spend the sumner with relatives in Garrett, Ind.

Misses Lou Moersch and Rosa Moersch, of Blue Mound Rd., are visiting friends in Milwaukee.

Miss Annetta Moersch, of Blue Mound Rd., went to Plymouth, Wis. to spend the fourth with her friend, Miss Adler,

Mr. and Mrs. P.G. Lewis, of Milwaukee, are visiting the Wm. Menninger home on Garfield Ave.

Mrs. Dr. Cairncross returned home from a visit to friends in Janesville.

Miss Nellie Englehart and Miss Agnes Brown entertained their Sunday school class.

Mr. and Mrs. A.L. Carlton will spend the summer with their daughter, Mrs. Mae Wasmansdorf, in Lewiston, Montana

Mr. J. Bryan will work for Paul Browne Railway Land Agency in Rhinelander, Wis.

Mrs. Jos. Lefeber and daughters will spend some time at Oak Dale, the summer home of F.W. Schneck in Okauchee.

Mr. H.O. Stone and bride, who were in Minneapolis, will be at the John Cushing home next week.

Miss Eliza Johnson is home for the summer from her teaching job in northern Wisconsin.

Mr. Abe Lefeber left for West Concord, Minn. to attend the funeral of Mr. R. Shepard, Mrs. Lefeber's father, who died July 1, 1903.

The H.P. Hemsing Co. have installed a machine to put tires on vehicles.

Mrs. Clinton Carter, assisted by Mrs. E.H. Clinton, and Mrs. Robert Sandford Perkins, of St. Louis, held a reception at her home in Graystone Park.

Mr. and Mrs. Jacob Johnson held the monthly missionary meeting of the Baptist church at their home.

Mrs. Clara Mittelstaedt and her daughter, Adeline Mittelstaedt, of Seaforth, Minn., are visiting her father, Rev. A.F. Siegler, along with Rev. R. Siegler, of La Crosse.

Miss Anabel Farries has gone to Janesville for a friend's wedding and to visit her sister, Mrs. R.M. Vaughan.

Misses Sadie Phillips and Winnie Phillips are going to visit their brother, Alvin Phillips in Ontonagon, Mich.

Some high schools girls will spend a week at Lake Keesis, near Merton. Among them will be: Calla Canright, Isabel Blodgett, Lida Mower, Florence Moore, Ethel Fisher, Fay Rogers, Gertrude Engelhart, Margaret Durbin, Jesse Waldie, Helen Kinney, and Faith Longfellow, with Mrs. J.B. Russell as chaperon.

A "Barn Dance" was given in Mr. Haney's new barn, the chaperones were: Mr. and Mrs. H.O. Wood, Mr. and Mrs. F.M. Keats, Mr. and Mrs. C.A. Haney, Mr. and Mrs. C.A. Crain, and Mrs. W.H. Landolt. Among those present were: Beth? Godfrey, Jane Keats, Gertrude Crain, Madeline Haney, Loleta Landolt, Hazel Harriman, Florence Bryne, Louise Landolt, Florence Adams, Edith Hooker, Blanche Landolt, Maud Knox, Lou Harriman, Walter Wood, Ray Greenwood, Frank Harriman, George Kershaw, Sterling Wood, Wm. Sanderson, Allister Currie, Geo. Adams, Geo. Rogers, Wm. Reuiie?, Tom Norton, and Jay Grosskopf.

Dr. H.F. McBeath, of Milwaukee, will be here to do dental work.

Mr. H.A. Propp, Margaret A. Propp, Edgar Bigsby, and Kate Bigsby were appointed letter carriers.

County Superintendent, Jesse F. Cory, Prof. W.H. Cheever, Prof. T.J. Jones, and Elnora C. Folkmar will conduct the Milwaukee County Teachers Institute.

# July 11, 1903

Wm. Davelaar and family are at Lake Keesus.

Jas. Lefeber is visiting friends at Pine River, Wis.

Miss Annette Dreutzer is visiting her sister, Mrs. Atwood, in Oak Park, Ill.

Mrs. C.G. Porter and son, Arthur Porter, are in Sun Prairie, Wis. visiting.

Miss Jane Keats went to Grand Rapids, Mich.

Will Maxon, of Cedar Lake, Wis., visited friends here.

Mr. C.G. Dreutzer and family will spend the summer in Sturgeon Bay.

Mr. and Mrs. E.B. Blake, of Chicago, spent Sunday with Mr. A. Landolt and family.

Mrs. W.A. Donahue, of Clinton Junction, is visiting relatives and friends.

Mr. W.G. Cutler, of Chicago, is visiting his son, Dr. J.S. Cutler, here.

Mr. and Mrs. C.C. Jacobus and children are at Beaver Lake.

Mesdames G.W. Sanford and W.B. Rice entertained at tea.

George Schroeder is at Sturgeon Bay for a couple months.

Misses Ruby Gilbert and Fannie Gilbert left for their home at Gilbert Station, Iowa.

Mr. and Mrs. Fred Orvis and son, of Ottumwa, Iowa, are visiting D.J. Hayes on Chestnut St.

John Potter is home from U.W. to stay with his parents for the summer.

Mrs. S.D. Johnson and daughter, Miss Edith Johnson, are spending time with Miss C.A. Warren.

Mrs. L. Rhodes was surprised by friends on her birthday, July 7.

Mrs. W.H. Landolt and daughter are visiting in Mich., Mr. Landolt went as far as Grand Haven with them.

Mrs. Arba M. Rice, her daughter, and Miss Alma Molltar, of Fond du Lac, are guests of Mrs. A. Rice, of W. Main St.

Mrs. Liebig and children, of Chicago, are visiting her parents, Mr. and Mrs. C.F. Bussewitz, of Greenfield Ave.

Rev. O.A. Williams, of Minneapolis, was at the Baptist parsonage.

Mrs. H.A. Sabin, of Whitefish Bay, Mrs. Henry Stiltz, of St. Louis, Mrs. F.C. Millard, and Miss Mary Sabine, of Milwaukee, were guests of Miss Carrie Warren.

Mr. and Mrs. O.E. Wilson entertained informally on the fourth.

Rev. C.T. Everett came home from Grand Rapids for a Baptist church meeting.

Miss Catherine Wheeler will entertain friends at the home of her parents Mr. and Mrs. L.C. Wheeler.

Mr. and Mrs. James Godfrey, of Calumet, Mich., are at the home of Mrs. Godfrey's parents, Mr. and Mrs. E.R. Godfrey.

Mrs. Max Rosenthal and daughters, Misses Gertrude Rosenthal and Cora Rosenthal, along with Miss Esther Blaesser, are visiting friends in Sheboygan and Manitowoc.

Miss Ruth Ellis assisted by Misses Florence Everett and Mary Hulbert, entertained at the home of her sister, Mrs. Putnam.

Little Lottie Austin, daughter of Mr. and Mrs. A.S. Austin, broke her leg at their farm in Sussex.

The Woman's Missionary Society of the M. E. church met at the home of Mrs. Olds on Church St.

Mr. Austin D. Crane, of Brookins, SD, called on Mr. Warren, superintendent of the sewer plant, to conduct an inspection.

**Marriage**

Mr. and Mrs. Frank M. Barnekow announced the engagement of their daughter, Alice Barnekow, to Fred Meahl, of Saginaw, Mich., the wedding will be July 18 at the home of the bride's parents.

**Death**

Mr. R.M. Brown died July 11, 1903, after an illnes of a year or more. He was 63 years of age and leaves a wife, friends and aquaintances.

Edward Marggraff, son of the late Mr. and Mrs. Herman Margraff, died at the age of eighteen, of a lingering illness, at the home of his aunt, Mrs. John Hamme, of Garfield Ave. The funeral was held at St. John's church with interment at Wauwatosa Cemetery, Rev. Rader officiated.

Mrs. Hannah P. Faries, wife of the late Dr. R.J. Faries, formerly of this city, died July 4, 1903 at Vandalia, Mich. at the age of 88 years. She was a Wauwatosa pioneer in 1855 and lived here until 1878. Dr. Faries had a dental office with the late Dr. Minor in Milwaukee. Mrs. Faries was born at East Hamburg, now a subburb of Buffalo, NY. She leaves one son, Royal P. Faries, of Wichita, Kas., and a daughter, Mrs. G.E. Rowe, of New York City, Frederick Heath, of Milwaukee, is a grandson. The interment was at Vandalia.

### July 18, 1903

Miss Bessie Horning is visiting in Illinois.

Miss Lucille Stout is visiting in Okauchee, Wis.

Miss Janet Smith is visiting in Chicago

Mrs. F.E. Hancock is visiting relatives in Chicago.

Walter L. Koenig left for a trip around the lakes.

Rev. S.T. Everett and family are in Grand Rapids, Wis.

Mr. L.B. Gregg went to Detroit on business.

Miss Margaret Hart has returned from Waukesha.

Miss A.E. Chamberlain went to Milwaukee for the summer.

Miss Armstrong, of Chicago, is visiting Miss Helen Kinney.

Miss Madeline Haney has returned from a Chicago visit.

Mrs. L.W. Hawley and daughter, Alberta Hawley, are visiting in Oshkosh, Wis.

Miss Beth Godfrey returned from Chicago.

Allen Williams and daughter went out east.

Misses Daisy Everett and Florence Everett are visiting in Sheboygan Falls

Miss Nellie Waldo, of Green Bay, visited Miss Margaret Mower.

Mrs. W.A. Hart returned from visiting her daughter in Fond du Lac.

Mr. and Mrs. S.D. Hoyt, of Fond du Lac, visited relatives here.

Mrs. I.M. Ames will spend time with friends in Hudson, Mich.

Mr. and Mrs. Harry Fuchs, of Chicago, are visiting Wm. Menninger, of Garfield Ave.

Mr. J.L. Morton and son, Fred Morton, have gone out east.

Miss Bea Rosenthal, of Milwaukee, is visiting Miss Sara Chatfield, of Greenfield Ave.

Mr. and Mrs. Edward M. McConnell, of Chicago, are visiting Mr. and Mrs. C.W. Damon.

Mrs. J.H. Muenster, of Port Washington, Wis., and Miss Adele Blake, of Ravenswood, Ill., visited Miss Louise Landolt.

Paul Warren went to Blackwell, Okla to work for Denver, Eold? & Gulf Railway Co.

Mrs. Henry Watner is visiting her sister, Mrs. Chauncy Goodrich, in Oberlin, Ohio before Mr. and Mrs. Goodrich return to their missionary work in China.

Misses Selma Higgins and Gertrude Higgins, of Chicago, are visiting E.M. Bussewitz, of Greenfield Ave. along with Mrs. Bussewitz's sister, Mrs. R.N. Allen, also of Chicago.

Stanton Taylor, of Winona, Minn., was here visiting relatives, his father, C. Taylor, went with him to spend some time at his son's home.

Mr. L.G. Wheeler is recovering from typhoid fever.

Rev. R.S. Walker, former pastor of the Baptist church here, now of Keokuk, Iowa, is taking treatment from a prominent Milwaukee Physician.

Misses Mildred Brockway, Mabel Lefeber, Lucile Stout, Elsie Hemsing, Lorena Chatfield, and Belle Gregg, of this city, and Miss Bartlet, of Pewaukee, are at Okauchee Lake

Adolph Lentz, of State St., has finished a summer home on Pewaukee Lake, where Miss Ida Lentz entertained Misses Lou Leutzow, Celia Lange, Ilma Winding, Emma Zunker, Bessie Foattler, Irma Boeder, Della Smith, Paula Reimer, Messrs. Oscar Lange, Walter Weifenback, Matt Sommers, John Toohey, John Deegaff, John Farchman, Henry Meyer, Charles Fisener, Fred Lentz, and Frank Lentz

Revs. O.P. Bestor and James Blake will preach at the Baptist church.

Wm. Baier will erect a building on a lot on State St. purchased from G.W. Sanford

An addition is being added to his building by Mr. Prentice for his growing business.

**Death**

Rudolph M. Brown died at his home on E. Milwaukee Ave. July 11, 1903. He was born in Elm Grove in 1839, he was the son of Silas Brown and Elizabeth Brown and moved to Wauwatosa about 1840 where he worked with his father on the home farm. He was village trustee in 1892 and 1893 and served as supervisor and member of the county board in 1897. He married Elizabeth Delpsch, of this city in 1894 after the death of his mother. His widow, two sisters, Mrs. Cyrds Pederick, of Wauwatosa and Mrs. John Warren, of Cumberland Mills, ME, and two brothers, Charles L. Brown, of Milwaukee, and Nathan A. Brown, of Cumberland Mills, ME, survive him. Rev. Horatio Gates officiated at the funeral with interment at Wauwatosa Cemetery.

**Letters uncalled for at the post office**

W. Eppenberger, Margaret Hines, Margaret Goodwin, Dr. J.V. Way, and George Witte

**Probate notices**

Lucy R. Underwood, deceased, late of the city of Wauwatosa, administration granted to Leverett C. Wheeler. Paul D. Carpenter, County Judge

Johann F. Schell, deceased, late of Wauwatosa, application for testamentary by his son, Wilhelm Schell, of Wauwatosa. Paul D. Carpenter, Co. Judge

## July 25, 1903

**Advertisements**

I am adding some of the large advertisements so you can see the types of businesses the people found in this book were involved in.

Robert Cain, painter and paper hanger, 62 Vine St., Wauwatosa, Wis.

"The Cash Meat Market", first door east of P. O.

Nettleton's "The Grocer" Greenwood Block, N. Main St.

W.B. Morse, dealer in flour, feed, grain, hay, straw and shavings, wood, coal, coke, 28 W. Main St., next to Electric plant

"The Chas. Leutzow Market" offers a choice line of best meats

"Dearsley Bros.", practical plumbers and gas fitters, 433 Milwaukee St., Milwaukee

"Schwaiger Pharmacy" next to bridge, Wauwatosa

"Lefeber Brothers Co." All American brand shoes

"Hirsh - Silverstone Co.", popular price tailors, 387 Water St., Milwaukee

"Wauwatosa Sash & Door Factory", Adolph Lentz, Proprietor, cor. State and Sixth Ave, Wauwatosa

G. Steinhagen, civil engineer and surveyor, room 19, Metropolitan Bldg., Milwaukee, Wis.

Dr. E.B. Fuller, dentist, cor. Wells and W. Water St., Milwaukee

"J.B. Judson & Co.", undertakers and funeral directors, State St.
opposite Depot, Wauwatosa

L.R. Gridley, Insurance, Real Estate, Renting

C.F. Eckstein, carpenter & builder, cor. ? and Chestnut Sts.,
Wauwatosa

A. John Wagner's, shoemaker and repair, Church St. in Schwaiger
Bldg.

Jno.M. Dunlop, florist, cor. Church St. and W. Milwaukee Ave.,
Wauwatosa

A.C. Kuchynski, harness, lap robes, horse blankets, Pabst Bldg.,
State St.

"Henry P. Hemsing Co.", general repairing and tool sharpening,
electrical supplies, etc., 207 N. Main St., Wauwatosa


Miss Nettie Smith is back from Chicago.

Miss Marjorie Hart is in Fond du Lac on a visit.

Mr. E.M. Lewis is in Racine, Wis.

Miss Pearl Evans, of Stoughton, Wis., is visiting Mrs. J.S. Allen.

Miss Evelyn Gilbert is back from Chicago.

Elbert Blodgett and family moved to West Allis, Wis.

Miss Gretchen Stout?, of Stevens Point, Wis., is visiting Miss
Mable Lewis.

Miss Rosie Bryan is in Williams Bay, Walworth Co., Wis. with the
William Netherent family.

Mrs. Elizabeth Clansen, Third Ave., has returned from
Delafield, Wis.

Mr. and Mrs. F.M. Keats will take a trip to Yellow Stone Park.

Walter Kaltenborn, of Merrill, Wis., is visiting the Wm.
von Baumbach home.

Roy Lillibridge has returned from his trip out east.

Mrs. Edward Coulthard is visiting friends in Kenosha and Somers, Wis.

Mrs. M.S. Hayden, of East Hartford, Conn., is visiting her sister, Miss Carrie Warren,

Miss Viola Poeck, of Milwaukee, is visiting her cousin, Miss Norma Phillips.

Rev. C.E. Goldthorp is vacationing with friends in Minnesota.

Mr. and Mrs. C.E. Curtis are taking a trip to Niagara Falls.

Mrs. Arthur Koenig and son Walter Koenig are at Mt. Clemens, Mich.

Mr. and Mrs. Walter Dearsley, of Milwaukee, are visiting the E. Coulthard home.

Hugo Schubel, of Chicago, is visiting his sister, Mrs. D. Phillip, Seventh Ave.

Mr. F.H. Bark and son, Edgar Bark, were in Chicago for a furniture exposition.

Mrs. Dr. Green and Miss Gussie Sewell, of Detroit, Mich., have been spending time with Captain and Mrs. A.P. Foster.

Mrs. F.A. Butterworth and son, Ned Butterworth, and daughter, Bessie Butterworth, have returned to their home on Wauwatosa Ave.

Mr. and Mrs. L. Brockway are going to Ft. Atkinson, Wis. to visit Mr. Brockway's sister.

Mr. and Mrs. J.O. Myers, Mrs. S.S. Lewis, her daughter, Mabel Lewis, Mr. and Mrs. C.G. Wade and Mrs. J.L. Morton are going to Lake Geneva.

Dr. Richard Dewey will build a house on Garfield Ave.

Mrs. H. Theo. Hanson, Greenfield Ave., entertained for Mrs. Helen Bates, of Albany, NY.

Mrs. Thomas De Swarte gave a party for her five year old son, Lawrence De Swarte, July 24, 1903

Mrs. W.A. Godfrey gave a luncheon, guests: Miss Smith and Miss

Hinckley, of Kansas City, MO, Mrs. R.C. Witte, of Milwaukee, Mrs. N.L. Kneeland, and Miss. Kneeland, of this city.

Mrs. Henry Watner, the misses Grace Goodrich, Elinor Swann, Grace Watner, Mr. and Mrs. C.S. Clark and children, of this city, and Mrs. O. Rogers, of Milwaukee, went to Oak Dale on Okauchee Lake.

Harry Fucus, a Lieutenant of the Chicago Fire Dept., who has been visiting Wm. Menninger, was the guest of honor at the Firemen's monthly meeting.

E.M. Darling, Cor. Sec. of W.C.T.C., Good Templars announced a picnic.

Deputy Sheriff Fred Schultz was notified of the serious illness of his brother, Sergeant Louis Schultz, from cancer, he is in the hospital at the Washington Barracks, D.C. Louis was in Troup C, Sixth Calvary and has been in the US Army for nineteen and one half years.

The sheriff of Milwaukee County, Wis., Fred Trotmeyer, will hold a sale of property for the amount due plaintiff, Carrie A. Kneeland. The defendant was the Young Men's Christian Association of Wauwatosa, attorneys for the plaintiff, Wheeler & Perry.

**Death**

Ella Bostwick, ten year old and eldest daughter of Mr. and Mrs. H.E. Bostwick, died July 18, 1903. The funeral was at their home on W. Main and Greenfield Ave. with interment at Wauwatosa Cemetery. Rev. F.S. Gray officiated.

## August 1, 1903

Miss Mary Thompson is the guest of Miss Thain.

Miss Mary Myers was at Lake Geneva.

Miss Blanche Landolt is visiting in West Bend, Wis.

Mr. T.E. Chatfield returned from his Waupaca trip.

Mrs. Geo. Prest, Sixth Ave., is visiting in Pontiac, Mich.

Mrs. H.M. Brown, of Chicago, is visiting Mrs. William Gauger.

Mr. and Mrs. Jefferson Gregg are in Madison, Wis.

Mr. T.E. Zimmerman was in Edmund, Wis. on business.

Miss Loleta Landolt is going to Cedar Lake.

Mrs. W.H. Landolt and daughter, returned from South Bend.

Miss Susie Minnehan or Gusie Minnehan is visiting her sister, Mrs. C.C. Jacobus, on Wisconsin St.

Mrs. S.S. Lewis, and daughter, Mabel Lewis, and Mrs. J.L. Morton are at Lake Geneva.

Miss Bessie Phillips returned from a Milton Junction, Wis. visit.

Miss Flora Garvens, of Waukesha, is visiting her brother, Ed. Garvens, W. Main St.

Misses Mamie Taylor and Rosa Reichardt were visiting relatives in Chicago.

Miss Harriet E. Moan returned from a Pine River, Wis. visit.

Mrs. H.W. Zimmerman has returned after three years in Hamburg, Germany.

Mr. V.V. Vining's mother is seriously ill in Pomeroy, Ohio.

Mrs. L.C. Wheeler gave a birthday party for her son, Laurence Wheeler, who was seven on July 30, 1903.

Rev. P.W. Longfellow, of the Baptist church will preach at the Soldier's Home.

William Wodertz, of Chicago, called on Wm. Menninger.

Cussius Sercomb and family were visiting his cousins, Mrs. W.B. Rice and Mrs. G.W. Sanford.

Mr. and Mrs. J.P. Thompson, of Ft. Atkinson, are visiting his sister, Mrs. Chauncy Morris on W. Main St.

Mr. and Mrs. Geo. Ambrose and grand daughter, of Oak Park, Ill., were guests of Mrs. H.E. Mower.

Mr. Geo. M. Ambrose, editor and publisher of the Oak Park Argus, paid a call at the News office.

Mr. and Mrs. Thos. De Swarte and children were in Plymouth, Wis. to visit Mr. and Mrs. Huson.

Mr. and Mrs. Andrew Portz and daughter Irma Portz, of Hartford, Wis., were guests of D.F. Philipp on Seventh Ave.

Mr. A. Harden sold his home on Second Ave. to Alfred Smith and family, of West Allis.

Mr. and Mrs. Fayette Stevens and daughter, of Glen Park, Ill., are visiting C.W. Damon.

Clarence Loomis almost drowned in the mill pond, but Martha Wenzel gave the alarm and two men came to the rescue.

Misses Ella Henke and Lizzie Henke and guest, Miss Gertrude Johnson, of Madison, and Miss Anna Larson are going on a visit to Chicago.

Martin Henke, of Vista Ave., was given a surprise party, July 25, for his 15th birthday.

Mr. W.A. Godfrey and family are going to Lewiston, Mich. to visit Mrs. Godfrey's brothers, the Messrs. Kneeland.

Mr. and Mrs. Chauncy Morris and daughter will visit relatives and friends at Stoughton, Deerfield, and Ft. Atkinson, Wis.

Mr. L.B. Gregg has been in Elyria, Ohio because of the serious illness and death of his mother, Adeline Gregg, which occured July 27, 1903.

Mr. H.W. Glasier will be moving his family to Glendale, a suburb of Cleveland, Ohio.

Rev. Cook, of All Saints Cathedral, will conduct services at Trinity church while Rev. Gray is on vacation.

Rev. A.F. Siegler, pastor of Friedens Lutheran church, will visit relatives in West Salem, Wis.

The Common Council meeting was attended by President von Baumbach, Mayor Hoyt, and Mr. L.S. Pease.

Town Board meeting was attended by Chairman Fred Harturng, Aug. M. Siegfried, and M.H. Adams. Catherine Goldsmith made application for a saloon license for the corner of Blue Mound and Barnekow Rd. There being some opposition, the matter was held over. John M. Regan resigned as town clerk, Geo. P. Dousman was appointed to replace him, H.P. Bradley to assist him. Mr. Dousman was also appointed health officer.

Rev. E.S. Ingreham, of Simpson M. E. church, Milwaukee, will be at the Wauwatosa M. E. church..

Judson Hulburt will lead the B. Y. P. U. at the Baptist church.

## Marriage

Mrs. J.E. Pierce gave a party in honor of her guest, Miss Quintal, of New York City, and Miss Alice Sanderson, of Milwaukee, who is to be married next week.

## Death

E. Payson Johnson, dropped dead at the Meinecke Toy Co., Milwaukee, July 30, 1903, from heart failure. He was the son of the late Mr. and Mrs. W.W. Johnson, of Greenfield, he was aged 55 and resided at 957 Beecher St, Milwaukee, where he had a grocery business. He is survived by a widow and four children. Services were at Simpson M. E. church, Milwaukee.

Franz Schleantek's body was recovered from the Monarch stone quarry where he committed suicide, Saturday, July 25, 1903, by jumping into the pond. Burial was at Calvary cemetery.

Jens Soe, a farmer from Audubon, Iowa, who was taking treatment at the sanitarium, died July 29, 1903, from an overdose of morphine taken to induce sleep. He was 47 years old and leaves a wife and three children. His brother, Dr. Soe, of Elkhorn, Iowa came to take charge of the body.

Mrs. I.C. Lillibridge is back from Ollvet, Mich., where she attended the funeral of her father, Luman Sheppard, who died in Iowa last week.

## Letters uncalled for at the postoffice

Nina Burdish, Mrs. Olle Clarus, Wm. De Swart, Mrs. M. Hotchkiss, Margerite Pegler, Mrs. Wm. L. Cox, Miss Dexter,

Miss D.H. Hays, Louise Neubauer, John P. Scholler, and Wm. Stafford

**Probate Notices**

Edward Margraff, of Wauwatosa, deceased about July 7, 1903, William Margraff petitioned to have Christoph Richert, of Wauwatosa appointed administrator. Richard J. Hennessey, 1st Assistant Register of Probate

Mary Ann Turner, of Wauwatosa, deceased, letters testamentary granted to Charlotta A. Turner and Hannah A. Little by the court. Paul D. Carpenter, County Judge

## August 8, 1903

Mrs. C.E. Roberts is visiting in Clinton, Wis.

Mrs. A.J. Wood is visiting her son in Janesville

Miss Marga Hart has returned from Fond du Lac, Wis..

Miss Frances Wilcox is vacationing in Cadillac, Mich.

Dr. W.C. Wendel and family went to Devils Lake.

W. Broker and family, W. Main St., moved to Milwaukee.

Miss Meta Kroesing is visiting her sister, Mrs. Greengo, in Chilton, Wis.

Rev. F.S. Gray is visiting friends in the state.

E.M. Lewis returned to work at the postoffice after his vacation.

Mr. A.H. Owens was in Port Washington on business.

Mrs. J.A. Fisher, of Kilbourn City, is visiting her son, E.E. Fisher.

Joseph Lefeber and his family were at Okauchee.

Miss Ida Leegson, of Milwaukee, is visiting the C.W. Damon home.

Mrs. I.B. Smith is visiting her daughter, Mrs. S. Breese, in Waukesha.

Mr. and Mrs. Chas. Brussatt were at the A.G. Becker home on Third Ave.

Misses Jessie Waldie and Florance Waldie have returned from Chicago.

Mrs. Claude E. Canright and son Eldon Canright have returned from Chicago and Oak Park.

Harry L. Doble and Arthur Brown, of Chicago, visited the W.H. Landolt family.

Myron Fowler, of Chicago, visited his parents, Mr. and Mrs. G.H. Fowler, Third Ave.

Miss Flora Menish and Milwaukee friends went to Beaver Lake.

Mr. and Mrs. F.G. Moritz, Greenfield Ave., returned from Cedar Lake.

Arthur Banky is visiting his parents in Columbus, Wis.

Misses Calla Canright and Blanche Canright are spending the summer with their grandparents in Battle Creek, Mich.

Mr. and Mrs. Jefferson Gregg leave for Madison, Wis. where they will again take up residence.

Albert Leutzow, who works at his father's meat market here, plans to open a market in West Allis.

Mrs. Elizabeth Helgesen, of Eagle, Wis., will spend the summer with her son, Oscar Helgesen, on St. Charles St.

Mrs. M.J. De Graff, her son and daughter, of Omaha, are visiting relatives, the A.F. Kellogg and M.B. Potter families.

G.P. Dousman, town clerk, has been cleaning and having the town hall painted.

Capt. A.P. Foster was injured severely when he slipped and fell.

Mrs. Chas. Fingado is having work done on one of her dwellings on Garfield Ave. by Contractor Yehle.

Mr. and Mrs. A.R. Gridley and Miss Grundy, of Janesville, Wis., visited Mr. Gridley's parents on Greenfield Ave.

Mr. F.W. McRavey, W. Main St., went to Summit Lake, Wis. for his health.

Mr. and Mrs. H.L. Moore left to attend a meeting of the Good Templars at Camp Cleghorn.

Mrs. H.P. Bradley and daughters, Edith Bradley and Helen Bradley, went to Chicago to visit relatives. Mr. Jere. Blodgett accompanied them.

Mr. Stickney and others are putting down cement near the library.

Rev. and Mrs. P.W. Longfellow are going to Granville, Ohio where Rev. Longfellow will preach at Denison Univ..

Dr. and Mrs. White and Reginald White leave on the "Northland" for a tour.

The school district voted to purchase a site from the A.M. Dickson estate for a new school house.

Mr. H.P. Bradley who purchased the Marggraff acreage recently has been offered an interesting price.

**Marriages**

Miss Martha Hamme married Charles Heideman and Miss Lydia Hamme married William Zimmer in a double wedding in Waukesha at the German Reform Methodist church. A reception was held at the home of the brides' parents, Mr. and Mrs. John Hamme, on Highland Park Ave., Waukesha. Guests included Ald. Hamme, brother of the brides, and Mrs. John L. Hamme, of Wauwatosa. The couples will live in Waukesha.


Mr. and Mrs. Harry Schafer, of Chicago, are spending a part of their honeymoon with Mr. and Mrs. Wm. Menninger.

**Probate Notices**

Louisa Kossow, dec'd, Christoph Rickert, executor, petitions court to examine his accounting and assign the residue of said estate. Richard J. Hennessey, Assist. Reg. of Probate

Joseph A. Warren, deceased, application for testamentary by Carrie G. Warren. John C. Karel, Reg. of Probate

### August 15, 1903

Mr. L.G. Wheeler was in Chicago.

Mrs. Agnes Roddis is visiting friends in Detroit, Mich.

Mr. Mart Taylor has gone fishing.

Mrs. H.O. Wood and family are at Cedar Lake.

Miss Madeline Haney is at Cedar Lake.

Assistant Postmaster Lewis is laid up with neuralgia.

Miss Daisy Wilder, of Elyria, Ohio, is visiting L.B. Gregg.

Frank Peake is visiting H.B. Hunter at Pine Lake.

Miss Hilda Rosenthal is spending time in Waukesha.

Mr. and Mrs. Chas. R. Davis were in Sheboygan.

Miss Nettie Smith is back from visiting friends in Sparta, Wis.

Mr. and Mrs. C.V. Burnside were in Ripon, Wis.

Misses Evelyn Gilbert and Mabel Gilbert were in Evanston, Ill.

Mrs. P.C. Clausen and Winifred Clausen are in Hartland, Wis.

Mr. H.P. Morse is moving to Milwaukee.

Miss Eva Thain, assisted by Miss Thompson, entertained at tea.

Mayor Hoyt was in Fond du Lac visiting his son.

Miss Helen Meyers, Mrs. S.S. Lewis, and Miss Mabel Lewis are back from Lake Geneva

Miss Lucile Stout will visit her home in South Haven, Mich.

Mrs. Elizabeth Carter, mother of Mrs. Gregg, who has been ill is improving.

Mrs. S. Coulter, of Duluth, Minn., was the guest of Margaret Mower, Wauwatosa Ave.

Mr. and Mrs. Gus Gregg have returned from Ripon and Green Lake.

Mrs. J.W. Martin and daughter, Gertrude Martin, formerly of Wauwatosa, visited here.

Mrs. C.R. Wells, of Racine, is visiting Mrs. W.A. Gilbert, Western Ave.

Mr. Luening and family, Sixty-First Ave., are at Elkart Lake.

Miss Lucy Case, of Milwaukee, is visiting Mrs. H.S. Temple, Center St.

Mrs. L.M. Curtis and grand-daughter, Miss Lucy Curtis, of Chicago, are at Mrs. C.A. Curtis's home.

Misses Edith Bradley and Helen Bradley returned from Chicago.

Mr. and Mrs. Ferdinand Bark returned from a Chicago visit.

Dr. Wendel and family returned from Devil's Lake.

Mrs. Hugo Schubel and son Walter Schubel, of Chicago, are visiting D.F. Phillips, Seventh Ave.

Dwight Lewis was home from Indianapolis with a friend, Charles Stevens, of Chicago.

Miss Mary Armstrong, of Portage, will be a teacher at the high school.

Mrs. Emma Orr and daughter, Mary Orr, of Park Ridge, Ill have been visiting Mrs. Orr's sister, Miss Mary Earls.

The Methodist church Foreign Missionary Society met at Mrs. H. Schoonmaker's home.

Mrs. M.J. De Graff and daughter have returned to Omaha after visiting here.

Mrs. F.H. Bark, Garfield Ave., gave a party for her son, Edgar Bark, Aug. 13.

George Hooley and daughter, Florence Hooley, were at the J.H. Hooley home.

Mrs. John Heiden, formerly of Wauwatosa, mother of Dr. F.M. Heiden, is ill with typhoid fever at her home on Greenfield Ave., Milwaukee.

Rev. Dr. Thain is visiting in Massachusetts.

Miss Dorothy Allen, daughter of Mr. and Mrs. G.G. Allen, entertained her little friends at her birthday party, Aug. 14, Second Ave.

Mrs. Linden Morehouse and daughters Miss Morehouse, Miss Lizzie Morehouse, and Mrs. Meacham will give a reception at Mrs. Meacham's home in Milwaukee.

Misses Agnes S. Allen, of Boston, Mass., Mary B. Stewart, and

Harriet M. Dillingham, of Passadena, Cal., cousin, aunt and sister respectively, are guests of Mrs. H.P. Bradley, Chestnut St.

Cement sidewalks are being laid at residence of F.E. Loveland and E.R. Godfrey, Sr.

J.L. Morton, Jas. Lefeber, G.A. Kurtz, O. Helgesen, Wm. Menninger, and J.D. Warren went to Wind Lake fishing.

Fred Digman, son of Hubert Digman, Vine St., had his hand caught in a machine at Geuder & Paeschke Tin Works and will probably lose several fingers.

Rev. D.W. Hulburt will represent Wauwatosa at the Baptist convention.

C.E. Armin, of Waukesha, Hon. W.H. Stafford, of Milwaukee, and Head banker A.N. Bort, of Beloit will deliver addresses at the annual outing of the Woodmen of Waukesha Co.

**Marriage**

Henry Watner, his family and relatives from Wauwatosa and Milwaukee, will attend the wedding of Roy Rherman Watner to Miss Ottilie Louise Graunke, at Watertown, Wis. They will live in a home on Thirty-Fifth St. in Milwaukee.

**Death**

Mr. V.V. Vining has returned from attending his mother's funeral in Indiana.

**Letters uncalled for at the postoffice**

Mrs. S. Gates, Miss Caroline Kopp, Miss Isabel Reuter, Jos. Carde, C.H. Hanks, Mrs. John Moss, Mable Reynels, Minard Mastinbrook, and Mrs. H.J. Rider

I am adding the directory that appears in every paper. I am adding it once for the year.

### Wauwatosa Directory

City Officials

Mayor, Emerson D. Hoyt; Alderman: William von Baumbach, J.W. Kennedy, C.A. Breed, Jas. Lefeber, John Hamme, Wm. Menninger, D.P. Jones, C.A. Gunn; city treasurer, A.F. Kellogg;

clerk, Edward Coulthard; assessor, C.W. Damon; attorney,
Chas. B. Perry; street commissioner, J.D. Warren; Weed Commissioner, Matt. Goebel; commissioner of health, D.G. Hathaway,
M.D.; Justices of the Peace, Edward Coulthard, and W.S.
Notbohm; marshal, Frank Herriman; ward supervisors, J.B.
Thomas, John F. Dittmar, G.E. Reichardt, and John Armstrong;
board of education, W.R. Netherent, president; Dr. J.S. Cutler,
vice president; Dr. J.W. Cairncross, L.G. Wheeler, G.A. Kurtz,
Ferdinand Bark, and F.E. Woller; Edward Coulthard, secretary;
A.F. Kellogg, treasurer; water commissioners, Charles Stickney,
president; Adam Currie, Charles Luetzow, C.A. Breed, and
Emerson D. Hoyt; public library directors: A.W. Smith, president;
J.O. Myers, secretary; Mrs. C.G. Porter, Mrs. L. Brockway,
John B. De Swarte, E.R. Godfrey, Sr., F.M. Merica, and Mrs. J.L.
Foley; fire department: Chief, J.D. Warren; assist. chief, H.E.
Leister; hose company: J.B. Russel, C.C. Jacobus, Joseph Keeler,
Joseph Schwaiger, John Hamme, J.F. Dittmar, J.C. Lefeber, B.F.
Hemsing, and H.P. Hemsing; truck company: James Lefeber,
Capt.; Walter Harden, 1st lieutenant; A.I. Smith, 2nd lieutenant;
F.E. Loveland, 3rd lieutenant; F.H. Bark, Chas. Curtis, F.M.
Heiden, Wm. Menninger, G.A. Kurtz, W.H. Engelhardt, Fred
Prudish, Jr., and Ed. Garvens

## Town Officials

Town board: Frederick Hartung, chairman; August M. Siegfried,
and M.H. Adams; town clerk, John M. Regan; treasurer, Albert L.
Story; assessor, W.E. Fisher; Justices of the Peace, R.J. Mathias,
Eug. Braunschweiger, Otto Breitkrentz, and John M. Reiter

### August 22, 1903

Mrs. Geo. A. James is visiting friends in Iowa.

Miss Mabel Gilbert is in Chelsea, Wis. visiting.

Mrs. Fred Picker is visiting relatives in Dubuque, Iowa.

Carl Rix, of West Bend, is visiting friends here.

Miss Hattie Moan is visiting relatives in South Bend, Ind.

Miss I. Jones, of Racine, is visiting Miss Ella Guile.

Geo. P. Bauer and family are camping.

Miss Lill von Baumbach is in Oconomowoc, Wis.

Frank Schmidt is going to Okauchee.

Mrs. A.M. Peck, of Waukesha, is visiting Mrs. G.G. Allen.

Mr. and Mrs. W.F. Humphrey are at the Soo.

Miss Ione Wharton, of Appleton, is visiting Miss Mary Jones

Rev. Dr. and Mrs. Thain are home from the east.

Mrs. Lillibridge and sister, Mrs. Bally, are in Michigan.

Mr. and Mrs. Abe Lefeber are at Okauchee.

Mrs. F.E. Loveland and daughter, Laura Loveland, were in Chicago.

County Sup't of Schools, J.F. Cory, visited the News.

Miss E. Birkett, of London, Canada, is the guest of Miss Bessie Butterworth.

Miss Kate West, of Chicago, is visiting Mrs. Agnes Rice.

Howard Cummerford, of Manchester, Iowa, is visiting his cousin, Mrs. C.A. Curtis.

Edwin Lefeber, Abe Lefeber, Wm. Buck, and Glen Gilbert went camping at Lake Keesus.

Miss Lottie Hart will spend the winter in Pennsylvania.

Mr. and Mrs. Thomas and children, of Waukesha, are staying with C.S. Clark.

F.E. Hancock and family went to Wausau, Wis.

Mr. and Mrs. L.C. Wheeler and family are in Ludington, Mich.

Ethel M. Currie, of Merrill Park, visited Hazel Harriman.

Mrs. Brownwich, of Boston, was at Mrs. L. Rhodes this week.

Mrs. G.W. Ringrose and daughter, Mrs. Davis, are going to Pewaukee.

Mr. Wm. Bark and sister, Miss Lily Bark, are in Chicago.

J.S. Allen and family moved to Thirty-ninth St.

Mrs. T.M. Hammond and son, Loring Hammond, have been in Southern Wis.

Mr. and Mrs. Geo. E. Wells, Harry Wells and Miss Florence Wells are in Shawano, Wis.

David M. Swan is at his aunts, Mrs. P.R. Earling, in Chicago.

Miss Helen Stickney entertained friends at her home.

Mrs. E.M. Guile and daughter Ella Guile are back from Northern Wis.

Miss Myrtle Stearn, of Elkhorn, returned home from visiting Mrs. A.B. Myers.

Mr. H. Cutler and family and Miss Cutler, of Chicago, were visiting at Dr. Cutler's home.

Mrs. G.S. Armstrong, of Port Washington, was visiting her brother, Albert Landolt, here.

Miss Sophie Volz, Greenfield Ave., entertained at coffee.

Mr. and Mrs. A.L. Carlton are back from Montana.

Miss Zoe Codding visited her aunt, Mrs. Leighton at the Wells' home on Greenfield Ave.

Mr. and Mrs. Alson Booth, of Seattle, Wash., were guests of C.E. Nettleton.

J.A. Schwaiger, G.F. Reichardt, Rich Henke, and Chas. Walters were fishing at Pewaukee Lake.

Justice and Mrs. W.L. Notbohm are visiting his cousin, Frank Denton, in Wyoming, Ill.

The Misses Errickson entertained at their home on Wauwatosa Ave.

Mr. and Mrs. G.W. Hunt are back home on E. Milwaukee Ave.

Mr. and Mrs. E.R. Blake, of Ravenswood, Ill., were here for Mr. and Mrs. A. Landolt's silver anniversary, August 21.

Miss Helen Stickney returned from visiting her sister, Mrs. Gregg Connell, in Colorado.

Mrs. C.P. Bussewitz went to Columbus, Wis. where her daughter, Mrs. Banky, is seriously ill.

Mrs. N.T. Curth, of Chicago, has returned there from a visit with with Mrs. H. Theo. Hansen, of Greenfield Ave.

Prof. and Mrs. F.M. Merica have returned from visiting relatives in Garrett, Ind.

Mr. and Mrs. Charles Rice, of Blue Springs, Neb., are visiting his sister, Mrs. H.E. Mower.

Mrs. W.A. Godfrey gave a luncheon for her children, the Misses Ives, her neices, and other cousins and friends.

Mrs. Geo. F. Leonard, of Lawrence, Kansas, is visiting her father, Frank Harriman on Wauwatosa Ave.

Mr. and Mrs. Duane Mowry, of Milwaukee, and Irwin W. Hosmer of St. Joseph, Mo., were guests at the Rich. Tennant home.

Mrs. Charles Farnham, of Milwaukee, was brought home after sustaining serious injuries from falling down stairs in Sparta.

Mrs. Mary Daen has returned to her Chicago home after a visit at Ch. Kropp home, Mrs. Kropp went with her.

C.E. Goldthrop will remain pastor of the Wauwatosa M. E. church for another year.

Mr. O.F. Lee, of Milwaukee, bought a lot from C.W. Damon for a residence on W. Main St.

Miss Miriam Hoyt gave a luncheon for fifty guests at her home on N. Main St.

John M. True, Secretary of the state board of agriculture, and members of the Milwaukee Automobile club made plans to hold auto races in connection with the state fair.

Rev. Eisfeld, general superintendent of the Lutheran Orphan society in Milwaukee, and Rev. Zollmann, assistant superintendant, is in charge of the home here.

Patents were granted to J.W. Dearsley, of Racine, molding machine and Simon Volz, of Milwaukee, bottle soaking machine, both former residents of Wauwatosa.

## Marriage

Hally E. Prentice, daughter of Mr. and Mrs. G.W. Prentice, of W. Main St., married Harry E. Hurlbut, Aug. 16, 1903, at the home of the bride's parents. Rev. C.E. Goldthorp performed the ceremony. The couple will live in Omaha, Neb.

### Letters uncalled for at the postoffice

Mrs. David Barndt, Miss Mae Dunn, Lieut. Thos. Cecll, Bir.Geo Cecll, Herman Gutsch, Mr. Hetkis, Miss Margaret Kieler, Paul Osten, Miss Maud Stickney, Miss Mira Dexter, Miss Jannette Caway, Miss Anna Haubert, Miss Minnie Larson, George Sell, and Wm. F. Schmidt

### August 29, 1903

Mrs. J.P. Gregg is visiting in Omro, Wis.

Miss May Foley is in Fond du Lac.

Mrs. C.F. Schneck is visiting in Scranton, Pa.

Mrs. Estella Wilcox is visiting in Wausau, Wis.

Miss Louise Landolt was in West Bend, Wis.

Miss Lill von Baumbach is going to Chicago

Mr. and Mrs. C.E. Curtis are going to Madison.

Mr. C.S. Clark and family are going to the Dells.

Miss Helen Rhodes was in Waterloo, Wis.

H.B. Hunter and family moved to Milwaukee.

Miss Florence Crandall is vacationing in Idaho

Miss Lulu Rix, of West Bend, is visiting Miss Blanche Landolt.

Mrs. A.B. Collins and son, Mark Collins, are going to Green Bay.

Miss Harriett E. Rice is at Lake Five, Wis.

Miss Maud Parkinson, of Madison, is visiting Mrs. C.E. Curtis.

Mr. and Mrs. J.D. Crandall are in Sheboygan Falls.

Master Archibald O. Walker, of Monroe, Wis., is visiting Rev. F.S. Gray.

Mrs. G.G. Allen and son, Donald Allen, are going to Minneapolis.

Mrs. Ann Morris was visiting her son, Chauncy Morris.

Mrs. A.J. Wood and family are back from Janesville.

Miss Della Brucehart, of Manitowoc, is visiting her cousin, Miss Ida Lentz.

Rev. P.W. Longfellow will preach at the Tabernacle in Milwaukee.

Miss Carrie Warren is moving into Mrs. Rhodes' house.

Mrs. Harrison Ludington gave a birthday party for her son, Sylvester Ludington, August 28.

Mrs. Lois Warren, of Portland, Me., was visiting Mrs. C. Pedrick.

Mr. and Mrs. Kaltenborn, of Waupun, were visiting Wm. von Baumbach.

Capt. and Mrs. W.H. Landolt and Mr. A. Landolt were in Pt. Washington.

Misses Bell Gregg and Grace Gregg and cousin, Miss Wilder, are going to Chicago.

Capt. A.P. Foster and family moved into the H.B. Hunter house on E. Milwaukee Ave.

Miss Edith Glasier was given a surprise shower by friends.

Mrs. Louisa Rhodes and daughter, Helen Rhodes, are going to Farmington, Wash. for the winter.

Wm. S. Rose, of Mancelona, Mich., formerly of Wauwatosa, was here.

Miss Nellie McCormack returned from her trip.

Miss Edna Winters has been visiting Miss Minnie Garvens.

Joseph Keeler and family will occupy a flat in the Wittenberg Bldg.

Miss Clara Englehart entertained at her home on Alice St.

Wm. Davelaar and family will return to their home, Spring Hill, soon.

Rev P.W. Longfellow and wife returned from their Ohio visit.

Mrs. Chas. B. Perry and children are visiting her parents, Mr. and Mrs. M.M. McNair in Brodhead, Wis.

T.E. Zimmerman is going to Peru, Ind. to promote his new potato digger.

Misses Helen Browne and Katherine Browne, of Waupaca, were here visiting their aunt, Mrs. J.D. Warren.

Nelson Munger, of Waterloo, Iowa, visited his aunt, Mrs. Wm. Moore, and friends here.

Gustav Hedtke and family are moving to a farm he purchased in Brookfield, Waukesha County.

Mrs. R.A. Viall and daughters, Misses Grace Viall and Charlotte Viall, of Chicago, are visiting Mrs. Viall's cousin, Mrs. Longfellow.

Mr. and Mrs. Chas. Foster, of Chicago, are visiting Mrs. Foster's father, J.M. Wheeler.

Frank Harriman will hold a family reunion in honor of his daughter, Mrs. Leonard, of Kansas.

Blacksmith, Albert Grunewald, of Lisbon Ave., is quite ill from blood poisoning, as the result of a scratch from a horseshoe nail.

Mr. H.W. Glasier and family will be leaving for their new home in Glendale, near Cleveland, Ohio, where he will work for Trolley Line Co.

New sidewalks are being layed for Rich Tennant, and Dr. Fisk.

Misses Olive Lefeber, Fern Ames, Lena Loveland, Messrs George Schneck, Cornelius Lefeber, and Everrett Hart chaperoned by Mrs. Inez Ames are taking a boat trip to Chicago.

The teachers appointed for 1903 school year are Francis M. Merica, Principal; Miss Mary Armstrong, Miss Ethelyn Bloedorn, Mrs. Grace Welch, Miss Janet M. Smith, assistants at the high school; Miss Eva May Acker, 8th grade; Miss Gertrude P. Dodd, 7th grade; Miss Jeanette L. Sage, 6th grade; Miss Henri Etta Aken, 5th grade; Miss Ethelyn Colwell, 4th grade; Miss Marion Pritchard, 3rd grade; Miss Katherine M. Wood, 2nd grade; Miss Ella Lillibridge and Miss Winifred E. Jones, 1st grade; Miss Myrtle Farnham, connecting class; and Miss Maud Pearce, kindergarten.

Rev. R.M. Vaughan, of Janesville, is visiting his family at the home of William Earries (probably Farries), he will preach at the Baptist church, Miss Janet Smith will lead the B. Y. P. U.

**Death**

Hiram Morse died August 25, 1903, aged 76 years, at the home of his son W.B. Morse, on Blue Mound Rd. He was a native of Maine, where he was a businessman. He served as an officer in the 20th Reg. Maine Vol. during the war of '61. Rev. A.R. Thain conducted the service with interment at Forest Home Cemetery.

## September 5, 1903

J.J. Angus and family are in Waldo, Wis.

Mr. A.F. Hasse went to Baraboo, Wis.

Miss Ella Lillibridge went to Elkhorn, Wis.

Rev. C.J. Rogers is back fron Indianapolis, Ind.

Ed Pavy has been ill.

G.E. Wells and family are back from Shawano, Wis.

Harold Rogers is vacationing in Minnesota.

Albert Hansen is home from his trip.

Rev. J.O. Ward, of Menasha, visited friends here.

J.B. De Swarte is visiting F.W. Schneck at Okauchee.

Mr. Hanson rented the Benson residence on Church St.

Mrs. T.S. Grassie and Miss Grassie are back from La Pointe, Wis.

Misses Louise Rhodes and Helen Rhodes went to Washington.

Jefferson Gregg purchased the Seymour residence on Church St.

Misses Harriett E. Rice and Theresa Mower are in Fond du Lac, Wis.

Maud H. Barnes returned to school in Westby, Wis.

Mrs. John Parkinson, of Menasha, Wis. is visiting her daughter, Mrs. I.W. Kennedy.

Mrs. Chas. B. Perry and children returned from visiting her folk in Brodhead, Wis.

Mr. and Mrs. T.H. Scott, of Chicago, are at the J.H. Waldie home.

Miss F.M. Sherin is visiting in Toronto and Woodstock, Canada.

Miss Jeanette Bush, of Evanston, Ill., visited Miss Marie Kennedy

John H. Taylor and family will move into the Brockway house where Mr. Glasier lived.

Mrs. M.J. Benoy, of Boscobel, Wis., is at the home of her son, John R. Benoy.

Mr. and Mrs. J.H. Waldie entertained at cinch.

Mr. and Mrs. John Dunlop were at Waukesha Beach with Scotch friends.

Mrs. De Leiuw and daughter, Marie De Leiuw, left for Rotterdam, Holland, to live with her father.

Rev. P.W. Longfellow has been at the Univ. of Chicago on business.

Mrs. R.M. Vaughan, of Janesville, visited her parents, Mr. and Mrs. William Farries.

Mr. and Mrs. G.W. Sanford left for a trip to Nebraska.

Mrs. D.G. Hathaway gave a picnic for her son, Newton Hathaway, and little Ethel Frisbe, of Pine Lake, their guest.

Mr. J.P. Dysart and family moved into the Morehouse residence on Kavanaugh Pl., he is the superintendent of the Children's Home Society of Wis.

Mrs. H.P. Bradley entertained for Miss Allen, Miss Stewart and Miss Dillingham, who are returning to their Pasadena, Cal. home.

Allen Williams, son of Mr. and Mrs. Allen Williams, was burned and cut by a powder explosion.

Fred Hartung, C.T. Fisher, Frank Foley, O.J. Swan, E.A. Swan, Aug. M. Siegfried, and Geo. A. James had telephones put in their homes.

August Ahrendt, who was employed at Englehart barbershop leaves for Hartford, Wis. to open his own shop.

Mrs. H.E. Mower, formerly of Wauwatosa, is a teacher at the Browning home in Camden, NC.

Rev. Perey Clibborn, a missionary, will preach in Good Templars' hall.

Prof. Max A. Bussewitz, who was seriously injured by a chemical explosion while he was experimenting is the cousin of C.F. Bussewitz.

Dr. H.V. Taylor will lead the B.Y.P.U. at the Baptist church.

R.M. Brown residence for rent, includes 12 room house, bath, electric lights, gas, city and cistern water, large grounds with large barn room, chicken houses, garden, fruit and ornamental trees at 241 E. Milwaukee Ave.

Pasturage available from W.A. Clapp.

Mrs. O.A. Fehling will do plain sewing.

**Death**

Friederica Heiden, wife of John Heiden, formerly of Wauwatosa, died at the home of her daughter, Mrs. Wm. Bark, Milwaukee, after a short illness on August 31, 1903. She was 64 years old and a resident of Wauwatosa for many years. She is survived by her husband, a son and daughter, Fred M. Heiden, of this city, and Mrs. Wm. Bark. She was interred at Wauwatosa Cemetery.

**Letters uncalled for at the postoffice**

P.F. Bowling, E.J. Loew, Frank Genske, Miss Katie Noonan, Abner Hampton and Miss V. Fowler

**September 12, 1903**

Chas. Godfrey is in New York on business.

Walter Wright, Jr., of Waukegan, is visiting friends here.

Miss Helen Stickney will enter Downer College this fall.

Miss Margaret Mower has returned to school in Wausau, Wis.

Mr. and Mrs. G.W. Sanford are in Council Bluffs, Iowa, visiting.

Miss Lill von Baumbach has returned from Chicago.

Capt. and Mrs. H. Leisk have returned from their trip.

Mr. and Mrs. Wm. Maxon, of Cedar Lake, Wis., were here.

Miss Mabel Lefeber is visiting Mrs. Wm. Donahue at Clinton Junction, Wis.

Miss Jessie Cundall is back from her trip out west.

Miss Chisholm, of Chicago, is visiting L. Brockway.

Mrs. R.A. Eggleston, of Houghton, Mich., is at the Methodist parsonage.

D.F. Philipp and family are back from Chicago.

Mrs. L.E. Hawley and daughter, Alberta Hawley, plan to move to Fond du Lac, Wis.

Miss Clara Myers, of Chicago, was visiting Mrs. W.R. Cundall.

Miss Ora E. Teal, of Chicago, was visiting Mrs. F.M. Keats.

Messrs. E. Carter and L. Carter, of Waupun, were at the Irvington with their mother.

Postmaster Landolt has been at a convention in Milwaukee.

Mr. M. Schlenger, of Cresco, Iowa, formerly of Wauwatosa, was here.

Miss May Taylor gave a party for friends.

Mr. M.L. Roberts, of Ft. Atkinson, Wis., was at the L.L. Gridley home.

A.L. Story has returned from his trip.

Miss Flora E. Doty, of Madison, Wis., is visiting her sister, Mrs. C.E. Curtis.

Wm. Tuck, of Whitewater, visited his sister, Mrs. R. Delpsch.

Carroll Webo, of Beaver Dam visited his aunt, Miss Myrtle Farnham.

Arthur W. Brockway took charge of the night office at McFarland station.

Mr. and Mrs. Kimball, of Grand Rapids, Mich., visited the A.P. Foster family.

Mrs. A.M. Lucus, the guest of Mrs. G.G. Allen, returned home to Dubuque, Iowa.

Mrs. R. Davis, son, Ralph Davis, and Mrs. Frye, of Milwaukee, visited Mrs. C.R. Davis.

Mrs. W.B. Whittaker, of Cook, Neb., was visiting her sister, Mrs. W.S. Falkner, of Second Ave.

John Ritchie, of Sun Prairie, Wis., visited C.E. Curtis and family.

The Ladies Aid society of the M. E. church met with Mrs. W.B. Rice.

Mr. and Mrs. Demerit Hoyt and Mr. Lester Pavy, of Fond du Lac, visited relatives here.

Mr. and Mrs. Ernest Butters, of Adell, Wis., have been visiting Mrs. Elizabeth Curtis.

Misses Ada Shields, Ella Shields, and Rena Chatfield returned from their trip.

Misses Laura Delpsch and Margaret Delpsch have returned to school in Omaha, Neb. and Shawano, Wis.

Mrs. C.F. Bussewitz is back from a visit with her daughter, Mrs. Banky, in Columbus, Wis.

Mr. and Mrs. J.W. Thickens, of Appleton, Wis., visited his sister, Mrs. L.R. Gridley.

Mrs. H.E. Mower and daughter, Carrie Mower, are leaving for Camden, S.C. to resume work at Browning institute.

Oscar Ebberthart and daughter, Mathilda Ebberthart, and Miss Frederick, of Plymouth, Wis. were at the Garvens bro's home, Blue Mound Rd.

Rev. C.E. Goldthorp is going to a conference in Green Bay.

Mr. and Mrs. Duxborrow, Mrs. Chas. Ringrose, and Mrs. Wheaton, of Alma Center, Wis., visited with Mr. and Mrs. G.W. Ringrose.

Mr. and Mrs. Smith McCormack had a family reunion, all their children, four daughters and two sons and their families attended.

Mayor A.S. Douglas, Aldermen Dr. C.W. Bennett, and John Connery, of Monroe, Wis., were here to examine the sewage plant.

Mr. J.B. Thomas, of Wausau, Wis., formerly of Wauwatosa, was here with Chas. Cramer and G.G. Knolle, trustees of the Marathon Co. Assylum, where Mr. Thomas is superintendent.

W.F.M.S. of the M. E. church met at J.B. De Swarte's home, Mrs. F.W. Schneck was elected president and Mrs. H.E. Mower, gave a speach.

Prof. Adolph Hoenecke celebrated his silver jubilee at a gathering of Lutheran ministers.

J.O. Myers' bike disappeared from in front of the Milw. Public Library and was found later on Grand Ave. rather worse for wear.

Michael Schmidt sustained minor injuries when the bridge over the Menomonee River colasped while he was driving a threshing outfit across it.

### Death

Henry Garvens died Sept. 8, 1903 at his home, he was 70 years old and an early settler, the funeral was from his home with interment at Honey Creek Cemetery, Greenfield. (His name on his tombstone is spelled Garvin, there is also a Wilhelmenia Garvens buried there, her death date is 14 Jul 1921.)[1]

### Letters uncalled for at the postoffice

Miss Gertie Bark, Mr. A.P. Gustafson, Miss Handley, Miss Lilie Lass, Mr. A. Van Ellis, Miss Eleanor Barrett, Mr. A. Grider, M.D., Herman Jager, Jos Pritchard, Miss Clara Walker, and Geo. Zimmermann

### Probate Notice

Charles Hart, dec'd, letters of testamentary to Mary E. Hart and Charles B. Hart. Paul D. Carpenter, County Judge

### September 19, 1903

C.T. Everett is in Grand Rapids, Wis.

Charles H. Godfrey is in New York on business.

Mrs. H.E. Leister and son were in Elkhorn, Wis.

---

[1] Old Cemetery Burials of Milwaukee County Wisconsin, by Elizabeth Doherty Herzfeld, published by Heritage Books, Inc., Bowie, MD., 1995.

Miss Agnes S. Tennant is visiting friends in Waukegan, Ill.

Mrs. W.S. Faulkner, Second Ave., entertained at tea.

Miss Elizabeth Butterworth went to London, Canada.

Rev. P.W. Longfellow will preach in West Bend.

Misses Florence Delpsch and Ida Delpsch left for San Antonio, Texas.

Miss Mabel Lefeber is back from Clinton Junction, Wis.

Mrs. H.E. Mower and daughter left for Camden, SC.

The Kensington club met with Emily Seamans.

Mr. and Mrs. T.W. Hart have returned home.

Mrs. J.W. Gilman, of Rockford, Ill. visited Mrs. M. Horning.

Wm. Palmer, of Chicago, visited Wm. Menninger

Mrs. Demerit Hoyt, of Fond du Lac, visited W.A. Hart and family.

Mr. E.E. Hanks, of Quebec, Canada, visited Rev. F.S. Gray.

Mrs. Lucy Fisher, of Chicago, visited her aunt, Mrs. C.A. Curtis.

Miss Katharine Cooper, of Racine, visited Miss Thompson.

Gilson Glasier and family returned home to Madison.

Mrs. M. Horning entertained informally.

Mrs. M.G. Heath, of Elkhorn, Wis., will spend the winter with Frank Harriman and family.

Thomas Helgesen, of Tomah, visited his parents here.

Mr. W.G. Taylor visited his brother in Kilbourn, Wis.

The Baptist missionary dept. met with W.A. Smith.

Thomas Marston, of Oconomowoc, was the guest of Mr. C.G. Norton.

Miss Emily Seamans returned to school at St. Mary's in Knoxville, Ill.

Mr. S.A. Wasburn and family will occupy Mrs. T.M. Potter's house.

Alderman, James Lefeber and son, Ernest Lefeber, are going to northern Wis.

Misses Mary Clapp and Helen Myers leave for college in Oberlin, Ohio.

Willis Watson and family are coming back after a year in California.

Rev. C.T. Everett is doing missionary work in Grand Rapids, Wis.

L.A. McElroy, of Milwaukee, rented the R.M. Brown residence.

Mr. W. Lincoln and family, of Milwaukee, rented the Hunter dwelling on Mower Ct.

H.P. Morse has rented his property to Mr. Gray, of Milwaukee, who is with the American Bridge Co.

An Auction will be held at the J.A. Warren farm.

Mrs. Reyher, of Garrett, Ind. and daughter, Grace Reyher, of Fond du Lac, Wis. are visiting Prof. and Mrs. F.M. Merica.

Mrs. C.S. Clark entertained in honor of Miss Mary Percilla Clapp, who is leaving for Oberlin.

Mr. J.B. Russell sold his interest in Smith-Russell Co. to Mr. Smith and left for South Dakota where he may locate.

Ed Pavy is improving from typhoid fever.

Miss Mary Menten was surprised on her birthday Sept. 18.

Mrs. E.A. More entertained the Woman's Missionary society of the Congregational church.

Mrs. James Fordham, of Chatfield, Minn., and niece, Mrs. Chas. Koessler, of Milwaukee, visited the Rich Tennant home.

Mrs. George Francis Leonard, of Lawrence, Kansas, who has been visiting her father, Frank Harriman, is returning home with Miss Hazel Harriman, who will spend the winter with her and probably take courses at the Kansas State Univ.

The Twentieth Century club will meet at the president, Mrs. Joseph Wood's home.

Rev. J.P. Dysart will preach at the M. E. Church while the pastor is gone.

Rev. Mr. Noyse, the M. E. pastor at West Bend, will preach at the Baptist church.

Present at the common council meeting were: Mayor Hoyt, Alder-men Baumbach, Kennedy, Breed, Hamme, Menninger, Gunn, and Jones. Notice is to be serviced on P.D. Pilgrim concerning a drain cave-in.

The board of directors for the Advancement club are: T.J. Ferguson, C.G. Porter, G.G. Allen, vice president, T.M. Hammond, president, Arthur S. Gregg, A.C. Hanson, secretary, and J.L. Hooley, treasurer.

**Marriage**

Miss Myrtle Nettleton attended the wedding of her brother, Carroll Nettleton to Lucie Freysinger at Rock Island, Ill., Sept. 16, 1903.

**Death**

Mrs. Margaret Breed, widow of A.O.T. Breed, died Sept. 12, 1903, at her daughter, Mrs. William F. Wesson's home. Services were at the First Baptist church with interment at Forest Home Cemetery. Mrs. Breed was born in Homer, NY, in 1818. She came to Milwaukee in 1836 from Manlius, Onondaga Co., NY with her brother-in-law and sister, Mr. and Mrs. Joseph Williams, in a covered wagon incurring many hardships. She married A.O.T. Breed, who had the first dry goods store in Milwaukee. Mrs. Breed is the last of a family of eleven children and is survived by one son and three daughters, Charles A. Breed and Mrs. George H. Fowler, of Wauwatosa, Mrs. William F. Wesson, and Mrs. Richard C. Sherwin, of Milwaukee, and seven grandchildren. After leaving the dry goods business Mr. Breed farmed land he bought on Vliet St. in the town of Wauwatosa which was sold to Milwaukee and is now Washington Park.

**Letters uncalled for at the post office**

Mable Gringam, Mrs. F. Humphreys, Rosa Kratz, H.R. Lee, Emma Marken, Angela Palm, Rosa Razorina, W.H. Titus, Lilli Oenow, Dorathy Huder, Mrs. Lois Long, Julius Meyer, Moritz Rudolph, Mable Quimby, Chas. Scheffler, and Otto Sassauske

**City Budget**

Aug. Henke, street sprinkling; G.E. Zimmermann, water mains; Math. Goebel, cutting weeds; J.W. Highley, guard; H.N. Andrews, calcimining city hall; D.T. Pilgrim, paving stone; G. Reuter, gutter paving; J.C. Zimmermann and Son, stone; Fred Voetz, pumping septic tank; C.B. Perry, legal; H.D. Hallett, plans for Electric Light plant; E.D. Etnyre, sprinkling wagon and freight; C.W. Damon, meeting; John Armstrong, repairs; Edward Coulthard, postage; A.F. Kellogg, postage; D.R. Brewer, gravel; S.D. Ringrose, gravel; W.H. Moore, gravel; O.L. Packard, bench vise; Adolph Lentz, lumber; J.F. Dittmar, repairs; J.D. Warren, salary; H.N. Andrew, painting; H.A. Propp, painting; August Boldt, mason work; Ernst Werner, hauling; A.E. Sieloff, paper; H. Niedecken, supplies; E.H. Schwaiger, supplies; H. Digman, cleaning school; H.P. Hempsing, scissors; A.S. Robbins, apparatus; A.B. Fuller, G.E. Smith, Henry Watner, L.R. Gridley, and G.H. Fowler, insurance; J.M. Smith. M. Farnham and others, books; Mrs. Roddis, librarian; H.A. Digman, janitor; D.W. Howie, coal; H. Nieuemarn, glass; F.H. Sporleder; repairs; Geo. Brumder, A.R. Thain and Miss McDermott, books; J.O. Myers, sundries.

### September 26, 1903

Albert Taylor was in Chicago.

Loleta Landolt was visiting in Chicago.

Miss Lou Landolt is visiting in Indianapolis, Ind.

Mrs. Gilson Glasier is back home in Madison.

Chas. Kroesing was in Chilton.

Mr. W.E. Poppleton and family moved to Montgomery, Ala.

Mr. C. Winkenwerder and family are in Menomonee Falls, Wis.

Miss Eveline Ellis is attending Wayland academy in Beaver Dam.

Ralph Kneeland is visiting his sister, Mrs. Morse Ives, in Chicago.

Miss Maude Parkinson, of Madison, visited Miss E. Colwell.

Miss Lottie Hart returned from Pennsylvania.

Mr. Stickney, of Milwaukee, rented the Jacobs' house on Fifth Ave.

J.B. De Swarte is in northern Wisconsin on business.

Mr. J.A.R. Tompkins went to Two Rivers, Mich. on business.

Rich Hayes is home from Thomson, Ill for a few days.

Albert Taylor, telegraph operator, is vacationing in Chicago.

Mr. J. Gray and family moved into the Morse house on First Ave.

Mr. J.B. Russell will be working for a South Dakota land company.

Louis Wright, of Cleveland, O, visited his cousin, Mrs. L. Brockway.

Mrs. M. Horning and daughter, Bessie Horning, and Mrs. Ella Smith were in Waukesha.

The W.H. Wright place was sold to Mr. Miller, of Milwaukee.

Mrs. John W. Sercomb, of Chicago, is visiting Mr. and Mrs. W.B. Rice

Miss Madeline Haney visited Miss Myrtice Cochrane in Tippecanoe, Wis.

Mrs. D.G. Hawley moved to Fond du Lac.

Mr. and Mrs. John P. Gregg and Miss Lou Landolt were in Grand Rapids, Mich.

Mrs. Henry Watner entertained her Sunday school class.

Miss Mary E. Hurlburt left to enter the Univ. of Chicago.

Fred Hartung left for a trip out west.

Miss Edith Hooker, of Milwaukee, visited Miss Florence Adams.

Mr. and Mrs. G.G. Allen left for a trip to North Dakota and Montana.

The baptist young people had a social at Stanley Waton's.

Walter Garvens, who has been living in Tennessee for two years, is here to visit his folk.

Mr. and Mrs. C.E. Curtis and Maude Curtis are going to visit Mrs. Frances Ritchie and family in Sun Prairie.

Geo. H. Rogers has returned to Wauwatosa to live with his daughter-in-law, Mrs. E.A. Rogers.

Mr. and Mrs. C.A. Nettleton, of Chicago, are visiting his parents.

Mr. Werner reports good progress in putting the sewage disposal plant at the County Farm.

Allan Phillips, of Ontonagon, Mich., is visiting his parents, Mr. and Mrs. John Phillips of Western Ave.

William Farries expects to be home soon from his lumber interests in Price Co.

Mrs. Irene Wallace, of Ogden, Utah, and Miss Elizabeth Holliday and Miss Sterling, of Milwaukee, were visiting Mrs. H.O. Wood.

Roy Wheeler, who has been vacationing with his parents in Milwaukee, is returning to the state univ.

Irwin Shepard, of Winona, Minn., was visiting his sister, Mrs. I.C. Lillibridge.

Mr. and Mrs. J.P. Rust, of Meadville, Pa. will visit her father, Mr. L. Brockway.

Miss L. Wiese is home from the National Dressmakers' Assoc. convention.

Mr. and Mrs. E.M. Bussewitz went to visit relatives and friends in Dodge Co.

Prof. and Mrs. Merica were surprised by the W.H.S. Class of 1902.

Rev. C.E. Goldthorp will be pastor at the M. E. church for another year.

Mr. C.A. Copeland and family are returning home. Mr Trever, who has occupied their home for the summer will remove to Milwaukee.

The Twentieth Century Topic club will be held at Mrs. Joseph Wood's home, Green Gables, on Grand Ave.

Messrs Ellis Rhodes, J.H. Waldie, C.A. Pettibone, and Carl Hasse will sing at the Congregational church.

Miss Julia Brown will lead the B.Y.P.U. at the Baptist church.

D.J. Hayes advertises for a girl for general housework.

**Death**

Gustav Lentz died Sept. 23, 1903, aged 52 years, 11 months, at his home on Fifth Ave., after a lingering illness. He is survived by his wife, five children, two brothers, Adolph Lentz and Emil Lentz, and a sister, Mrs. Chas. Radtke. The funeral will be at St. John's Lutheran church.

**Letters uncalled for at the postoffice**

Chas. Allen, George Brier, W.P. Carpenter, Adolph Fraham, Adam Krauss, Chas. Masch, Emma Rodehl, Nathan Seed, Mrs. W. Brady, M.P. Carpenter, Anna Filgge, Ethel Gilmette, Wm Kochsick, M Schneider, and Lille Zeldell

### October 3, 1903

Miss Louise Landolt is in Chicago.

Mr. H. Watner is in Portage on business.

Mrs. F.A. Butterworth went to London, Ontario

Miss Winifred Jones will visit her home in Racine.

Miss Ethel Colwell will spend Sunday at home in Rome, Wis.

Miss Lehmann, of Neosho, is visiting J.T. Van Vecton's home.

Arthur Brockway was home from McFarland.

Russell Faulkner was in Menomonee Falls on business.

Burley Allen will be the night operator in Waukesha.

Everett Hart's health is improving.

Mrs. A.J. Moan went to Iowa.

L.L. Gridley has been confined to bed because of a fall.

Mrs. H.E. Frisbie, of Pine River, Wis., is visiting James Lefeber.

Mrs. C.W. Damon went to Palmyra to visit friends.

Miss Edna Hooley went to Madison to visit friends.

C.C. Jacobus was in Iowa County to look after his mining interests.

Mrs. L.S. Cutler and daughter, Mary Cutler, visited relatives at Cedar Lake.

Miss Katherine Wood is back from Janesville and will resume teaching next week.

Miss Nellie Ross, of Sioux Falls, Dakota, is visiting the Smith McCormack home.

Mrs. Hadfield and Mrs. Rhodes, of Waukesha, are visited Mrs. Agnes Rice.

Dr. and Mrs. Walton Perkins, of Milwaukee, visited the L. Brockway home.

C.T. Everett and family moved to the Barkhausen residence on E. Milwaukee Aves.

Dr. J.S. Cutler moved to his new home on Second and Milwaukee Ave.

Miss La Homadien, of Detroit, Mich., visited her aunt, Mrs. C.G. Norton.

Rev. Mr. Oliphant and mother, of Milwaukee, visited Rev. F.S. Gray.

Agnes S. Tennant returned from visiting friends in Waukegan, Ill.

The West Side Neighborhood club met at Mrs. W.F. Humphrey's home.

Mrs. Abram Lefeber entertained for Mr. and Mrs. T.D. Rust, of Meadville, Pa.

Miss Elizabeth Foley, Geo. Kershaw, and G.W. Garvens left to attend UW Madison.

Miss Harriet Lehmann, of Evanston, Ill., visited her grandfather, J.T. Van Vecten.

Albert Link and Miss Carrie Link, of New Berlin, are guests of the Garvens.

Otto Zilmer moved to Marrinette, Wis. where he purchased a farm.

Rev. and Mrs. Goldthorp were given a reception at the M. E. church.

Mr. A.G. Rice, of St. Paul, visited his brother, W.B. Rice.

Alderman James Lefeber returned from visiting friends at Pine River, Wis.

Mr. O.F. Lee is building a new residence on W. Main St.

Mrs. Chas. Davis attended the Culture club at Mrs. C.B. Whitnall's home on Humbolt Ave. in Milwaukee.

Mr. and Mrs. Rust, who have been visiting her father, Mr. L. Brockway, returned home to Meadville, Pa.

Mrs. J.H. Tuttle returned home to Decatur, Mich. after spending the summer with her daughter, Mrs. A. Landolt.

Mrs. C.S. McLean and Mrs. Maurice Hess, of Milwaukee, were here for the Harvest Home supper.

Mr. Morris and Mr. Warner, of Milwaukee, are erecting four cottages on Sixth Ave.

Rev. Dr. Thain, Mr. and Mrs. W.R. Netherent and Mr. J.O. Myers will attend the Congregational church convention.

Alderman and Mrs. Charles Breed, with his sister and husband, Mr. and Mrs. Wm. Wesson, of Milwaukee, are going to French Lick, Springs, Ind.

There was a fire at Mr. G. Hedtke's home on St. James St. in the rooms occupied by Mrs. Wilde.

James L. Foley is confined to his bed after a fall at his farm.

The H.P. Hemsing Co. reports a large demand for the wiring residences and businesses.

Mary E. Moxcoy, the state secretary of the Young Woman's Christian Assoc., will speak at the Baptist church.

D.W. Hurlburt, C.T. Everett, P.W. Longfellow, Miss Belle Farries, and Miss Sylvia Lefeber will attend the Baptist convention.

**Death**

Michael Trottner was killed by a car Monday, Sept. 28, 1903, when returning to his home at the almshouse after celebrating his seventy-eighth birthday in Milwaukee.

**Letters uncalled for at the postoffice.**

Mr. Baldwin, W.S. Dillan, Mrs. G. Garrison, Ehtel Harvey, Ernst Hoth, H.J. Henniky, Miss Justice, Art Johnson, Jacob Jager, H.A. Loery, Elizabeth Ludwig, Mrs. F.A. Pigeon, and Chas. Protzmann

### October 17, 1903

Captain Landolt was in Waukesha.

Alex Rogers, of Minneapolis, called on relatives here.

Len Gridley was at Cedar Lake.

Mrs. Richard Tennant has been at her mother's in La Valle, Wis.

Mr. and Mrs. John Farries, of West Bend, are visiting here.

Mrs. C.A. Copeland and daughter returned home to Fargo, ND.

Mrs. A.F. Kellogg has been visiting her daughter, Mrs. G. Glasier, in Madison, Wis.

Harold Rogers, Blue Mound Rd., will engage in the milk business.

Mr. and Mrs. A.A. Fairweather were at the H.E. Rose home.

Miss Belle Farries is back home.

Walter Koenig gave a kitchen shower for Alice Kershaw and Mr. A.C. Hanson.

Wm. Prouditt, of Denver, Colo., formerly of Wauwatosa, visited C.T. Fisher and other friends.

Mr. C.E. Canright was the leader of the Missionary Dept. of the Baptist church that met at H.N. Andrew's home.

Frank Harriman returned from a hunting and fishing trip.

Mrs. E.H. Cornwall entertained for her sister, Miss Alice Kershaw, at the home of her mother, Mrs. J.H. Kershaw.

Paul Warren returned from Blackwell, Okla. where he was working.

Mrs. George Allanson, of Milwaukee, is visiting her daughter, Mrs. C.G.B. Schenk.

Mrs. R.W. Schneck is entertaining Mrs. Jos. Lefeber, Mrs. C.F. Schneck, Miss Tennant, and Mr. and Mrs. F.M. Merica, of this city, at Okauchee Lake.

Rev. B.H. Moore, Rev. James Blake, pastors in So. Milwaukee and West Allis, visited the Baptist parsonage.

Rev. Kunth and Rev. Doenfield, of Milwaukee, will deliver addresses at Friedens Lutheran church's Missionary Festival.

Mrs. L. Brockway returned from the Woman's Foreign Missionary society convention of the M. E. church.

Mrs. Richard Dewey hosted the Twentieth Century club. Mrs. Lillibridge read a paper on Green Bay and Miss Isabelle Skinner, Mower Ct., gave musical numbers. Mrs. W.F. Beutler will entertain the club at the next meeting.

Mr. and Mrs. Charles Breed have returned from Indiana.

Mr. A. Harden is back from a business trip.

John Hamme and family were at his father's home in Waukesha.

Rev. Henry Holmes, of Minneapolis, Minn., former pastor of the Congregational church here, will be the guest of Mr. and Mrs. A.F. Kellogg, Church St. Friends are invited to meet him at Mr. and Mrs. W.A. Hart's on Warren Ave.

Chas. O. Merica, of Warsaw, Ind., and Rev. Chas. A. Payne, will lecture at the B. Y. P. U. entertainment.

## Death

Gustave Hedtke was accidentally killed by a train near Waukesha on his way to catch the train. He was 44?(the numbers are difficult to make out) years old and resided in Wauwatosa about 18 or 20 years. His home was on St. James St. Mr. Hedtke is survived by his widow and six children. The funeral was held at the Baptist church with interment at Wauwatosa Cemetery, Rev. G. Ehrhardt officiated.

## Letters uncalled for at the postoffice.

H. Bauers, F. Bilfernicht, Mrs. Anra R. Boller, Frank Bribeckl?, Cora E. Eddy, Ernst Hoth, Dr. F.S. Keuter, C. Soendsch or C. Soendsen, Mrs. Wm. C. Smith, Pauline Frost, F.A. Traver, S.E. Wright, and George Witte

## Probate Notice

A.J. Wagner petitioned the court to admisister the estate of Michael Muller who died intestate about March (can't read the year). G.E. Morton is mentioned as guardian ad litem. Paul D. Carpenter, County Judge.

### October 24, 1903

J.T. Van Vechten and daughter are in Kewaskum.

Mrs. William Baier and children are in Ripon.

Mrs. Arthur Gregg is visiting in Oconomowoc.

Miss Miriam Hoyt is back from Reedsburg, Wis.

Mrs. Elizabeth Maxon is visiting her daughter, Mrs. J.S. Cutler.

Miss Mary Menton entertained some ladies.

Mrs. George Bennett, of Pewaukee, visited friends here.

Mrs. J.B. Freye, of Milwaukee, was at the G.W. Ringrose home.

M.E. Oertel and J.A. Schwaiger went duck hunting.

Mrs. G.C.B. Schenk entertained for her son, Allan Schenk.

E.C. Nettleton plans to take a trip through the south and west.

Mrs. F. Vandercook, Blanchard St., has been quite ill.

Miss Carrie Papie, of Sheboygan, visited Miss Elma Goldthorp,

Miss Lou Griffith, of Milwaukee, visited Mrs. Joseph Horle.

Mrs. Stanley Watson gave a shower for Miss Mabel Watson.

Mr. and Mrs. C. Melcher, of Chicago, visited at the D.W. Philipp home.

Mrs. J.E. Pierce and Mrs. H.O. Wood are going to New Orleans.

Mrs. Charles R. Davis attended the State Federation of Women's Clubs.

The Kensington club will meet at Mrs. Charles Stickney's home.

The T.C.T. club will meet with Mrs. W.F. Beutler, Mrs. Fowle assisting.

Rev. Henry Holmes returned to his home in Minneapolis.

C.E. Wilson and family, of Delafield, Wis., moved into the house recently occupied by C.A. Copeland.

Mrs. J. Benoy gave her son, Niely Benoy, a birthday party Oct. 22.

Arthur Banky is expected back from Columbus, Wis. soon.

Mrs. C.E. Roberts is back from visiting her daughter, Mrs. Donahue in Clinton Junction.

Mr. E.C. Werner has rented the house where the late J.A. Warren lived.

Mr. and Mrs. Fred Morton will entertain for their fifth wedding anniversary, Oct. 24.

Mrs. Elbert Blodgett, of West Allis, and Mrs. S. Breese, of Waukesha, were guests of Dr. Cairncross.

Mr. and Mrs. Charles Garvens, of Saylesville, visited their son, Louis Garvens.

Mr. and Mrs. H.E. Rose will attend the tenth wedding anniversary of Mr. and Mrs. Frank Phelps in Milwaukee.

Messrs Kroesing and Tennant were in Menomonee Falls.

Mrs. John Parker Gregg, Misses Louise Landolt, and Blanche Landolt gave a shower for Miss Alice Kershaw.

Misses Gertrude Dodd and Harriett Rice will entertain for Miss Alice Kershaw.

Mrs. Burnside, Mrs. Wright, and Miss Harriman attended the Federation of Woman's Clubs.

Mr. and Mrs. Joseph A. Kershaw sent out invitations to the marriage of their daughter, Alice Mabel Kershaw to Albert C. Hanson.

Charles O. Merica, of Warsaw, Ind., will lecture at the Baptist church.

The Outdoor Art club met with Mrs. Myers.

Rev. P.W. Longfellow, president of the Baptist Ministerial society, will honor Revs. O.P. Bestor and J. Heritage, who are leaving Milwaukee.

Mrs. C.T. Everett gave a dinner party in honor of her mother, Mrs. Clarke's birthday, Oct. 22. Guests were: Mr. and Mrs. J.H. Cushing, Mr. and Mrs. William Moore, Mrs. J.L. Pelton, Mrs. A.M. Hills, Mr. and Mrs. William Farries, Mr. and Mrs. Dr. Cairncross, Mrs. L.B. Smith, Mr. and Mrs. D.W. Hulburt, Mr. and Mrs. P.W. Longfellow, Mr. and Mrs. Kirk Putnam, Mrs. C.E. Tyler and Miss Katherine Leiske.

Secretary Charles Curtis, of the Fire dept., presented Chief J.D. Warren with a gold badge in appreciation of his work.

C.E. Canright will lead the B.Y.P.U. at the Baptist church.

C.W. Loomis has a phaeton for sale.

Charles Stickney and Charles Luetzow were elected water commissioners at the common council meeting.

Judge Ludwig's decision to probate the will of James Hanley was affirmed. This practically sustains the contentions of Joseph Krafezyk, the defendant in the suit brought by Michael Hanley, son of James Hanley. James Hanley once owned five acres of land in the city of Wauwatosa. His widow later married an old soldier named Dodge, and the property was purchased on a tax deed and divided and sold in parcels. Ejectment suit was brought by Michael Hanley to gain possession of the property. The case was brought before Judge Mann for probating of the will, the judge died before deciding it. Judge Pereles denied the will to probate. An appeal in circuit court before Judge Johnson affirmed the decision of probate court, but he died before signing the findings. Judge Ludwig gave the final decision.

**Marriages**

Miss Mabel Watson, of Wauwatosa married John Coon, of Milwaukee , Oct. 22, 1903, at the Watson home on Fond du Lac Ave.

Miss Stella M. Grassie married Lloyd Nelson, of Hibbing, Minn., Oct. 22, 1903 at the home of the bride's mother, Mrs. M.E. Grassie. Rev. A.R. Thain officiated.

**Letters uncalled for at the postoffice.**

Miss Hulda Busz, Miss Lizzie Franz, Ernst T. Fischer, Eliza. Forrer, Mrs. V.M. Goodrich, S. Holmes, Bettie Klatke, Lucy Kenister, W. Lipscomb, Wm. Mahnke, Minnie Wilmot, and J.W. Siefert

**October 31, 1903**

Miss Blanche Maloy is visiting in Pittsburg.

Mrs. J.B. Thomas, of Wausau, is visiting here.

Joe McNab, of Chicago, visited E.M. Lewis.

Miss Lulu Rix, of West Bend, is visiting Miss Gertrude Dodd.

Mr. J.B. Russell and family moved to West Allis.

Capt. and Mrs. W.H. Landolt were in Port Washington.

Mr. W.H. Goodall is in St. Paul on business.

Mr. and Mrs. B.S. Harris moved to Milwaukee.

Fred Lamont, who is in Chicago, was here.

Adolph Becker will work for A. Paulsen, grocer in Milwaukee.

Chas. Stafford is putting in a cement sidewalk.

Arthur B. Currelley is back from visiting friends.

Mrs. L. Brockway will be a delegate to the Woman's Foreign Missionary convention.

Mr. D.J. Hayes sold some land to Mrs. M.E. Laurner, of Chicago, for a residence.

Rev.'s T. Gensike and H. Hoffmann, of Milwaukee, will speak at St. John's Lutheran Mission Festival.

Messrs. H.F. Schultz, C.H. O'Neil, J.M. Doesburg and other residents of 35th St. between Grand Ave. and State St. protested the granting of a franchise to lay a track along that street by Milwaukee Street Railway Co.

Wm. E. Fisher was severely bruised when his wagon turned over and dragged him under the box, his father, C.T. Fisher, who was with him was thrown, but escaped injury.

Mr. L.B. Wickersham will lecture at the Congregational church.

Dr. Moses J. White, superintendent of the Milwaukee Co. Hospital for the insane, escorted inspectors and visitors through the asylum, after dinner trustees G.E.G. Kuechle, Robert F. McMynn, and W.F. Becker. District Atty. Benott addressed the group.

Hugo Frommann has found a gold Masonic ring.

Ada Winters will lead the B.Y.P.U. at the Baptist church.

Charles Kieckhafer, Jr. will not be a cadidate for re-election as superintendent of the county almshouse. He has taken an interest in and will manage the F.A.W. Kieckhefer Edgewood Dairy Farm at Pewaukee Lake, Wis.. Ferdinand Bark, of this city, is the most prominently mentioned person to replace him.

## Marriages

Mabel Watson, only daughter of Willis Watson, married John Roberts Coon, of Milwaukee, Oct. 29, 1903, at her family home. Miss Watson was born and raised in Wauwatosa, Mr. Coon grew up in Eau Claire. Rev. P.W. Longfellow presided. The couple will live in Milwaukee.

Miss Lizzie Cordle married Louis Schmeling, of Lisbon Ave., at St. John's church, Oct. 28, 1903. Rev. Rader read the service.

## Deaths

William Dierke commited suicide by shooting himself in the head at Schoonmaker quarry, Oct. 27, 1903. He had been an inmate at the county asylum for a month and was boarding at Mrs. Wolf's on State St. He had received a message from his brother, who is a telegraph operator in W. Chicago, to return home and it is thought he feared his family would put him in an asylum. He was about 30 years old and unmarried.

Jacob Berkstresser Johnson died at his home at Wells Farm, Wauwatosa Oct. 27, 1903, at the age of 68 years. Mr. Johnson was born Feb. 7, 1835 in Montgomery Co., Penn. and came to Milwaukee Co. at the age of twelve years. He married Miss Annie Campbell, Sept. 13, 1870, and several years later moved to South Dakota where he lived for nineteen years and returned to Wauwatosa in 1897. He had four children, three have survived him, George J. Johnson, of Wentworth, SD, Archie C. Johnson, and Mrs. M. Matheson, of this city. Mr. Johnson was a member of the Baptist church. Funeral will be from his home with interment at Forest Home cemetery.

Mrs. Ann Brown died Oct. 29, 1903, at the home of her daughter, Mrs. Mitchell, on State St. She was 82 years old. The funeral will be at Trinity church with interment at Forest Home cemetery. Rev. F.S. Gray will officiate.

**Letters uncalled for at the postoffice.**

Henry Engle, Alma Koegel, Minnie Martin, Jewel O'Connor, Amanda Olson, Annie Turynski, and Mr. and Mrs. Fred White.

**Probate Notice**

Auguste Hedtke petitioned the court to be appointed adminstator of the estate of her husband, Gustav Hedtke, who died about Oct. 15, 1903. Paul D. Carpenter, County Judge

**November 7, 1903**

Mr. G.G. Allen was in Chicago.

George Kershaw is back from Madison.

Mr. A.B. Fuller has been ill.

Miss A.K. Porter is wintering at C.G. Wade's on 2nd Ave.

Mrs. Catherine Hoyt is visiting her grandson in Fond du Lac.

Mrs. M.L. Young, N. Main St. is seriously ill with paralysis.

Mr. and Mrs. John Benoy were in Hartland.

Mrs. J.M. Nash and daughter, Mattie Nash, returned from Hudson, Wis.

Mrs. E.B. Pares will give a Kensington.

Mrs. C.G. Dreutzer will entertain at coffee.

Mrs. W.B. Lincoln will give a luncheon.

Mr. and Mrs. W.A. Godfrey entertained the Evening Circle club.

Miss Ella Kneeland is visiting her sister, Mrs. Morse Ives, in Chicago.

Mrs. James Rogers is visiting her daughter, Mrs Doig, in Wilmette, Ill.

Earl Rogers will entertain the Clay Hill club.

Fred Hartung and Charles Jacobus went to Iowa county to see to their lead mine.

John Farries, of West Bend, attended the funeral of Jacob Johnson.

Mrs. Catherine Haertel moved from North Ave. to Fifth and Pabst Aves.

Rev. and Mrs. Blakesly, of Milwaukee, visited J.O. Meyers.

Mrs. Fred Hancock will entertain the T.C.T. club assisted by Mrs. C.H. Shaw.

Mr. and Mrs. C.E. Morehouse, of Menomonee Falls, visited the W.S. Falkner home.

Mr. and Mrs. L. Brockway went to Clear Lake, Ia. to visit friends.

Gen. Ruggles, Gov. of the Soldier's Home in Washington DC, is visiting his son, C.H. Ruggles, of Church St.

Mr. and Mrs. Chas. Stickney are going to Leadville, Col. to visit their daughter, Mrs. Gregg Connell.

Messrs. F.E. Loveland, J.D. Warren, E.D. Hoyt, and W. Menninger went hunting.

George Johnson returned to his home in Wentworth, SD.

Mr. and Mrs. O.F. Wilson and daughter, Gertrude Wilson, returned from Racine where they attended the funeral of Mrs. Wilson's cousin.

The W.C.T.U. will meet with Mrs. J.W. Cairncross, E. Milwaukee Ave.

C.T. Everett, D.W. Hulburt and P.W. Longfellow are active members of the Baptist convention board.

Mrs. R.M. Brown returned from visiting relatives in Whitewater, but left immediately for Shawano to care for her sister, Margaret Delpsch, who is quite ill.

Miss Maude Lizette, of Minneapolis, assisted by local musicians will give a recital.

The Union Evangelistic meetings will be postponed until after Christmas to give Evangelist Lyon, of Chicago, a rest.

Mrs. Burnside read a report of the State Federation of Woman's clubs at the Woman's club meeting.

Mrs. Nickerson will conduct sewing classes in the public schools.

Hon. L.B. Wickersham gave a lecture at the Congregational Church.

Miss Faith Longfellow will lead th B. Y. P. U. at the Baptist church.

Rev. Mr. Hare will speak at the Congregational church.

## Marriage

Miss Alice Mabel Kershaw, daughter of Mr. and Mrs. J.A. Kershaw, of Wauwatosa, married Albert C. Hansen, Nov. 3, 1903, at the home of the bride's parents on Fifth Ave. Rev. Horatio Gates officiated. The bride's attendants were Miss Blanche Landolt, maid of honor, Misses Louise Landolt and Gertrude Dodd were bridesmaids. George Kershaw, brother of the bride, was best man, the ushers were Sterling Wood and Roy Shinner. Mr. and Mrs. Hansen will be at home on Church St. after Nov. 20.

The marriage of Miss Edith Glasier to J. Bosworth Dawson at Bedford, O. was announced.

## Deaths

Charles S. Farnham, formerly of this city, died suddenly. After taking sick in Ripon, he returned home to Twenty-first St. and died twenty-four hours later. Mr. Farnham has suffered with asthma and heart trouble for some time. He was 64 years old and is survived by a his wife, daughter, Katherine Farnham and son, Charles R. Farnham. He will be buried in Sparta.

John Van Uxem, a Wauwatosa boy who was a brakeman on the Milwaukee Road, fell off the engine of the train in Hartford, Nov. 2, the succeeding car ran over his legs and he died at Milwaukee Hospital Nov. 3, 1903. Mr. Van Uxem was 28 years old and lived with his parents, Mr. and Mrs. A. Van Uxem, on Hadley Ave. The inquest held by Coroner Broegman found his death to be accidental. The funeral will be from the family home with interment at Wauwatosa cemetery.

## Letters uncalled for at the postoffice.

P. Alexander, F. Bleifernicht, V.S. Barnes, E.E. Cavalere, Robert

Laird, Miss A. Moll, Lizzie Raby, Albert Thompson, A.H. Staube, Mr. and Mrs. H. Tory, Fred Wilke, Frank Webber, and P.P. Zoll

## November 14, 1903

Henry Rachow is visiting in Stoughton.

Rev. C.J. Rogers went to Greenville, Maine.

Mrs. John Parker Gregg went to Madison.

Mrs. H. Theodore Hansen is in rockford, Ill.

Mr. and Mrs. A.C. Hanson were in Hartford.

Niel Benoy has been ill.

Miss Isabel E. Skinner, Mower Court, is in Chicago.

Mr. E.W. Lindsay is in Campbellsport.

Mr. and Mrs. Louis Nickel entertained at cinch.

Mrs. A.W. Lehmann, of Neosho, visited J.T. Van Vechten

Uncle Fritz Barnekow has been ill.

Mr. and Mrs. John P. Gregg moved to Madison.

The Alex. Rogers' house has been sold.

Worrel Buck will work for Lefeber Bros. Co.

Messrs. A.E. Beecher and Fred Kocher will give a dancing party.

Mrs. L.G. Wheeler held a quilting bee for Mrs. John Parker Gregg.

Messrs. C. Leutzow, O. Helgesen, and V. Vining were hunting.

Miss Mertie Nettleton has returned home.

Mr. De Voe and family, Kavanaugh Pl., moved to Truesdale, Wis. to engage in farming.

Mrs. M.H. Hess, of Milwaukee, and daughter, Mrs. Bertha Radcliff, of Grand Forks, ND, visited friends here.

Miss C.G. Warren bought a lot on W. Main St. from Charles Stafford to build a home.

Contractor Benkendorf is laying the foundation for Pauls church.

Capt. and Mrs. W.J. Denny their daughter and her husband, Mr.

and Mrs. E.A. Knowlton, of Milwaukee, visited Richard Tennant.

Mrs. J.M. Knowles, of Dartford, visited her niece, Mrs. H.E. Rose, she gave a talk at the W.C.T.U. meeting at Mrs. J.W. Cairncross' home.

Mr. S.P. Croft was given the contract to grade part of Watertown Plank Rd.

Mrs. R. Gianella and Mrs. C. Taylor entertained the West Side Neighborhood club.

H.E. Leister, H. Ludington, Peter Schmidt, Fred Heiden, Peter Diedrich, C. Wadsworth, H. Buchman, W.E. Fisher, Nic. Nolz and Joe Sausen went hunting.

Miss Lizette, Mrs. Merica, Mrs. Burnside, Miss Sporleder, and George Schneck performed at a recital at the M. E. church.

Judge O.T. Williams, Vernon T. Wakefield, George H. Wright, O.W. Robertson, William Stark, and George H.D. Johnson are promoters for a new golf club called the Blue Mound club which will be located on the Wellauer farm.

Ferdinand Bark will succeed Charles Kieckhefer, Jr. as superintendent of the almshouse, sewerage plant, and waterworks with an annual salary of $1,500 and living expenses. Michael Schmidt, Adelbert Heise, and Dietrich Thiele were also considered. Mr. Bark was born in Germany in 1863, and came to Milwaukee with his parents at the age of sixteen. He worked at a company learning wood carving and then became foreman of the Milwaukee Chair co. After coming to Wauwatosa he started a furniture business, which he conducted for six years. In 1899 he was appointed assistant of the city poor. His family consists of his wife, a daughter, and a son.

Mrs. Allen Williams, who is interested in Texas and Louisiana real estate and oil fields, returned from that part of the country.

**Death**

Mr. J.C. Fairbanks, brother of Mrs. J.B. Judson, died at his home in Traverse City, Mich..

Mr. J. Emory Roberts, brother of the late Mrs. L.L. Gridley, died at his home in Belle Plain, Ia., Nov. 11, 1903. He will be interred at Ft. Atkinson, Wis., his former home.

Mrs. Mary Van Antwerp died at her home on N. Main St. after suffering a stroke, Nov. 10, 1903, at the age of seventy. She resided with her daughter, Miss M.L. Young. Mrs. Van Antwerp will be buried in Rochester, NY, her former home.

**Letters uncalled for at the postoffice.**

F. Bliefernicht, Geo. W. Ballentine, Anna J. Brady, F.L. Carmy, Fred Domers, Herman Miller, Alma Schuek, Geo. M. Wakefield, Harry Wenborn and E.J. Wagner

### November 28, 1903

Miss Mary Wales is visiting her sister in Saylesville.

Mrs. A.E. Barnes has a severe cold.

Mrs. S. Blaesser is visiting friends in Chicago.

Miss Claudia McPheeters was in Eau Claire for Thanksgiving.

Mrs. Nelson, Spring Hill, is quite ill with the grippe.

Earling Swan injured his foot in an accident.

Miss Mary Hulburt is home from Chicago Univ.

Mrs. H. Theodore Hansen went to California.

Miss Belle Farries visited Miss Mary Hulburt at the Univ. of Chicago.

Mrs. Ray Mann, of Chicago, visited her parents, Mr. and Mrs. Walter Griffith.

Mrs. E. Clinton Carter gave a musicale at her home at Graystone Park.

Mr. and Mrs. C.D. Barnes, of Lowell, visited Mrs. Agelena Barnes.

Mr. Dysart, assistant postmaster in Ripon, visited his parents on Kavanaugh Pl.

Mr. and Mrs. Charles Stickney are visiting their daughter in Leadville, Col.

George Kershaw, St. Clare McMillan and Miss Elizabeth Foley are home from the U W Madison.

Dr. E.B. Fuller, of Milwaukee, son of A.B. Fuller, fell and broke his arm.

Mr. J.A. Schwaiger has improved the interior of his drug store.

Earling Swann entertained the Freshman class of W.H.S.

Louis Nickel, Peter Nickel, and Otto Schwandt returned from hunting.

August Henke, Vista Ave., is doing some repairs on his house.

Mr. and Mrs. Henry O. Stone, of Bloomington, Ill., spent Thanksgiving with her parents, Mr. and Mrs. J.H. Cushing.

Dr. Cairncross, Messrs. G.E. Smith and A.L. Smith and families had Thanksgiving dinner with Mr. and Mrs. Elmer Blodgett, of West Allis.

Herman Hoppe was fined by Judge Neelen for opening the Schoonmaker dam.

Mr. and Mrs. J.I. Fairbanks and daughter, Mary Fairbanks, of Milwaukee, and Mr. J. Watts Judson, of Chicago, spent Thanksgiving with J.B. Judson.

Miss Jessie Gilbert was elected a director of the Wis. Humane society.

Wm. Jullet, of Lowell, and Louis Bussewitz, of Cumberland, visited E.M. Bussewitz.

Mrs. R.M. Brown is back from Shawano where she attended her sister, Miss Margaret Delpsch, who has been quite ill.

Superintendent Loveland, of the Pickle Co., reports they had a banner day shipping 400 barrels of pickles to New England and Albany, NY.

Gilbert Thompkins, Edward Pares, and Thomas Norton will give a dance.

Mrs. R. Delpsch will spend the holidays with her daughter and son, Mrs. Stanley Conway and Charles Delpsch in St. Paul, Minn.

Oscar Hartung accompanied the football team to Green Bay.

Rev. A.R. Thain will deliver an address at the Wauwatosa Lodge, I.O.G.T. meeting. B.F. Parker, Right Worthy Grand Secretary of the World, and Mrs. Altie Reed, Chancellor of the Course of Study, visited the last meeting.

Dr. Grosskopf's charges had a good meal at the County hospital as did Dr. Beutler's at the Chronic Insane asylum, Superintendent Kieckhefer's at the Alms house, and Superintendent Kringel's at the home for Dependent Children.

Thos. Bendelow, of Chicago, laid out the golf course for the Blue Mound Country Club.

George W. Sanford, veteran real estate dealer and long time resident of Wauwatosa, is very ill with heart trouble.

Miss Lily Pelton will lead the B.Y.P.U. at the Baptist church.\

Rev. G.A. Ehrhardt is the pastor in charge of Paul's church.

**Death**

Albert H. Krantz died Nov. 24, 1903 at the age of 34. He was buried at Forest Home cemetery.

**Probate Notice**

Letters testamentary on the estate of Gerhart Loerx, dec'd, have been granted to Mary Flizen. Paul D. Carpenter, County Judge

**Letters uncalled for at the postoffice.**

Willie Haase, Anton Kreutzberg, William Powell, and George Wherry

## December 5, 1903

Miss Belle Farries is visiting in Chicago.

C.K. Douglas, of Troy Center, was here.

Mr. and Mrs. Oscar Helgesen are in North Prairie.

Mr. and Mrs. Warren Woodmansee were in Chicago.

Mrs. G.W. Hunt and son were in Green Bay.

Mr. T.E. Zimmerman was in Chicago on Business.

Mrs. H.N. Andrew and son, Oliver Andrew, visited in Delavan.

Mrs. Mary Horning entertained the West Side Neighborhood club.

Mr. L.F. Potter, of Harlem, Ia., visited the M.B. Potter family.

Rev. F.S. Gray has taken rooms at the C.T. Everett home.

Miss Esther Landolt is having a Dollie party for friends.

Mrs. W.S. Faulkner was surprised by Milwaukee friends.

Henry Knapp is visiting his folks after an absence of fifteen years in Outagamie County.

Mrs. F.M. Keats entertained for her sister, Mrs. Craig, of Chicago.

Mr. Kearney and family moved to the house formerly occupied by Prof. Cornelius.

Miss Sylvia Lefeber's Sunday School class gave a social at the Baptist church.

Mr. and Mrs. H.P. Bradley entertained at Whist.

The Neighborhood club met with Mrs. J.H. Cushing.

Messrs. C.T. Fisher, E.D. Hoyt, and F.E. Loveland attended a stock show in Chicago.

Mrs. Sparling and son, of Trempeleau, visited at E.C. Nettleton's home.

Mr. J.W. Highley, who was home, returned to his job in Oshkosh.

Mmes. C.A. Curtis and E.E. Curtis entertained the Kensington club.

The W.C.T.U. will meet with Mrs. George Smith.

Edmond Hayes was surprised by friends on his sevententh birthday, Dec. 1.

The road grading by Contractor Croft is going slow because of cold weather.

Joseph Trost tendered his resignation as constable at the town board meeting.

Miss Blanche Landolt is visiting in West Bend.

Miss France Sanderson is visiting in Chicago.

Mr. J.B. Thomas, of Wausau, visited friends here.

W.D. Maxon, of Cedar Lake, visited relatives here.

Mrs. E. Smith was the guest of Mrs. Stanley Watson.

Mrs. D.B. Barnes is seriously ill.

Mr. T.E. Chatfield, is home from Waupaca, to visit his family.

Miss Nellie Ross is visiting her aunt, Mrs. Smith McCormack.

Mrs. D.F. Phillipps entertained friends at coffee.

Mr. G.W. Sanford is slightly improved, but still critical.

Mrs. Victor Lowe, of Palmyra, visited Mr. and Mrs. C.W. Damon.

Mr. and Mrs. E.C. Eldridge, of Neenah, visited the J.T.
Van Vechten home.

Mr. D.A. Lewis, of Baraboo, visited his mother, Mrs. S.S. Lewis.

Mr. E. Bigsby has recovered from injuries and is back on his postal
route.

Elling Opsal, sheriff of Lincoln County, SD, visited his niece, Mrs.
J.W. Highley, of Western Ave.

Grant Thomas, superintendant of the Wisconsin Dept. of the St.
Louis Exposition, visited Adam Currie.

Messrs. A.E. Beecher and Fred Kocher held an entertainment at
the W.A.C. hall.

Leslie A. Bollenbach entered into a printing partnership with Frank
Van De Kamp, of Milwaukee.

Charles A. Payne will lecture at the M. E. church.

Rev. Dr. Thain delivered an address at the Congregational church
convention in Kaukauna.

Louise J. Landolt is secretary of the Postal Board.

**Marriage**

William Kerber married Miss Ida Hardtke at St. John's church,
Nov. 30, 1903, with the reception at the home of the bride's
parents, Mr. and Mrs. August Hardke on North Ave.

**Death**

The infant son and only child of Mr. and Mrs. Charles McClintock died Nov. 29, at the home of Mrs. McClintock's parents Mr. and Mrs. M.H. Adams. The funeral was from the family home with interment at Calvary cemetery.

Mrs. Dorothea Barfooth, wife of Ernest Barfooth, Barnekow Ave. died Nov. 29, 1903. Mrs. Barfooth was seventy one years old and had been a resident of the town for almost forty years. She died suddenly from apoplexy. She is survived by her husband and four children. The funeral was at St. John's church with interment at Wauwatosa cemetery. Rev. William Rader officiated.

**Letters uncalled for at the postoffice.**

Jessie Alberti, Miss W.L. Adams, F. Bielfernicht, Cora Edwards, Mrs. M. Johnson, Miss F. Stokdyk, Johanna Schultz, and Herman Welms

### December 12, 1903

Arthur Koenig was in New York on business.

Mrs. Jemima Hart, of Zion City, is visiting relatives here.

Mrs. L.A. Warren is back from Minnesota.

Mrs. Anna Peck, of Waukesha, visited Mrs. G. G. Allen.

Gus Gregg purchased the Wakefield property.

Mr. A.L. Carlton is back from a three months business trip in California.

Miss Elinor Barrett, of Oshkosh, will winter with Mrs. D.B. Barnes.

Mrs. N.W. Hinckley, of Chicago, visited Mrs. Mary Horning.

Miss Lucile Stout moved to Evanston, Ill.

Mr. Fritz and family moved to the Hart House on N. Main and Park Sts.

Miss Mary Sabin, of Whitefish Bay, visited Miss Carrie G. Warren.

Harry Bennett, of Milwaukee, visited Rev. C.E. Goldthorp and family.

Judson Hulburt is home from agricultural college in Ames, Iowa.

Mrs. C.G. Dreutzer entertained at coffee.

Messrs. W.L. Notbohm, J.P. Bark, and Ferdinand Bark were witnesses at the grand jury.

C.A. Payne gave a lecture at the M.E. church.

The Epworth League met with Miss Mildred Brockway, the officers elected were: President, Miss Lou J. Pilgrim; 1st Vice-President, Miss Agnes Tennant; 2nd Vice-President, Mr. E.G. Nelson; 3rd Vice-President, Miss Nellie Engelhart; 4th Vice-President, Miss Olive Lefeber; Secretary, Miss Agnes Brown; Treasurer, Elmer Pilgrim; Organist Miss Florence Wells.

Officers elected at the meeting of the Modern Woodmen of America were W.H. Engelhart, G.A. Sylvester, J.J. Marquardt, L.R. Gridley, M. Casperson, D.P. Jones, L. Nickel, Ferdinand Bark, O. Helgesen, Dr. E.A. Schmitz, and C.B. Perry.

The Ladies Aid society of the M.E. church met with Mrs. G.W. Ringrose. They will give a Sock social at Mrs. L. Brockway's home.

Rev. Levi White, of Indianapolis, says Rev. Lyon is the greatest preacher.

Union prayer meetings have been held at the homes of Mr. Wilcox and Rev. D.W. Hulburt.

**Letters uncalled for at the postoffice**

Christian Doerfler, John Illiment, Charles Laning, Wm. Mahnke, Betty Klatke, Mrs. K. Peterson, Joseph Rundle, Miss Emma Spuhrieder, and Louis Thorp

### December 19, 1903

Capt. Henry Leisk returned from Chicago.

Miss Belle Farries has returned from Chicago.

Rev. C.J. Everett is in Oconomowoc.

Emil Fauerbach, of Madison, was here visiting friends.

Miss Ethelyn Colwell is vacationing at her home in Rome.

Mr. F.A. Fritz and family moved into the Hart house.

Charles Warren, of Minneapolis, is visiting his sister, Mrs. P.W. Longfellow.

G.W. Barrett had a sleigh ride party.

Miss Elizabeth Morris has returned home to Sheboygan after visiting H.P. Bradley.

Mr. A. Harden returned from buying wood in Pittsville.

Joseph Diedrich and family moved to Pewaukee, he will work on the Kieckhefer farm.

Liveryman, J.L. Morton, has added a Rockaway to his line of sleighs and cutters.

Rev. and Mrs. W.J. Patton, of Superior, former pastor of the M.E. church here, visited friends here.

The Wauwatosa street railway case will be brought before Judge Halsey today.

Misses Cora Hartung and Verna Nichols gave the Freshmen of W.H.S. a sleighride.

H.W. Dascomb, of Port Huron, Mich., praises Evangelist Lyon.

Union prayer meetings were held at Mr. Hubbard's and Mrs. Horning's.

Mr. J.B. Judson is quite ill.

Prof. and Mrs. Merica, went home to Garrett, Ind. for the holidays; Miss Wood to Edgerton; Miss Farnham to Beaver Dam; Miss Bleedorn to Janesville, and Miss Colwell to Rome, their homes.

Mrs. Charles T. Morris, of Berlin, was the guest of honor at a T.C.T. club meeting. Mrs. Arthur Gross, Mrs. John Romadka and Mrs. Burnside provided the music. Out of town guest were: Mrs. H.M. Youmans, Mrs. Thomas H. Brown, and Miss Lutie E. Stevens. The hostesses were: Mrs. Joseph Wood, Mrs. Will Godfrey, Mrs. Walter H. Wright, Mrs. James L. Foley, Mrs.

Horatio Gates, and Mrs. G.P. Dousman, assisted by Mrs. Grant, Mmes. V.B. Dunham, Joseph Flanner, and J.C. Stacy and the Misses Annette Dreutzer, Lou Harriman, Edna Hooley, and Ella Lillibridge.

The mayor and members of the city council were served with papers by Henry Leisk and others, the matter was turned over to the city attorneys.

Don Curtis will lead the B.Y.P.U. at the Baptist church.

### Death

Miss Tina Madsen, age 27, died of consumption, Dec. 13, 1903, at the County hospital. She had been employed at Dr. Hathaway's home for several years. The undertaker was Judson, funeral from the M.E. Church with interment at Wauwatosa cemetery. Rev. Goldthorp officiated.

Mrs. Werner, wife of Earnest Werner, died at her home on North Ave., Dec. 14, 1903. She was 72 years old. The funeral was from the Baptist church, Rev. Ehrhardt, of Pauls church officiated with burial at Wauwatosa cemetery.

Mrs. Angelina C. Barnes, widow of David B. Burhs(sic), a long time resident of Wauwatosa, died at her home on Wauwatosa Ave. of heart failure, Dec. 15, 1903.. She was 70 years old. The funeral was from her home with interment at Wauwatosa cemetery. Rev. Goldthorp officiated.

### Letters uncalled for at the post office.

Mrs. Louisa Bernbach, Lawrence Eere, G. Holliday, Wm. J. Kendrick, Nettie Millar, Harry Patter, O.W. Paine, Mrs. Herman Sherf and Steve Steinea; held for postage: Clarence Gunderman.

### January 2, 1904

John Young, who injured his foot, is up and around.

Miss Emily Seamans is home from Knoxville, Ill for a short visit.

Miss Mabel Gilbert, who was ill with quinsy, is better.

Dr. and Mrs. Hathaway entertained informally.

Ferdinand Bark will take charge of the county farm Jan. 4.

Mr. and Mrs. E.M. Petri, of Chicago, visited the Mr. and Mrs. Ferdinand Bark.

Mrs. Edward Temple, of Chicago, visited the H.S. Temple home.

The Evening Cinch club was entertained at the John Greenwood home.

Misses Florence Everett and Daisy Everett entertained at tea.

Dr. and Mrs. Claude Greengo, of Chilton, Wis., visited Charles Kroesing.

Miss Mary E. Marvin, of Philadelphia, visited her sister, Mrs. Charles Crain.

Mrs. Otis Kneeland and son, Fred Kneeland, of Lewiston, Mich., visited Mrs. N.L. Kneeland.

Master Jack Pierce gave a party.

Mrs. J.W. Cairncross and mother, Mrs. I.B. Smith, gave a family dinner.

Miss Edith Hooker, of Milwaukee, visited Miss Florence Adams.

Mr. and Mrs. Arthur Gregg and Mr. and Mrs. G.G. Allen will entertain the Evening Cinch club.

James Lefeber, who has been ill, is better.

Charles Stickney went to St. Louis, Mo. to attend the funeral of his cousin, Miss Fannie Stickney.

Mrs. J.L. Morton, Mr. and Mrs. Cross Twinem, and Miss Mary Clapp are ill.

D.T. Pilgrim, Jr. found a man's mitten.

The Country Cousins' Birthday club met at Mr. and Mrs. O.J. Swan's home.

Dr. and Mrs. H.G. Morton and Mr. and Mrs. C.H. Godfrey entertained at dinner.

Mr. and Mrs. J.T. Bossingham, of Oswego, NY, formerly of Wauwatosa, are visiting friends here.

Capt. Henry Leisk was elected president of the Milwaukee Shipmasters' assoc.

Miss N. Fairweather returned to Evanston, accompanied by Miss Nellie McCormack, after a visit to the S. McCormack home.

A fire destroyed the barn of Charles Eckstein on Wells St., but the house was saved.

C.B. Perry and H.P. Bradley were summoned before the grand jury.

The officers for the I.O.F. for 1904 are: E. Hurlbut, C.F. Eckstein, A. Riebe, John Taylor, W.H. Engelhart, A. Luetzow, O. Walters, Ben. Ackman, O. Ulrich, Chas. Luetzow, Ferd. Bark, and Dr. J.W. Cairncross.

The F.&A.M. officers are: W.R. McKowen, J.D. Shaw, O. Kroesing, F.H. Durbin, A. Landolt, Geo. Wepfer, L.C. Wheeler, S.M. Tibbits, C.T. Chandler, R. Tennant, and C.B. Perry.

A petition to close business early during the gospel meetings held by Rev. M.H. Lyon was signed by: Lefeber Brothers Co., Menninger & Bussewitz, Charles Luetzow, Fred. H. Bark, W.H. Englehardt, A.C. Kuchynski, G.W. Prentice, Wm. A. Hart, Smith-Russell Co., H.P. Hempsing Co. E.C. Nettleton.

C.R. Bachman was nominated a member of the fire dept.

### Marriage

Miss Edith Brownell married Frank Burkhart, of Milwaukee, Dec. 31, 1903 at the home of the bride's parents, Mr. and Mrs. J.C. Brownell, W. Main St. Rev. F.S. Gray read the service.

### Death

John B. Judson died Dec. 27, 1903, at his home. He was 83 years and one of the oldest undertakers in Milwaukee County. He was engaged in that business in Wauwatosa. Mr. Judson was born at Oxford, Chenengo County, New York on April 2, 1821. He came to Milwaukee in Oct., 1852 as an actuary for an

Mr. Morse, known as Judson & Morse. In 1888 Mr. Judson moved to Wauwatosa where he continued the business with his son, Charles E. Judson. He was active in the M.E. church and is survived by his wife and son, C.E. Judson.

### January 9, 1904

Miss Edna Hooley is in Hurley, Wis.

Mr. and Mrs. Barney Blum, of Forsyth, Mont., are visiting here.

Miss Louise Landolt is ill with a severe cold.

Mrs. Charlotte Wyman is in Chicago visiting.

Miss Lottie Hart is visiting friends in Zion City, Ill.

Arthur Hibbard, of Gloversville, NY, is visiting friends here.

Charlie Hausch was severely injured while coasting.

Mr. and Mrs. D.B. Lewis returned to Indianapolis.

Van Lehman, of Neosho, visited his grandfather, J.T. Van Vechten.

The Married Ladies' Cinch club will meet with Mrs. C. Noyes, Milwaukee.

Mr. Kearney will build a residence on Eighth Ave.

Mr. C.J. Millard, of Lake Mills, Wis., is visiting his daughter, Mrs. A.I. Smith.

Mr. and Mrs. James Godfrey are back from visiting E.R. Godfrey in Calumet, Mich.

Mrs. B.H. Meyer, of Madison, and Dr. E.P. Carlton, of Keyeser, Wis., were here for the funeral of their father, Mr. A.L. Carlton.

Mrs. Allen Moan and Mrs. H.B. Hunter will entertain the T.C.T. club.

Mrs. Joseph Wood and Miss Annette Dreutzer assisted at a tea given by Mrs. Arthur Cross, Milwaukee, in honor of Mrs. A.E. Copeland, of New York.

Messrs. Frank Mayer and son, Herman Voltz, F. Yehle, and Jos. Ginter returned from a fishing trip.

Mrs. L.C. Tisdale and Mrs. W.H. Hadley entertaind at cinch, Mrs.
M.H. Fisk won the prize.

Miss France Sanderson went to New Orleans where she will be
joined later by her mother, Mrs. J.E. Pierce and William
Maher, Miss Sanderson will make her social debut with Miss
Quentall.

At the county board meeting Supervisor Bell instructed the county
surveyor to survey the right-of-way of the Grand Ave. viaduct.

Messrs. A. Harden and J.D. Warren found the reason for the
stench in the river at the sugar beet plant in Menomonee Falls.

**Deaths**

Rufus G. Dreher died Jan. 1, 1904, at his home on Fifty-Fourth
St., Residence park, he was 28 years old. The funeral was from
his home with interment at Forest Home cemetery.

Mrs. Fred G. Lynds died Jan. 2, 1904, at her home on Franklin
St., Milwaukee, after a short illness. She was interred at
Calvary cemetery.

George W. Sanford, died at his home here, Jan. 2, 1904, of
heart disease and dropsy. He suffered a heart attack while
visiting his sister in Council Bluffs, Iowa three months ago and
returned home with his health completely broken down. Mr.
Sanford was a Milwaukee county pioneer, he was born in 1834, at
Constantine, Mich.. His parents died when he was 10 years old
and he went to live with his brother at Mineral Point, Wis. where
he attended public schools and later went to Lawrence Univ. in
Appleton. After graduating he joined a surveying institution in
northern Wisconsin and then engaged in the mercantile business at
Sparta. He came to Milwaukee in 1862 and soon married
Mary A. Secromb, the daughter of John Secromb, with whom he
became a business partner. In 1888 Mr. Sanford went into the real
estate business in Wauwatosa. He is survived by a widow.

Albion Leighton Carlton died Jan. 4, 1903, of apoplexy, at the home of his father-in-law, George Wells, of Greenfield Ave. Mr. Carlton was one of the oldest residents of Wauwatosa. He was born in 1840 in Bradford, Mass. and was a relative of Will Carlton, the well known poet, he was also a writer of considerable merit. Mr. Carlton was educated in Bradford and was valedictorian of the class of 1857, at Phillips' academy. He then spent three years at Brown Univ. in R.I. He subsequently learned the shoe business and came to Milwaukee at the age of 27 where he became a traveling salesman for several shoe firms, a position he held until his death. Mr. Carlton resided in Wauwatosa for thirty years after coming here in 1873, he had spent seven years in Madison. He married Miss Elizabeth R. Clark, of this city, who died in 1887, leaving three children. In 1893 he married Miss Catherine Wells, of Wauwatosa, who survives him. He is also survived by his three children, Mrs. Mary L. Wasmansdorf, of Lewiston, Mont., Mrs. Alice E. Meyer, of Madison, Wis., and Dr. E.P. Carlton, of Keyeser, Wis.. The funeral was from the Wells family home with interment at Forest Home cemetery. Rev. A.R. Thain officiated.

**Probate notice**

Letters Testamentary on the estate of Angelina C. Barnes were granted to Charles D. Barnes. Paul D. Carpenter, County Judge

### January 16, 1904

John F. Dittmar is in Madison on business.

Mr. J.C. Lefeber is ill with a severe cold.

Mrs. Smith McCormack is quite ill.

Miss Ada Maxon is back from an extended visit out east.

Miss Flora Stewart visited Joseph Lefeber.

Jerry Rogers lost a valuable team horse while hauling ice.

John Zimmerman will occupy the Ferdinand Bark home.

Charles Loomis and Austin Gregg will work the J.A. Warren farm.

Ned Keats is moving to California.

Alex. Rogers, of Minneapolis, was here to visit friends and relatives.

Miss Mabel Lefeber is visiting Miss Mabel Potter in South Milwaukee.

Mrs. J.D. Warren gave a Kensington at her home.

Geo. Smith has a severe cold.

Miss Inez Wright, of Milwaukee, is visiting Mrs. Eugene Wright.

Henry Rose, of Princeton, Wis., is visiting his son Mr. H.E. Rose.

Mrs. Chas. Sage, of Delavan, Wis., is visiting her parents, Mr. and Mrs. Smith McCormack.

Thomas Helgesen, of Tomah, is visiting his parents, Mr. and Mrs. Oscar Helgesen.

Mr. J.K. Hemphill, of Nashville, Tenn., visited the John Winters' home.

Mrs. H. Ludington gave a children's birthday party for her son, Harrison Ludington.

Mrs. J.A. Fetterly, Miss Peters, and Ellis Lamb, of Milwaukee, visited W.H. Lamb.

Mrs. May Butters, of Adell, Wis., will visit her mother, Mrs. Elizabeth Curtis.

Mrs. I.C. Lillibridge will entertain at a Kensington.

George Rogers and Ray Greenwood were in Winona, Minn. to visit Stanton Taylor, Mr. Rogers' uncle.

Miss Ethelyn Colwell resigned her teaching position, Miss Elizabeth Daly, of Boone, Iowa will replace her.

Mrs. Henry B. Hunter and Mrs. Allen J. Moan entertained the Twentieth Century Topic club. There were readings by Charlotte Parry Smith, Mrs. Richard Dewey, and Mrs. George Dousman with music by Mrs. Merica and Miss Haney.

The Woman's club will meet with Miss Miriam Hoyt, guests included: Mrs. Gudden, of Oshkosh, and Mrs. T.H. Brown, of Milwaukee.

**Death**

Mr. Tully, son-in-law of Richard Gilbert, died at his home in Baltimore, Md. of pneumonia. He leaves his widow, Mrs. Maude Tully and six children. Jesse D. Gilbert, brother of Mrs. Tully, left to attend the funeral.

The funeral of Patrick D. O'Brien, head news pressman for *The Evening Wisconsin* for thirty years, was held Jan. 14, 1904 at Gesu church in Milwaukee. Mr. O'Brien was a Wauwatosa boy.

**Letters uncalled for at the postoffice.**

F. Bielpernicht, W. Jacques, Miss Ida Krysch, Mrs. Clara Scott, G. Harris, Mrs. Ida May Thrall, James Kearns, Mrs. Schultz, and Mrs. F.L. Stewart

### January 23, 1904

Mrs. S.S. Lewis visited her son at Baraboo, Wis.

Miss Blanche Landolt is in Madison.

Ned Keats left for California.

Mrs. G.W. Sanford is quite ill.

George Wells, Sr., who had the grip, is improving.

Mrs. A.A. Roddis visited friends in Waukesha.

Mrs. Mary Horning is quite ill.

Mr. Joseph Keeler is leaving for Montana.

Mr. J.L. Hamme spent Sunday in Waukesha with his father.

Mr. and Mrs. E.R. Godfrey, Jr. are back from their trip.

Mrs. John Young visited friends in Milwaukee.

Mrs. W.R. Cundall gave a birthday party for her son, Roland Cundall's sixth birthday, Jan. 14, 1904.

Misses Lillian Sisson and Marian Smith, of Milwaukee, visited Miss Maud Curtis.

Miss Eliza Hunt, of West Bend, will visit the J.S. Cutler home.

Miss Helen Temple, of Milwaukee, is visiting her brother, H.S. Temple.

Mr. W.S. Faulkner and son, Russel Faulkner, are home because Mrs. Faulkner is ill.

Dr. and Mrs. M.J. White gave a dinner.

Rev. F.S. Gray visited Rev. G.S. Sinclair in Oconomowoc.

Miss Maud Curtis, Richard Hayes, Mr. W.B. Lincoln, and James Lefeber are ill.

Mrs. W.R. Robertson returned home to Chicago after a visit with Mrs. M. Horning.

Miss Helen Stickney is going to Leadville, Colo. to visit her sister, Mrs. Connell, who is quite ill.

T.F. Grover, of Fond du Lac, former superintendent of the electric plant here, was elected president of the Northwestern Electrical Assoc.

Mr. and Mrs. Abram Lefeber entertained at tea, their guests were: Mrs. Brockway, Mr. Lyon, Mr. Coultes, Rev. and Mrs. C.E. Goldthorp, and Rev. and Mrs. Edwin Hyde, of Milwaukee.

Mrs. M. Bauer is looking for work in private families.

The Woman's club met at Miss Miriam Hoyt's home.

A Wauwatosa branch of the Consumer's League was established, Mrs. C.B. Perry was chosen president and Mrs. Richard Dewey, secretary and treasurer.

**Letters uncalled for at the postoffice**

Miss Katy Kihman, L.M. LaFollette, Johann Polkow, Frank L. Peschman, Miss Frank(sic) Seymour, Henry Lench, John Peters, Miss Clara Schultz, and Miss Lydia Zieglmann.

### January 30, 1904

This paper is in poor condition and very hard to read, the names may be spelt wrong.

M.E. Oertel went for a visit to Oshkosh.

Mrs. Hans Koenig went to St. Paul to visit her parents.

Miss Ada Maxon has returned from Cedar Lake.

John Thomas, of Wausau, is here visiting friends.

Miss Mabel Gruet entertained informally.

Walter Keisen was in Lena, Wis. on business.

Miss Blanche Landolt is back from Madison, Wis.

The We Ten club will meet with Miss Blanche Canright.

Mrs. Oscar Pierce, of Milwaukee, is visitng her daughter, Mrs. D.G. Hathaway.

Miss Mabel Potter, of Bay View, was here visiting Miss Mabel Lefeber.

Rev. G.S. Sinclair, of Oconomowoc, visited Rev. F.S. Gray

Charles Fisher will enter a college of osteopathy in Missouri.

Miss Lill van Baumbach will resume her studies at the music conservatory.

Miss Thompson and Mr. Lewis entertained the Evening Cinch club.

Mr. and Mrs. L.S. Pease left to attend his aunt's funeral in Portage.

The Kensington club will meet at the home of Mrs. J.S. Cutler.

J.D. Gilbert accompanied by his sister, Mrs. Tully and children, returned from Baltimore.

Mr. and Mrs. E.O. Stumpf, of Milwaukee, were visiting the W.S. Faulkner home.

Mrs. A.T. Hubbard and Rev. P.W. Longfellow are ill.

The Woman's Auxillary of Trinity church will meet with Mrs. G.P. Adams.

D.F. Philipp and family have gone to Hartford to attend the funeral of Mrs. Philipp's uncle, A. Hacker.

Mr. and Mrs. L.C. Tisdale will spend a month with their son, Dr. E. Tisdale in Milwaukee.

Mrs. M.H. Fisk, C.G. Dreutzer, and Miss Annette Dreutzer will entertain the Married Ladies' Cinch club.

Charles Loomis will deliver an address at the agricultural dept. at UW in Madison.

Miss Emma Falk is back at her duties at the telephone central after having tonsilitis.

Miss Mary Hart lost a mink muff between Lefeber Brothers and the library.

Mmes. Henry Watner, D.G. Hathaway, and I.C. Lillibridge attended the meeting of the Kehnia club at Mrs. E.S. Streeter's home in Milwaukee.

Mrs. John Marquardt was surprised on her 71st birthday, Jan. 21.

Ald. Menninger was made aquainted with woodcraft at the M.W.A. meeting.

Prof. and Mrs. Francis M. Merica entertained in honor of Miss Reyher and Miss Teal. Those attending were: Misses Florence Lefeber, Florence Adams, Alice Smith, Laura Loveland, Olive Lefeber, Daisy Everett, Ruth Ellis, Messrs Perey Myers, George Schneck, James Lefeber, Charles Fisher, Walter Smith, ? Gridley, and Edward Pavy.

Barney Blum and Joseph Keeter went to Forsyth, Mona.

Burley Allen will resume work as night operator at this station and Arthur Brockway will go to Elm Grove.

**Births**

Mr. and Mrs. H.S. Temple, of Center St., had a daughter, Jan. 29, 1904

Mr. and Mrs. M. Meinder?, Blanchard St., had a son, Jan. 29, 1904.

**Letters uncalled for at the postoffice**

Mrs. Joseph Bushnell, Annie Brese, August Koeppen, Louis Kreger, Hughie McDonald, Edward Moore, James McHugh, Martin Taek, Mrs. Matti White, and Miss L. Wurderle

### February 6, 1904

Miss Lulu Shaw is visiting in Bangor, Wis.

Miss Alice Sherfy returned from Rockford, Ill.

Mr. E.C. Nettleton is taking a trip to Missouri.

J.B. De Swarte was in Chicago on business.

Mr. and Mrs. John P. Gregg, of Madison, visited friends here.

Jesse Hart, of Root Creek, visited the News office.

G.G. Allen and family are moving to Second Ave. and Center St.

Mrs. D.G. Hathaway will entertain in honor of her mother, Mrs. Oscar Pierce, of Milwaukee.

George Kershaw is home to visit his folks.

Miss Lou Pilgrim attended the Epworth league meeting in Sussex.

Miss Florence Lefeber entertained her normal school friends at tea.

John Ritchie, of Sun Prairie, visited C.E. Curtis.

Mrs. John Parkinson, of Madison, Wis., visited Miss Miriam Hoyt.

Mrs. E.R. Godfrey, Jr. entertained the Neighborhood club.

Mrs. J.W. Hyde, of Milwaukee, spent Sunday with Mrs. John Young.

Mrs. H.P. Bradley entertained the West Side Neighborhood club.

Mrs. J.E. Pierce, entertained at cards.

Mrs. Welch is recovered from her illness and will return to teaching.

Miss Pritchard visited the Milwaukee public schools.

The Evening Cinch club will meet with Dr. and Mrs. J.S. Cutler.

Frank Kalfahs, of Red Wing, Minn., is visiting his brother, A. Kalfahs, here.

Mrs. R.M. Brown left to visit her brother and sister in St. Paul, Minn.

Mrs. A.M. Blaeser has returned from visiting friends in Sheboygan.

Messrs. T.W. Hart and Richard Hayes, who have been ill, are improving.

Jos. Schwaiger was in Fond du Lac and Oshkosh.

G.W. Hunt and family have returned home.

Mr. A.T. Hubbard will move to a farm he purchased in Franklin.

Max Rosenthal was appointed foreman of the grand jury.

Mr. T.J. Ferguson and family will move into the house vacated by John T. Zimmerman.

Reuel C. Reed, of Lamont, Ill, is visiting his Civil War conrades at the Soldier's Home.

Dr. and Mrs. M.H. Fisk went to Fond du Lac to visit his aunt, Mrs. De Nevue.

Mr. and Mrs. Frank Conley, of Minneapolis, are visiting Mr. Conley's parents.

Mrs. M.G. Heath, who is spending the winter at the Frank Harriman home, has returned from visiting relatives in Elgin, Ill.

The appointment of Joseph Trost to constable was rejected by the town board.

Mrs. Pares, Mrs. James Lefeber, and Mrs. L.G. Wheeler presented papers at the Woman's club.

Mr. H.W. Bardenwerper will lead the Young People's Union at the Baptist church.

**Death**

Mrs. Frieda Gombert, wife of Victor L. Gombert, died at the age of 25 years after a short illness. She was a daughter of Mr. and Mrs. Max Rosenthal. She was married to Mr. Gombert Aug. 3, 1901. Mrs. Gombert came to Wauwatosa in her early childhood and spent most of her life in here. The funeral was from her home with interment at Wauwatosa cemetery.

**Letters uncalled for at the postoffice.**

Fred Baldwin, Mrs. Ida Downer, Robt Hahn & Wm Hahn, Jas Lynes, W.R. McKowen, Willie Mahnke, Henry Phillips, John Rosenthal, Leonora Turnsey and H. Zehen.

### February 13, 1904

Miss Loleta Landolt is visiting in Chicago.

Mrs. L.C. Wheeler entertained at tea.

Mrs. E.R. Godfrey entertained at dinner.

Mr. and Mrs. Chas. E. Curtis are going to Madison

Miss Margarette E. Lawrence went to Denver.

Miss Blanche Landolt will attend the Junior Prom in Madison.

Fred H. Bark was badly bruised in a run-a-way accident.

Miss Stella Nelson, of Oconomowoc, visited Miss Maude Curtis.

Miss J. Jones, of Racine, visited Mrs. W.S. Faulkner.

Rev. Richardson, of St. James, Milwaukee, visited Rev. F.S. Gray.

Mr. and Mrs. H.P. Bradley entertained Milwaukee friends.

Mrs. Abram Lefeber will entertain the West Side Neighborhood club.

Dr. and Mrs. J.S. Cutler gave a Hard Times party.

Mrs. A.P. Foster will entertain the Kensington club.

Miss Jean Huntoon, of Minneapolis, visited the Curtis home.

Miss Meta Kroesing was surprised by the W.H.S. Freshman class.

Miss Agnes Tennants' Sunday school class will give a Valentine social.

Mrs. Joseph Lefeber entertained the Epworth League.

Tom Helgesen, who visited his parents here, went to Denver, Col.

Mr. and Mrs. George Skillman are visiting her mother in Milwaukee.

The Womans' Missionary Society of the M. E. church met with Mrs. C.V. Burnside.

Charles Jacobus was in the western part of the state to look after his mining interests.

Mrs. Wm. B. Lincoln entertained at a luncheon.

Mr. E.C. Nettleton is taking a trip to the south.

Supt. Ferdinand Bark is attending lectures at the agricultural dept. of U.W. Madison.

Miss Isabelle Hulburt will visit her sister, Mary Hulburt in Chicago.

Mrs. John Parker Gregg returned to Madison after visiting friends here.

H.E. Smith, who is a United States meat inspector, has transfered here from Detroit and will live in the Underwood house with his family.

The Womans' Missionary society of the Congregational church will meet with Mrs. L.B. Gregg.

The T.C.T. club met with Mrs. G.P. Adams, the next meeting will be at Mrs. Clark's home.

Mr. and Mrs. George Brown, of Whitewater, and Mr. and Mrs. Nichols, of Chicago, were here to attend the funeral of Mrs. Nichols' half sister, Mrs. Sarah Smith Ferguson.

Miss Matilde Kroesing and Oscar Kroesing entertained friends.

Charles E. Curtis, two National Guard officers, a Major and Capt. Frietche, will judge a drill competition of the Minute Men.

I.O.G.T. Wauwatosa Lodge No. 203 entertained friends with a program. Miss Ruth Sporleder gave an instrumental selection, Miss Schleifer, and Miss Everett gave recitations, Miss Skinner performed a vocal solo, and Mr. Skinner delivered an address.

Miss Haney, Prof. W.H. Cheever, Miss Frances A. Wuerst, Miss Alice Marshall, Miss Edith Harney, and Miss Rose A. Cook participated in the program of the Milwaaukee County Teachers' Meeting sponsored by Jesse F. Cory, County Superintendent.

The St. Agnes Guild met with Miss Maud Curtis, officers elected were Mrs. Ruggles, president; Mrs. Lincoln, vice-president; Mrs. Sanderson, second vice-president; Miss Morehouse, treasurer; and Miss Haney, secretary.

Miss Florence Everett will lead the B.Y.P.U. at the Baptist church.

Rev. Kellogg gave a lecture at the Union Bible Study at the Baptist church.

**Marriage**

Otto A. Zillmer will marry Miss Stella Moore at the home of her parents, Mr. and Mrs. W.H. Moore, North Ave., Feb. 17, 1904. They will reside in Ringle, Marathon Co., Wis. where Mr. Zillmer farms.

**Death**

Mrs. Sarah Smith Ferguson died as a result of a surgical operation in Chicago. She lived on a farm in the town of Wauwatosa until her marriage to James Ferguson about twenty-six years ago. The funeral was from the Baptist church, Rev. Longfellow officiated.

Rev. Goldthorp went to the funeral of Miss Bickel, of the Deaconess Home, at Trinity M. E. church in Milwaukee.

**Letters uncalled for at the postoffice.**

Willig Boetcher, Mrs. Julia Boetcher, A.B. Currelley, Arthur Currelley, Miss Louisa King, Dolly Reynolds, Mrs. Nick Teeths, and Miss Rena Weid.

### February 20, 1904

Mrs. J.P. Gregg, of Madison, is visiting friends here.

Miss Ella Lillibridge is going to Elkhorn, Wis.

Sterling Wood is in Iowa on business.

Miss Maude Curtis is visiting friends in Madison.

The St. Agness Guild met with Mrs. W.B. Lincoln.

C.F. Bussewitz was in Juneau, Wis. on business.

Mrs. J.E. Pierce leaves for New Orleans next week.

George Thompson, of Sun Prairie, visited the J.F. Rood home.

Mrs. J.I. Fairbanks and daughter, of Milwaukee, visited Miss C.G. Warren.

Mrs. G. Sanford is considerably improved.

Major A.B. Crombie, of Milwaukee, visited Mr. C.E. Curtis.

Mrs. George Kuehltan, of West Bend, visited Miss Blanch Landolt.

The Lake Keesis campers will be entertained by Miss Jesse Waldie.

Mrs. Fred Barneknow, Sr. is seriously ill.

Mrs. Fred Koch, Sr. fell and broke her arm.

Christian Koenitzer, of Waukesha, visited his sister, Mrs. Jacob Gunderman.

Mr. M. Wietschak broke his leg when he slipped on ice in his yard.

Mr. and Mrs. Vernon Scribner, of Rosendale, Wis., visited Mrs. Wm. R. Curdall.

Mrs. H. Leisk gave a party in honor of her husband, Capt. Leisk.

Fred Hartung returned to his business trip in Iowa county after a few days at home.

Mrs. Harold Nickerson will be a matron at Milwaukee Downer college.

Mrs. L.B. Gregg gave a family lunch in honor of her mother, Mrs. Elizabeth Carter's 86th birthday, Feb. 14.

The Ladies Aid society of the M. E. church met with Mrs. N.L. Kneeland, their next meeting will be with Mrs. F.W. Schneck.

Mrs. O.B. Pond, of Seattle, Wash., visited Mr. and Mrs. O.F. Wilson.

G.A. Kurtz has resigned as secretary and retired from the Metropolitan Coke Co., Milwaukee.

Mrs. Max Rosenthal, Mr. J.L. Morton, and Mr. Adam Currie are threatened with pneumonia and confined to their homes.

Mrs. C.S. Clark and Miss Lou Harriman will entertain the T.C.T. club. Sketches and papers will be read by Mrs. Tisdale, Mrs. H. Morton, Mrs. Charles Godfrey, Mrs. W. Beutler, and Mrs. A.J. Moan.

Mrs. Andrew met with a serious accident when returning to Mrs. Dexter's house, where Mrs. Dexter has been very ill. She arrived at the Dexter home in an unconcious condition. It is supposed that she fell on jagged ice near the Dexter home where blood was found. She is rapidly improving.

Mr. A. Riel, state organizer of the United Order of Foresters instituted a court here. The following officers were elected: Julius Becker, August H. Kealies, Jacob W. Neib, John C.

Gable, Bertha Schleifer, Catherine Wilson, Otto C. Barnekow, Leonard J. Wolf, and Dr. D.S. Hathaway.

Everett Hart won the Hoyt medal which is given by the Minute Men to the person who proved the best in military discipline and drill.

## Marriage

Miss Jennie Estelle Moore and Otto Augustus Zillmer were married at the home of Mr. and Mrs. Wm. H. Moore, Feb. 17, 1904. Rev. P.W. Longfellow officiated. Mr. Zillmer was born in Germany and reared principally in Brookfield. Miss Moore was born and raised in the home in which she was married. They will live on a farm Mr. Zillmer purchased in Marathon county.

## Death

Mrs. Harriet D. Underwood, widow of Rev. Enoch D. Underwood, died at her son's home in Chicago, Feb. 14, 1904, at the age of 86 years. She was the mother of Fred D. Underwood, president of the Erie Road, and W.J. Underwood, assistant general manager of the Milwaukee Road. Until a few years ago Mrs. Underwood resided at the Underwood homestead, here. She spent the last two years with her daughter, Mrs. Gray, in Cumberland, Md. While visiting her son, W.J. Underwood, in Chicago she was taken ill with the grippe which developed into pneumonia and caused her death.

Mrs. Underwood, whose maiden name was Denny, was born at Leicester, Mass. in 1818. She came to Wisconsin in 1837, first living in Lisbon, Waukesha county, near Pewaukee. She married Enoch D. Underwood in 1842. Rev. Underwood, who died in 1888, settled in Wauwatosa in 1835, coming from Virginia with his father. Mrs. Underwood was a teacher in Wauwatosa in 1840. They were pioneer residents having settled in Wauwatosa over sixty years ago. Rev. Underwood was the pastor of the Baptist church here for nearly forty years. Mrs. Underwood will be interred at Wauwatosa cemetery. She is survived by her sons, F.D. Underwood and W.J. Underwood, grandson, E.W. Underwood, of Minneapolis, son of F.D. Underwood, two daughters, Mrs. Thos. S. Gray, of Cumberland, Md., and Mrs. Sarah Curtis, of Minneapolis, and grandson Frederick Curtis.

Mrs. Mary J. Dexter, widow of Lieut. D.H. Dexter, died Feb. 17, 1904, at the age of 77 years. She was an early settler in Wauwatosa and lived on the home farm on Lisbon Rd. for many years. She has spent the past two years at the home of her daughter, Mrs. R.A. Witte in Waukesha. She came here to reside in December and was ill for only ten days before her death. She is survived by a son, Frank Dexter, of North Dakota, and a daughter, Mrs. R.A. Witte, of Waukesha. The funeral will be from the Baptist church with interment at Wauwatosa cemetery.

Robert Thompson died at the home of his nephew, Richard Tennant, Feb. 16, 1904, at the age of 87 years. Dr. Thompson came to Wisconsin in 1852 from England after graduating from the London College of Physicians. His practice was in Friendship and Avon for about twenty-five years. He has made his home with the Tennant family for the past six years. The funeral was from the home of his nephew, with interment at Wauwatosa cemetery. Rev. Goldthorp officiated.

**Letters uncalled for at the postoffice.**

Arthur Connelley, W.S. Coe, Dr. A.B. Grider, Hans Jacobson, Otto Kruger, Katie Kihnow, Mrs. Gertrude Kolba, and A.J. Willis.

**February 27, 1904**

Miss Lena Loveland is ill with the grippe.

Mr. and Mrs. Bollenbach are visiting in Milwaukee.

Mrs. R.M. Brown is visiting relatives in St. Paul, Minn.

Arthur Brockway visited friends in Rhinelander, Wis.

Hugo Fromman is laid up with rheumatism.

Miss Maude Curtis is visiting friends in Chicago.

Mrs. Sam Leister is quite ill.

Mr. J.L. McNab, of Chicago, is visiting E.M. Lewis.

Mrs. Ed Bussewitz is visiting relatives in Chicago.

George Schneck is going to Waco, Texas to visit friends.

Mrs. Richard Tennant, who has the grippe, is improving.

The Woman's Auxillary of Trinity church met with Mrs. W.H. Landolt.

John Parker Gregg returned to Madison.

Mrs. J.K. Douglas, of Troy Center, visited the Van Vechten home.

Jefferson Gregg, of Madison, is visiting his daughter, Mrs. L.G. Wheeler.

Mrs. Morse Ives and children, of Chicago, are visiting her mother, Mrs. N.L. Kneeland.

Wm. Menninger and family moved to Greenfield Ave. and Brazee St.

Mr. and Mrs. W.R. Netherent have returned from Lake Geneva, Wis.

Mrs. J.O. Meyers entertained the north side Neighborhood club.

Rev. G.A. Ehrhardt, pastor of Pauls' Ev. congregation will occupy H. Siegart's house on Hadley Ave.

Mrs. J.K. Davis returned to Evanston, Ill., after a visit with Mrs. Burnside.

Mr. A. Harden is in northern Wisconsin to purchase wood and lumber.

Mr. E.C. Nettleton is ill with grippe.

Mr. and Mrs. S.D. Hoyt, of Fond du Lac, were here visiting friends.

Mrs. N.L. Kneeland and daughter, Mrs. W.A. Godfrey, entertained at a Kensington.

A petition is being circulated to ask E.R. Godfrey, Sr. to run for mayor.

Miss Alice Stacey, of Milwaukee, will replace Mrs. Nickerson as sewing teacher.

Miss Lilli von Baumbach has been appointed substitute piano teacher at the Conservatory of Music in Boston.

Friends have convinced Mr. G.P. Dousman to become a candidate for town supervisor.

Mrs. J.E. Pierce was called to New Orleans because her son, Will Sanderson, needs an operation to remove his appendix to save his life.

At a cinch smoker given by the firemen the music was furnished by A.F. Weber, Burt Cope, John Schwada, and Walter Harden and Henry Hemsing gave selections using one of his talking machines.

M.E. Launer and wife, of Chicago, were here to look at the lot where they plan to build a house.

The fifth and sixth grades of Milwaukee Normal school enjoyed a sleighride to C.G. Porter's home where Mrs. Porter entertained for her son, Chester Porter, a student at the school.

The officers chosen at the Men's Club of the Congregational church are: W.R. Cundall, president; Henry Watner, vice-president; E.T. Wright, secretary and treasurer.

The trustees of the Insane Asylum are: Mr. Truss, Mr. Haisler, Mr. Mayhew, Mr. Oswald and Mr. Seidel. The superintendent is Dr. Wm. F. Beutler.

Mr. F.C. Bussewitz and son, E.M. Bussewitz, are severing their connection with their partner, William Menninger, in the Cash Meat Market in order to take up farming near North Lake in Waukesha County.

C.J. Crilley was the successful bidder on a contract to put in sewer and water mains.

Miss Winifred Phillips will lead the B.Y.P.U. at the Baptist church.

**Death**

Mrs. M. Barnekow, wife of Frederick Barnekow, died Feb. 28, 1904, at her home. She was 80 years old and an old resident of the town of Wauwatosa. Mr. and Mrs. Barnekow came here from Germany in 1858. She is survived by her husband, three sons, John Barnekow, Frank Barnekow, and Ernest Barnekow and a daughter, Mrs. Nauerts, of Iowa. The funeral was at the Congregational church with interment at Wauwatosa cemetery. Rev. Rading, of St. John's Lutheran church, Milwaukee, officiated.

**Letters uncalled for at the postoffice.**

August Breblow, E. Hartung, Daziel Matias, Clara Seisser, Walter Schern, George Seflute, and Albert Hughs

### March 5, 1904

Mrs. V.V. Vining is visitin relatives in Columbus, Ohio.

Miss Bessie Horning visited friends in Milwaukee.

St. Agnes Guild met with Miss Louise Landolt.

Arthur Brockway has been assigned as operator at Edgerton, Wis.

George Bennett, of Milwaukee, visited Wm. Baier.

Miss Stella Nelson, of Oconomowoc, visited Mrs. C.E. Curtis.

Mr. and Mrs. George Prest have returned from Michigan.

Mrs. C. Winkenwerder entertained friends.

John Kerin and K.C. Dousman, of Waukesha, were in town.

The W.C.T.U. will meet with Mrs. D.A. Cooley.

Mrs. Henry Watner gave a Kensington.

Mr. and Mrs. Wm. Cundall will entertain the Evening Cinch club.

Mrs. J.S. Cutler and daughter, Mary Cutler, attended the Old Settlers meeting.

Miss Lillian Sisson and Miss Marian Smith, of Milwaukee, visited Miss Maude Curtis.

If anyone asks, H.B. Bradley will be our next town clerk. From an OLD SOLDIER

Miss Helen Temple, of Milwaukee, visited her brother, H.S. Temple.

Mr. and Mrs. A.L. Smith entertained the young people of the Baptist church.

Miss Ida Schlichter lost a gold watch between Lefeber Bro's store and school.

Roy Wescott and Arthur Walter were charged with vagrancy before Judge Neelen and sentenced to the the house of correction.

Mrs. Cooley, of Milwaukee, will address the meeting of the Womans' Missionary Society of the Congregational church at the home of Mrs. H.G. Wheeler.

H.P. Bradley and family are moving to Hawley Rd. near Wells St.

The W.H.S. junior class had a leap-year party given by the girls consiting of a sleigh-ride with refreshments at the home of Miss Lillian Bark.

Mr. and Mrs. R.B. Griffith and son, Paul Griffith, of Grand Forks, ND, visited Rev. Longfellow, who was their pastor in Dakota.

Dr. Moses J. White has not admitted visitors at the insane asylum because of a case of Varioloid traced to Jacob Beaman, who was placed in a detached cottage for isolation purposes.

At the city board meeting S.P. Croft and L. Mannegold were paid by the city for grading and stone. C.J. Crilley was the lowest bidder to do street improvement.

Alice Smith will lead the B.Y.P.U. at the Baptist church.

**Death**

Thomas Watson Hart died March 1, 1904, suddenly at his home on Church St. of Heart disease. Mr. Hart was one of Wauwatosa's earliest settlers. He was born in Lennox, NY, March 4, 1835 and came to Wauwatosa with his parents in 1838. In 1866 he married Isabel Rogers, of Milwaukee. As a young man he was the superintendent of the Watertown toll road. He later became owner of what is now Monarch stone quarry and then engaged in the real estate business. He is survived by his wife, three brothers, Oliver W. Hart, of Charles City, Iowa, Judson G. Hart, of Waukesha, Wis., and Jesse Hart, of Root Creek, Milwaukee Co., Wis.

The funeral was held from his home with interment at Wauwatosa cemetery. Rev. Thain, officiated.

William Sanderson died in New Orleans as a result of an operation to remove his appendix. He was the son of Mrs. J.E. Pierce. Mr. Sanderson was 23 years old, he was married last spring in Madison and was engaged in business in New Orleans. He is survived by his wife, his mother, his sister, Miss France Sanderson, and a half brother, Jack Pierce.

The funeral was from the family home with interment at Forest Home cemetery. The pall-bearers included: Messrs. Harold Rogers, Edward Pavey, George Kershaw, George Rogers, Walter Wood, and Sterling Wood. Rev. E.P. Wright, chaplain of the Soldiers' Home, assisted by Rev. F.S. Gray, officiated.

**Letters uncalled for at the postoffice.**

Mrs. George Garrison, Geo Gloed, Mrs. Lizzie Loomis, M.J. Murphy, Jacob Scharver, Chas Servis, Alice Tralil, E.A. Travis, Chas Witcher, Adelaide Warner, Frau Juilana Wagner, Herrn Edward Wagner, and Miss Gerty Yank

**March 19, 1904**

Miss Hattie Scherer is visiting in Nenah, Wis.

Mrs. W.C. Wyman is ill.

Miss Blanche Landolt is visiting in West Bend, Wis.

Mr. and Mrs. C.G. Norton have been in Chicago.

The H. Loomis family have been ill with the grippe.

Mrs. T.S. Grassie has returned from her winter stay in La Crosse, Wis.

Mrs. H. Theo Hanson visited her mother in Los Angeles, Cal.

Mrs. Cyrus Pedrick entertained the Neighborhood Club.

Mrs. Jefferson Gregg, of Madison, is visiting her daughter, Mrs. L.G. Wheeler.

Mrs. Chas. Shaw entertained informally.

Miss Jesse Hibbard (sic), of Milwaukee, is visiting the A.P. Hubbard home.

Mrs. Spooner, of Green Bay, Wis., visited her daughter, Mrs. Geo. Hunt.

Mrs. Agnes Rice is visiting her son, Arba Rice, in Fond du Lac.

Mrs. L. Brockway was given a birthday surprise, Mar. 15.

Mrs. Abram Lefeber will entertain the young married people of the M. E. church.

The West Side Neighborhood club will meet with Mrs. L. Brockway.

Mr. and Mrs. John Netherent, of Lake Geneva, are visiting Wm. R. Netherent.

Rolland Morrison, of Morrisonville, Wis., visited C.E. Curtis.

Capt. and Mrs. A.P. Foster are moving to Milwaukee.

Mr. E.C. Haash and family moved to the Van Vecten house.

Mr. O.F. Lee and family moved into their newly built house on W. Main St.

The H. T. Cinch club will meet with Dr. and Mrs. H.G. Morton.

Russell Faulkner moved to Marquette, Mich. to work for a business house.

Mrs. D.F. Philipps entertained the Jolly Nine club at cinch.

Mrs. Ann Morris is visiting her son, Chauncey Morris.

T.M. Hammond will give a talk at the Men's Club of the Congregational church.

Mr. and Mrs. Smith McCormack celebrated their fifty-seventh wedding anniversary March 18.

The W.C.T.U. will be held at the home of Mrs. Cairncross.

The results of the Republican caucuses in the city were: Charles Curtis, C.R. Davis, F.E. Loveland, Wm. Farries, Wm. von Baumbach, J.J. Marquardt, H. Prust, F.L. Morton, C.C. Jacobus, A.J. Moan, F. Buch, John Hamme, L.R. Gridley, G.F. Beichardt, Wm. Menninger, Max Rosenthal, Fred Prudisch, F. Woller, John Armstrong, and Charles Leutzow.

The following nominations were made at the town Republican caucuses: Charles T. Fisher, M.H. Adams, John Barnekow, Herbert P. Bradley, Albert L. Story, George R. Jeffrey, R.J.

Matthias, Gilbert J. Davelaar, Max Arnauld, J.P. Williams, Herman Koepp, Wm Hanley, and John Reuter.

Miss Elsie Moore will lead the B. Y. P. U. at the Baptist church.

Information on a special tourist excursion to Houston, Texas this month can be obtained from Mrs. Allen Williams, 28 Hadley Ave.

**Death**

Mrs. Matilda Griffith, wife of Walter Griffith, died March 17, 1904 from bowel trouble at the age of 55 years. She was born in Rochester, NY where she married Mr. Griffith in 1872. They came to Milwaukee in 1880 and have lived in Wauwatosa since 1901. She is survived by her husband, a son, Lewis J. Griffith, of Milwaukee, a daughter, Mrs. Ray Mann, of Chicago, her parents, Mr. and Mrs. H.W. Welsher, of Walworth, Wis., and three brothers, William Welsher, of Madison, Frank Weslher, of Walworth, and Herbert Welsher, of Delavan.

The funeral will be from her home on Alice St. with interment at Forest Home cemetery.

**Letters uncalled for at the postoffice.**

S.B. Drake, Adolph Frahm, Mrs. Emilla Kallths, J. Sampson, Mrs. Ida McDonald, Laura Peters, and Henry Messre

### March 26, 1904

Mrs. H. Bostwick is visiting friends in Tomah, Wis.

Mrs. Miller, of Racine, is the guest of Mrs. E. Coulthard.

Mrs. E.H. Schwaiger moved to Milwaukee.

T.H. Grover, of Fond du Lac, visited friends here.

Mrs. E. Collins will occupy a flat in the Schwaiger Building.

Mrs. Ella Smith visited friends in Milwaukee.

Mr. H.O. Wood and family are moving to Milwaukee.

Mrs. Adam Currie will entertain at a Kensington.

H.E. Bostwick and family are moving to Milwaukee.

W.S. Faulkner is going to Chicago.

Miss Fern Hurlbut, of Winifred, SD, is visiting friends here.

Capt. A.P. Foster and family moved to Milwaukee.

John Foley is in Mt. Clemens, Mich.

Miss Ada Maxon went to St. Louis for a few days.

Mr. and Mrs. Stanley Watson visited the James Lefeber home.

Fred Frisbee, of Pine River, Wis., visited James Lefeber.

Mr. G. Sanford, of Oshkosh, is visiting the W.B. Rice home.

Mrs. A.W. Lehman, of Neosho, visited the J.T. Van Vecten home.

Mr. and Mrs. Chas. Jacobus visited friends in Chicago.

Mr. F.S. Sturges and family moved into the Hart house.

Dr. C.T. Chandler will entertain his mother, Mrs. S.A. Chandler, and his son, Phil Chandler, of Monroe.

Miss Fannie Moore, of Fond du Lac, visited her parents, Mr. and Mrs. H.L. Moore.

Miss Harriet Secrombe, of Milwaukee, is visiting Mrs. W.B. Rice.

Mrs. F. Barnekow gave a birthday party for her son, Albert Barnekow, Mar. 20.

Mrs. A.I. Smith entertained the Neighborhood Club.

Miss Dysart is home from Chicago University.

Dr. Walter Perkins and family, of Milwaukee, will move into one of the Braun flats on Garfield Ave.

Mrs. J.B. Johnson has rented the Hilty house on Park St.

Mr. and Mrs. L.B. Allen, of Cedar Rapids, Iowa, visited G.G. Allen.

Mrs. M. Horning entertained for her daughter, Bessie Horning, on her birthday, Mar. 21.

Miss Laura Sage, of Oregon, Wis., is visiting her sister, Miss Janette Sage, and her grandparents, Mr. and Mrs. S. McCormack.

Mrs. I.C. Lillibridge, Miss Lillibridge, and Mrs. W.F. Humphrey will entertain the T.C.T. Club.

Miss Lena Niese attended a convention of dressmakers in Chicago.

Herbert E. Prest and George Shenk went to St. Louis on business.

C.F. Eckstein and Julius Guentner will be independent candidates for supervisors in the upcoming election.

Rev. P.W. Longfellow preached in West Allis.

Mr. and Mrs. A.L. Smith entertained friends.

The entertainment by Mr. R.S. Baird was posponed because of weather.

Mr. Morse lost a cord or two of wood to the flood Wednesday.

The Hon. G.A. Gearhart will lecture at the Congregational church.

Mr. G.E. Smith will lead the B.Y.P.U. at the Baptist church.

**Death**

Willis E. Story, of the firm of Story Brother, stone quarry, brother of town treasurer, A.L. Story, died of heart disease at his home on Blue Mound Rd., March 21, 1904, at the age of 47 years. Mr. Story was the son of the late William F. Story, an early settler in Wauwatosa. He was born here and graduated from the Milwaukee high school in 1875. He graduated from Yale college in 1879. He then entered the law office of Wells, Brigham & Upham, where he worked for four years, and after passing the bar he practiced law for himself. In 1887, when his father died, he went into the quarry business with his brother A.L. Story. He married Miss Alice Tichenor, of Milwaukee, in 1884. He is survived by his wife and two children, a son, aged 13 and a daughter aged 10. Mr. Story was a member and trustee of the Grand Avenue Congregational church.

The funeral was from his home conducted by Rev. C.H. Beale, with interment in Forest Home cemetery.

**Probate Notice**

Agnes S. Tennant and Edward Coulthard, of Wauwatosa, executors of Robert Thompson, dec'd, asked that his last will and testament be admitted to probate and letters testamentary be granted to them. Paul D. Carpenter, County Judge

**Letters uncalled for at the postoffice.**

Miss L. Bagley, Henry S. Berringer, Edward Frink, Lyman Evans, James B. Lewis, Minnie Schreiber, and Fred Weisel

### April 2, 1904

Dr. C.T. Chandler is going to Chicago.

Mr. E.M. Lewis is ill.

Miss Katherine Davis is the guest of Miss C.G. Warren.

Miss Myrtle Farnham is home in Beaver Dam, Wis.

Mrs. Miller, of Whitewater, is visiting Mrs. Edward Coulthard.

Arthur Brockway, of Edgerton, Wis., visited his parents here.

Mrs. I.C. Lillibridge visited friends in Winona, Minn.

Miss Beth Allen is at the A.M. Lucas home in Dubuque, Iowa.

Mr. and Mrs. S.D. Hoyt, of Fond du Lac, were in town.

Adolph Becker will work at Nettleton grocery.

Lester Pavy, of Fond du Lac, visited his folks here.

Mrs. Joseph Lefeber is taking a trip to Gunther, Oklahoma.

Mrs. A.M. Blaesser has returned from visiting relatives in Sheboygan.

Mr. W.L. McPherson, of Tullahoma, Tenn. is visiting A.H. Owens.

Mr. and Mrs. Ed Bussewitz, of North Lake, are visiting Wm. Menninger.

Mrs. W.A. James, of Tennessee, is visiting Mrs. M. Hornings.

Miss Maud Pearce is vacationing at her home in Waukegan, Ill.

Mrs. E.J. Kearney is back from visiting in Milwaukee.

Mrs. Wm. von Baumbach will entertain at cinch.

Mrs. Abram Lefeber entertained some Milwaukee friends at dinner.

Miss Gertrude Dodd entertained her Sunday school class.

Julius Scholtka has rented the Pabst farm and will engage in the horse keeping business.

Mr. Jean Phillips and daughter visited the home of his son, C. Phillips.

Mrs. M. Tulley and family will occupy a house on E. Milwaukee Ave.

Misses Jeannette Donnelly and Jeannette Smith, of Milwaukee, visited Miss M. Hoyt.

The Ladies Aid Society of the M. E. church will meet with Mrs. Richard Hayes.

Mr. and Mrs. Edward Wells, of New York, are visiting his father, George Wells, Sr.

Miss Mary Hulburt has returned to Chicago University.

Miss Mary Belle Netherent, of Lake Geneva is visiting her uncle, W.R. Netherent.

James Laurie, father of Mrs. G.A. Kurtz, is not expected to recover.

Mrs. R. Relpsch (sic) has returned from her winter stay with her daughter, Mrs. S.O. Cowan, in St. Paul, Minn.

Everet E. Hatch resigned from Nettleton's to fill the vacancy left by Miss Louise Landolt at the post office.

Misses Edith Everett, Isabel Hulburt, and Helen Williams attended a birthday party April 1, for Leslie Travis in Milwaukee

Mrs. Frank Davidson and daughter, Margaret Davidson, of Fox Lake, Miss Rodger, of Packwaukee(sic), and ? Johnson (the paper is damaged), of Milwaukee, were at Miss Carrie Warren's.

Henry B. Hunter, who now lives in Milwaukee, is trying to get five cent street car fares for Wauwatosa.

The musical program at the Baptist church will be rendered by: Mrs. H.V. Taylor, Mrs. G.E. Smith, Miss Janet Smith, Mr. A.W. Smith, Miss Campbell, and Frank Smith.

Republican candidates for office: Emerson D. Hoyt, mayor; Alonzo F. Kellogg, city treasurer; Cyrus W. Damon, assessor; Frank Harriman, constable; William von Baumbach, Allen J. Moan, William Menninger, Charles Luetzow, and William Farries, aldermen; Charles C. Jacobus, Gottlieb F. Reichardt, and John Armstrong, supervisors.

Individual nominations for offices: E.R. Godfrey, Sr., mayor; J.D. Gilbert, city treasurer; P.C. Clausen, T.J. Ferguson, John H. Taylor, William Picker, aldermen; C.F. Eckstein, and Julius Guentner, supervisors.

**Death**

Dwight C. Watson died March 29, 1904 in Santa Cruz, Cal.. He was 57 years old and lived in Wauwatosa most of his life. He went to California with his wife in hopes of recovering his health. It is expected his remains will be brought here for burial.

### April 16, 1904

Miss Louise Landolt was in Port Washington.

A.R. Gridley, of Janesville, made a short visit here.

Mrs. John Parker Gregg, of Madison, is visiting friends here.

Walter Wright, Jr., of Waukegan, was here.

Will. Hawley, of Fond du Lac, was here.

Mr. and Mrs. L.W. Gridley are taking a trip through the south.

Miss Louise Landolt will entertain those assisting at her wedding.

Misses Gertrude Dodd and Harriet Rice gave a shower for Miss Louise Landolt.

Miss Loreta Landolt will entertain in honor of her sister, Louise Landolt.

Mrs. T.J. Franklin and daughter, Doris Franklin, of Appleton, Wis., are visiting the L.R. Gridley home.

Mr. C.C. Jacobus and Paul Hartung were in the western part of the state.

Mr. J. Fuller and family, of Milwaukee, moved into the Hunter house on E. Milwaukee Ave.

Mrs. A.C. Hanson and Miss Blanche Landolt entertained for Louise Landolt.

Mr. and Mrs. D.J. Scully went to Green Bay to attend her brother's funeral.

Mr. and Mrs. Henry Rose, of Princeton, and Mrs. F.O. Phelps, of Milwaukee, visited Mrs. H.E. Rose.

Mr. A. Wespetal and Miss Mamie Harter, of Racine, visited the home of Mr. and Mrs. O.T. Wilson.

Mr. Everett, Miss Ruth Sporleder, Archie Johnson, and ? Rose (this paper is in poor condition) attended the Good Templars' convention.

The dancing party given by Clarence Wolf and N.E. Newstab has been postponed.

In the Memphis paper dated Apr. 15: a drunken painter named Wise was arraigned before Recorder, Frank Davis, for attacking Matt J. Ehrlicher, formerly of this city. Mr. Ehrlicher was attacked in his office by Wise, his coat and shirt were torn to ribbons by the knife and he encurred several wounds. No reason was given for the attack. Mr. Ehrlicher and his brother appeared against Wise.

Kirk Putnam will lead the B.Y.P.U. at the Baptist church.

The April Missionary social will be held at the home of Mrs. J.H. Cushing, Miss Ruth Ellis is in charge of the program.

Rev. P.W. Longfellow was unable to preach Sunday because of hoarseness. The chorus gave a musical program instead.

Robert Marston, of Chicago, Mr. J.J. Regan, of Milwaukee, Mrs. C.G. Morton, Mrs. C.V. Burnside, and Miss Loraine Wright entertained at a Twentieth Century Topic Club musicale. The hostesses were Mrs. G.C. Murphy, Mrs. Wm. Landolt, Mrs. J. Tompkins, Mrs. C.G. Norton, and Miss Morehouse.

Lyman G. Wheeler gives a sterling testamony for Emerson D. Hoyt, who lost the election for mayor.

Mayor elect E.R. Godfrey, Sr. held his first common council meeting. Mr. Kennedy was elected president; Mr. Coulthard, clerk; Mr. Perry, attorney; Mr. Harriman, marshall; Mr. Warren, street commissioner; Mr. J.D. Warren, superintendent of the sewerage plant and the chief of the fire department; Dr. E.A. Schmitz, health commissioner; P.C. Clausen was appointed a member of the water commission; and Matt Goebel, weed commissioner. The judiciary committee will be: Moan, Gunn, and Lefeber; the rules and ordinance committee: Gunn, Haunne (sic), and Picker.

**Birth**

A son was born April 14, 1904 to Mr. and Mrs. Charles E. Curtis.

**Marriage**

George Lund, of Wauwatosa, and Miss Elizabeth Barry, of Madison, will be married in Madison, April 19, 1904. They will reside here.

Miss Louise U. Landolt, daughter of Mr. and Mrs. W. Landolt, will marry Charles Smith, of Chicago, April 20, 1904. Rev. F.S. Gray will conduct the ceremony. (the rest cannot be read because of damage to the paper)

**Letters uncalled for at the postoffice.**

Peter Cordy, W. Brobratz, Mrs C.P. Franklin, Mrs. Ed Lutzen, Mrs. Susan Milier, Mame McDonald, Max Nader, Leonard Neetrel, Mrs. A. Rieck, E. Schiltz, and Mrs. Geo. Witte

### April 30, 1904

Lea L. Gridley has the grippe.

Miss Lottie Hart is visiting in Brookfield, Wis.

Mrs. Little went to Chamberlin, SD.

Capt. W.H. Landolt was in Port Washington.

Mrs. O.L. Shearer, of East Troy, is visiting Mrs. H.E. Rose.

Rev. F.S. Gray will attend a clericus in Nashotah.

G.W. Schroeder is moving to Milwaukee.

Mr. D.R. Brewer is improving and able to be up.

Miss Cox, milliner with Lefeber Bro's, has pneumonia.

Herman Siegert is up and about at home.

Miss Lila Pease, of Marinette, Wis., is visiting Miss Olive Lefeber.

H.E. Bostwick and family is moving to Milwaukee.

Mrs. Chas. Barnes, of Lowell, Wis., is visiting friends here.

Sam Leister purchased the Kalfahs house.

Mrs. J.R. Benoy went to visit her sick mother in Muscoda, Wis.

Mrs. F.W. Schneck was in Oak Dale and Okauchee, Wis.

Mrs. Joseph Lefeber returned from visiting relatives in Oklahoma.

H.S. Loomis and family, of Chicago, will occupy the Brown house.

D.M. Jones was called to Ohio because his mother is very ill.

Mrs. Gregory Connell, of Leadville, Colo., is visiting her parents, Mr. and Mrs. Chas. Stickney.

William Tschergi and family have returned from Dubuque, Iowa to live on Blanchard St.

Sam. Cameron, of Waukesha, formerly of Wauwatosa, had a stroke of paralysis.

John McCulloch, of Madison, Wis., is visiting his niece, Miss Katharine Wood.

Mrs. Stacy and family will occupy the house vacated by H.O. Wood on Center St.

George Prest sold his place to a Milwaukee party and will move to Milwaukee.

Morton Casperson and family will move into the house on Chestnut St. vacated by Mr. Bradley.

Chas. Gillett, Mr. Bigsby, and families will live in the house vacated by H.E. Bostwick, W. Main St.

Dr. W.A. Perkins, of Milwaukee, will occupy one of the flats in the Braun Building., Chestnut St.

James McAdams, who has been ill, is improving.

Capt. Ward's Military Band will give a band concert at the Soldiers' Home.

Mrs. J.T. Greenwood and Miss Thompson entertained the ladies of the Evening Cinch club in honor of Mrs. G.G. Allen who is leaving for Oelwein, Iowa.

Miss Lizzie Van Vechten, J.R. Benoy, Miss Lillie Pelton, Rex Sporleder, ..bel Skinner (paper damaged), Wm. Bark, and Miss Nellie Engelhardt were elected officers of the Good Templars.

Mr. and Mrs. John Moss and daughter, Ethel Moss, Mrs. G.W. Sanford, Mrs. W.B. Rice, and Rev. C.E. Goldthorp went to Los Angeles, Cal. to attend the Methodist conference.

The city delegates elected to the state republican convention were: Fred. L. Morton and F.E. Loveland, the delegates to the congressional convention are: L.R. Gridley, E.M. Lewis, C.H. Godfrey, and D.M. Jones, to the assembly convention are: W.L. Notbohm, T.E. Zimmerman, Fred. Bark, and Charles Curtis.

The town delegates to the state convention are: C.A. Carter, Orlin J. Swan, Patrick O'Connell, Wm. E. Fisher, G.J. Davelaar, F. Bark, and J.A. Berg, to the assembly convention are: Fred Schulz, G.R. Jeffrey, Jas. Crowley, Wm. Reichert, Max Arnauld, C. Wahl, E. Harman, F. Boddenhagen, A.L. Story, Al Baker, F. Behling, and Chris. Sommer, to congressional convention are: L.J. Davis, N. Colte, E. Langdon, C. Van Buren, Fred Rogge, J. Fitzgerald, H. Losburg, M. O'Regan, W.H. Hassinger, M. Delaney, T. Mason, and Swain Gunderson.

Miss Julia M. Brown will lead the B.Y.P.U. at the Baptist church.

Wm. Scully, Greenfield, has eggs for sale.

**Letters uncalled for at the postoffice.**

Edith Bates, Sophia Christiansey, R. Farrer, Louis Gross, G.Y. Koeppel, Frank Lemits, E.J. Loew, Ed Mueller, Mrs. Alice Warner, Fred Nedean, Mrs. J.H. Reid, Arthur L. Ruanie, Mrs. C. Surges, and Thomas Walter

### 1904 Wauwatosa Directory

City Officials

Mayor, E.R. Godfrey, Sr.; Aldermen: I.W. Kennedy, P.C. Clausen, Jas. Lefeber, A.J. Moan, John Hamme, Wm. Menninger, C.A. Gunn, and Wm. Picker; Treasurer, A.F. Kellogg; Clerk, Edward Coulthard; Assessor, C.W. Damon; Attorney, Chas. B. Perry; Street Commissioner, J.B. Warren; Weed Commissioner, Matt.

Goebel; Commissioner of Health, E.A. Schmitz, M.D.; Justices of
the Peace, Edward Coulthard and W.L. Notbohm; Marshal, Frank
Harriman; Supervisors, Wm. Farries, C.C. Jacobus, G.F.
Reichardt, and Julius Guentner

Board of Education: W.R. Netherent, Dr. J.S. Cutler, Dr. J.W.
Cairncross, L.G. Wheeler, G.A. Kurtz, Ferdinand Bark, Fred
Prudisch, Edward Coulthard, and A.F. Kellogg.

Water Commissioners: Charles Stickney, Adam Currie, Charles
Luetzow, P.C. Clausen, and E.R. Godfrey.

Public Library Directors: A.W. Smith, J.O. Myers, Mrs. C.G.
Porter, Mrs. L. Brockway, John B. De Swarte, E.R. Godfrey, Sr.,
F.M. Merica, and Mrs. J.L. Foley.

Fire Department: J.D. Warren, H.E. Leister, C.C. Jacobus, Jos.
Schwaiger, John Hamme, Fred Bark, J.F. Dittmar, J.C. Lefeber,
B.F. Hempsing, H.P. Hempsing, James Lefeber, A.I. Smith, F.E.
Loveland, G.A. Kurtz, C.E. Curtis, F.M. Heiden, Walter Harden,
Wm. Menninger, W.K. Engelhart, Rudolph Buchman, and Fred
Prhudis (sic).

Town Officials

Town board: Chas. T. Fisher, M.H. Adams, and John Barnekow;
Town Clerk, H.P. Bradley; Treasurer, Albert L. Story; Assessor,
Geo. R. Jeffrey; Justices of the Peace: R.J. Matthias, G.J.
Davelaar, J.P. Williams, and Max Arnauld; Constables: William
Hanley, Herman Koepp, and John Reuter; Board of Health:
Chas. T. Fisher, M.H. Addms(sic), John Barnekow and H.P.
Bradley; Postmaster, W.H. Landolt

**Death**

Mrs. Ernst, mother of Martin Ernst and Mrs. Jacob Tennessen,
died at her home on Kenyon St., April 27, 1904.


Mrs. Sangston, youngest daughter of Mr. and Mrs. E.W. Fowler,
of Chicago, formerly of Wauwatosa, died at her home in
Mt. Sterling, Ill., April 25, 1904. She will be interred at Forest
Home cemetery, Rev. P.W. Longfellow will read the service.

## May 7, 1904

Arthur Koenig is quite ill

Miss Nellie Ross is visiting Smith McCormick.

Mr. Wellinghurst and family moved to the Ludington farm.

Miss Flora Doty, of Madison, Wis., is visiting her sister, Mrs. C.E. Curtis.

Miss Lena Siegler is visiting her sister, Mrs. Jno. Mittelstadt, in Seaforth, Minn.

H.A. Nolte and family have taken the Barkhausen place.

Mr. and Mrs. Edwin Hyde visited the John Young home.

The Woman's Club met with Mrs. E.W. Grant.

W.B. Lincoln and family, Mower Ct., are moving to Wichita, Kan.

Lee Rose will entertain young friends.

Frank Doty, state high school inspector, visited the high school and his sister, Mrs. Chas. Curtis.

Misses Carrie Warren and Allison Armstrong will attend the reception in honor of Miss Elizabeth Banks, authoress, at Milwaukee Downer College.

Mr. W. Kavanaugh and family moved into the house they purchased from George Prest.

The Foreign Mission Society of the M.E. church will meet at the George E. Wells home.

The Ladies Aid Society of the M. E. church surprised Mrs. C.E. Goldthorp on her birthday, May 6.

Steph. Croft received the contract for graveling a portion of Chestnut St.

A lecture was given by Gen. Chas. King at the Congregational church sponsored by the Wauwatosa Minute Men.

Dr. E.C. Groskopf, superintendent of the county hospital, denies charges made against the manner in which the hospital is conducted.

Harold Angus is a photographer in Wauwatosa.

**Letters uncalled for at the postoffice.**

Mrs. Mary Everhart, H. Foelske, Bildes Grimming, Mrs. Nettie Miller, Ed Miller, Wm Neef, C.L. Parker, Mrs. Rockel, Lrs.(sic) Josephine Rusk, Miss Je... Tullar (paper damaged), Miss Tess Wickers, and E.E. Zillmer

Common Council

Mayor Godfrey nominated J.L. Hooley to fill the vacancy as alderman left by Mr. Moan, from the Second ward. C.A. Breed was also nominated, but rejected. Arthur McGill and Fred Prudisch were nominated for school commissioner. Mr. Prudisch was elected. Applications for pool table and bowling alley licenses were presented from C.C. Jacobus, G.F. Reichardt, John Hausch and Fred Picker.

**Sheriff's** sale of the estate of Harriet F. Warren, dec'd. Carrie G. Warren, administrix, plaintiff against Thomas Greenwood and Rosalie Greenwood, his wife, C.A. Higgins, Frank B. Golley, Louis Coorsen, Jr., D.W. Howie and Marine National Bank, defendants. Fred Tegtmeyer, Milwaukee County Sheriff

**Sheriff's** sale of the estate of Oliver Harwood. Joseph A. Warren, Nathaniel J. Swann and Edward W. Robbins, trustees, plaintiffs against Thomas Greenwood and Rosalie Greenwood, his wife, Frank B. Golley, Louis Coorsen, Jr., D.W. Howie and Marine National Bank, defendants. Fred Tegtmeyer, Milwaukee County Sheriff

## May 14, 1904

C.E. Crain and family moved to the Wells farm.

Mrs. C.W. Damon is quite ill.

Chas. Davis was in Chicago on business.

Mr. Lindow, of Milwaukee, has taken the August Sporleder house.

Mrs. A.H. Swan, who has been ill, is improving.

Mrs. Richard Dewey is giving a reception at her home.

C.G.B. Schenck and family will occupy the G.H. Rogers house.

Mrs. Arthur Gregg entertained the Evening Cinch club.

Miss Gyda Erickson will give a musicale at her home.

Will Maxon, of Cedar Lake, Wis., visited Dr. Cutler.

Rev. Oliphant, of St. Edmonds, Milwaukee, visited Rev. F.S. Gray.

Miss Annie Munns, of Madison, Wis., visited her sister, Mrs. L.S. Pease.

Ralph Ellis, of U.W. Madison, visited his sister, Mrs. Kirke Putnam.

Miss Carrie Warren was in Milwaukee to visit Mrs. Johnson.

The Woman's Club will be entertained by Mrs. N.L. Kneeland.

Mr Stockdale and family, of Minneapolis, moved into the residence of the late G.G. Allen.

Dr. Dewey is having a stone lodge and gate erected at the entrance to the Sanitarium grounds.

Fred Smith, of Chicago, formerly of Wauwatosa, visited relatives here.

Mrs. W.A. Godfrey and son, Dudley Godfrey, leave to visit relatives in Faribault, Minn.

Mrs. C.S. Clark entertained the Missionary Society of the Congregational church.

Mr. J.F. Dittmar sprained his ankle severely.

Mrs. E.R. Godfrey entertained Mesdames G.G. Allen and W.B. Lincoln.

Miss Mav Foley, who has a short vacation from her school work in Sheboygan, is visiting her parents, Mr. and Mrs. J.L. Foley.

Mr. and Mrs. Wm. Menninger visited her parents, Mr. and Mrs. C.F. Bussewitz, in North Lake, Wis.

Mrs. Shields, of Howell, Mich., visited her father, John Foley, here.

Mr. and Mrs. Clarence Schneck and George Schneck visited relatives in Rodger's Park, Chicago.

Rev. Edwin Hyde, of Milwaukee, will preach at the M. E. church.

Frank Woller was severly bruised in a fall when his ladder broke.

Mrs. Ann Morris returned to Milwaukee after visiting her son, C. Morris.

Mrs. L.C. Tisdale assisted by Mrs. W.J. Hadley, of Milwaukee, entertained the Afternoon Cinch club.

W.B. Lincoln and family moved to Wichita, Kan. Mr. A.C. Hanson has rented the house they vacated.

Mrs. C. Wyman, assisted by Miss Charlotte Rogers, entertained the T.C.T. club.

Mr. J.D. Warren sold his mill and water privilege to Mr. Harden and Mr. Helgesen for $15,000.00.

Miss Abigail Cook, of Petoskey, Mich., is visiting Miss Evelyn Gilbert.

Chas. Godfrey is building a home on E. Milwaukee Ave. Bachman Bro's will do the carpentry and Mr. Ducco, of Milwaukee, the mason work.

Edward A. Bauer, manager of the E. Harrison Cawker estate, Milwaukee, purchased the Phillips furniture factory to manufacture enamel ware.

Att'y G.E. Morton, of Milwaukee, represented the superintendent of highways of Dist. 10, at the town board meeting, taxpayers in that district want the superintendent removed.

Miss Ruth Ellis will lead the B. Y. P. U. at the Baptist church.

**Marriage**

Charles E. Judson, of Wauwatosa, married Miss Bessie Hamilton, of Milwaukee, in Chicago, May 4, 1904.

**Letters uncalled for at the postoffice**

Christian Coerder, Mrs. Mary Everhardt, Ella Hasse, Wm. Hasse, Gladys Hanke, Herman Kiemert, Mr. Kempser, Max Lindower, Mrs. Susan Miller, and Frank Rinehardt

### May 21, 1904

Mrs. Bruno Zinn is visiting friends in Sheboygan.

Mrs. N.L. Kneeland was in Chicago.

Mr. L. Brockway was in Palmyra, Wis.

Mr. and Mrs. L.V. Gridley, of Racine, were here.

Mr. F.W. Schneck and family were in Okauchee, Wis.

Miss Durby, of Shannon, Ill., is visiting her aunt, Mrs. Richard Hayes.

Charles Barnekow, of Chicago, was here to visit relatives.

Mr. Myer, of Chicago, is the guest of Mrs. M. Horning.

Mr. G.F. Reichardt, of Wauwatosa, will run for sheriff.

Mr. and Mrs. Chas. Judson have returned from their wedding trip.

Messrs. Chas. Stickney and E.D. Hoyt are taking a trip to northern Wis.

The Woman's Club was entertained by Mrs. N.L. Kneeland.

Miss Katherine Farnham, of Milwaukee, is ill in the Knowlton hospital.

Mr. and Mrs. Fred C. Nash, of Pasadena, Cal., are visiting Mr. and Mrs. Gus. Gregg.

Arthur Brockway, who has been visiting his parents, returned to Edgerton.

Mrs. Grassie and daughter, Elizabeth Grassie, have returned from Milwaukee.

The Epworth League of the M.E. church met with Mr. and Mrs. Joseph Lefeber.

Miss Cox is well and returned to work at Lefeber Bros.

Mrs. Peter Nauertz, who was here during her father's last few days of fatal illness, is returning to her home in Waucoma, Iowa.

John Dunlop, the florist, has rheumatism, Donald McFadden will run the greenhouses in his absence.

David Swan had an operation to remove a carbuncle on his neck.

The W.C.T.U. will meet with Mrs. L. Brockway.

L.G. Wheeler, E.D. Hoyt, and C.B. Perry attended the Republican State convention.

Rev. W.D. Cox, of Milwaukee, will lecture at the Methodist church.

Fire destroyed a hen-house at the Luening place.

Warden H.H. Jacobs, of Wisconsin University Settlement, gave a talk at the meeting of the Men's Club of Congregational church, held at the home of Mr. W.R. Cundal.

District Attorney William H. Bennet and his assistant, Edward T. Fairchild will conduct the investigation against Superintendent Grosskopf, of the county hospital.

James L. Foley, Marshal, requests school children and friends to bring flowers to decorate graves for Memorial Day.

Claude Cairncross will lead the B. Y. P. U. at the Baptist church.

Rev. P.W. Longfellow will preach the annual sermon to the G. A. R. at the Baptist church.

Rev. C.A. Payne will preach at the M. E. church.

At the common council meeting, the contract concerning water pipes, with C.J. Crelley, was brought up, the need for more room for school purposes. The following bills were paid: Mil. Trac. Co., C. Kropp, John Blum, Wauwatosa Milling Co., Mrs. Hosford, Mrs. E.C. Matheson, and R.H. Bark. Pool table licenses were granted to C.C. Jacobus, Hausch, and Reichardt and a bowling alley license to Fred Picker. J.L. Hooley was nominated for alderman and rejected. The following people were present: E.E. Hatch, J.F. Harriman, E.A. Schmitz, Frank Harriman, J.D. Warren, L.S. Pease, John Taylor, L.R. Gridley, C.R. Davis, Frank Keats, C.T. Chandler, Chas. Stafford, Geo. Wilcox, and Henry B. Hunter, of Milwaukee.

Supt. August F.W. Kringel, of the home for dependent children, emphasizes the need for an isolation hospital because of over-crowding. The number of children at the home has been steadily increasing since it's establishment in 1898 there have been 831 children committed, of that number 127 have been indentured or adopted and 437 have been returned to their parents, 180 children were placed in the home during 1903.

Among endorsers for a correspondence course advertised in the News were: N. Meyer, advertiser "The Hub" Milwaukee; Geo. L. Waetjen, Canadian Atlantic Trans. Co., Milwaukee; M.L. Jenkins, Supt. Allis Chalmers Works; S.B. Harding, Pres. Modern Structural Steel Co., Waukesha; Chris. Hanson, West Allis, Wis.; J.T. Mason, Gas Works, Milwaukee.

## Death

Frederick Barnekow, a veteran of the Civil War and the German army, died at his home, May 16, 1904, at the age of 77 years. Mr. Barnekow, Sr. was a native of Mecklenburg, Germany, he entered the german army when he was 22 and served the king for six years and was discharged in 1854. He married in the spring of 1858 and left for America. He came directly to Milwaukee where he lived for a year then moved to Wauwatosa where he spent the rest of his life, forty-six years. In 1862 Mr. Barnekow enlisted in the Twenty-Fourth Wisconsin volunteers and was with that regiment during the Perryville and Stone River engagements. At Stone River he was taken prisoner and sent to Libby prison, where he endured it's horrors for six weeks, contracting ailments from which he never recovered. After being exchanged he was found unfit for further service and honorably discharged. He then returned to Wauwatosa and purchased a farm where he lived ever since. His wife died Feb. 20, 1904, he is survived by three son, John Barnekow, Frank Barnekow, and Ernest Barnekow, all of Wauwatosa and one daughter, Mrs. Peter Nauertz, of Waucoma, Ia. He had thirty grandchildren and fifteen gr-grandchildren.

The funeral was from his home to St. John's Lutheran church, Milwaukee, with interment at Wauwatosa cemetery. Rev. Dr. J. Rading officiated.

## Letters uncalled for at the postoffice.

C.A. Beeter, Lawrence Eckerd, Nona Gaffney, A.E. Jens, and Henry Schuster

## May 28, 1904

Rev. C.E. Goldthorp will be home from California soon.

Mrs. Wm. Baier was at Holly Hill in Washington County.

Lester Pavy, of Fond du Lac, visited relatives here.

Miss Henri Etta Aiken will visit her folk in Whitewater.

Mr. and Mrs. H.D. Colby are going to Chicago to visit.

Mrs. C.F. Bussewitz, of North Lake, is visiting her daughter, Mrs. Wm. Menninger.

Wm. Bullock, of Chicago, visited his cousin, Albert Taylor.

President J.B. Russell, of West Allis, visited the News office.

Mr. Harden and Mr. Helgeson are making repairs to their dyke and mill.

Mrs. S.W. Sanborn, of Milwaukee, visited the H.D. Colby home.

Oscar Kroessing and Miss Matilda Kroessing entertained at cinch.

Mr. J.W. Craven is going to Hull, England to visit relatives.

Mrs. J.R. Benoy is back from visiting her mother in western Wisconsin.

Messrs. and Mesdames F.W. Schneck, C.E. Wilson, Abe Lefeber, and F.M. Merica are going to Okauchee.

Mr. C.C. Chubb, of Algona, Iowa, is visiting his brother, O.S. Chubb.

Joseph McNab and John McNab, of Chicago and Mexico respectively, were here to visit friends.

Mr. J. Kennedy and family, of Racine, will occupy the Underwood house.

Rev. A.R. Thain will deliver a lecture at the Congregational church.

Morton Casperson, local agent for Wood's laundry (this is probably the Veterans Hospital, AKA, Old Soldiers Home), purchased two lots on Greenfield Ave.

H.P. Bradley, the health officer, ordered the school in District No. 1 closed because of scarlet fever.

Mrs. Lockmann sang a solo at the Milwaukee Missionary Union at the Baptist Church.

Mrs. G.P. Dousman was invited by her daughter, Mrs. Charles Sooysmith, of New York, to accompany her on a trip through Europe.

The Missionary meeting and social was held at the home of Dr. Cairncross, Miss Anabel Farries was in charge of the program.

Rev. and Mrs. G.A. Ehrhard and children are going to visit relatives in Harriettsville, Ohio.

Mrs. Bergoman, the aged mother, of Mrs. Miller, dislocated her arm when stepping from the street to the curbstone she lost her balance and fell. Mr. Bergoman was with her at the time.

John Marquardt was set upon by dogs that were running loose, they frightened his horse, causing it to run and bringing injury to his horse, wagon and left him shaken badly.

The town board took up the matter of the petition for the removal of Louis Jung as superintendent of road Dist. 10. A contract for sprinkling part of Watertown Plank Rd. was awarded to Wallis Theis.

Capt. Amos P. Foster will give the address at the Memorial Day Exercises.

Miss Janet Smith will lead the B.Y.P.U. at the Baptist church.

Rev. Albert A. Martin, of the Children's Home Society of Wisconsin will preach at the M.E. church.

Judge George W. Burnell, of Oshkosh, handed down his decision in the case concerning the extension of the street railway, brought by Atty. Lynn S. Pease, of this city, for Imre Boos, Dr. Wendel, and Captain Leisk.

**Marriage**

Miss Cynthia Krafcheck married Stanly Polarek, May 24, 1904, at the home of the bride's parents, Mr. and Mrs. Jos. Krafcheck, 61st St.

**Death**

Miss Bertha Florence Delpsch, daughter of Mrs. Robert Delpsch, died May 28, 1904. Mrs. Stanley Cowan and Chas. Delpsch, of St. Paul, Miss Laura Delpsch, of Omaha, and Miss Margaret Delpsch, of Shawano, brother and sisters of the deceased were here to attend the funeral. Rev. F.S. Gray officiated at the funeral.

Lillie Seuberth, age 14 and Lyda Seuberth, aged 8, drowned in the Schoonmaker quarry while fishing. Lyda slipped on the bank, falling into the water and Lillie tried to rescue her. Their three brothers were also fishing and seeing what was happening ran home to get their father, who managed to pull the children out, but it was too late to save them. The Seuberth family lives on Eighth Ave., a short distance from the death hole. They are survived by their parents, three brothers, Edward Seuberth, aged 15, Roy Seuberth, aged 9 and Victor Seuberth, aged 4 and one sister, Hazel Seuberth, aged 12. Mr. Seuberth is employed by Signalphone Company. The funeral was held from the family home with Rev. E.W.A. Meyer, of the Second Baptist German church, Milwaukee, officiating, with interment at Wauwatosa cemetery.

Coroner Broegemann and the Coroner's jury recommended that the Schoonmaker quarry pond be enclosed by a fence and signs posted warning of the danger, because of the number of deaths every summer.

# INDEX

# Index

**A**

Abbott, Mr. 10
Acams, M.H. 122
Acker, Eva May 89
Ackman, Ben. 127
Adams, Charles Kendall 42
Adams, Florence 38, 48, 64, 100, 126, 135
Adams, G.P. 134, 139
Adams, Geo. 64
Adams, M.F. 8, 18
Adams, M.H. 3, 8, 15, 75, 83, 149, 160
Adams, Mrs. 56
Adams, W.L. 122
Addms, M.H. 160
Adell, Wis. 131
Adler, Miss 63
Ahrendt, August 91
Aiken, Henri Etta 168
Aken, Henri Etta 89
Akin, Henrietta 58
Albany, NY 72
Alberti, Jessie 122
Albertine, Kurt 13
Albion, NY 36
Alexander, P. 114
Algona, Iowa 168
Allanson, George 105
Allen, Agnes S. 82
Allen, Anna May 60
Allen, Beth 153
Allen, Burley 61, 102, 135
Allen, Chas 102
Allen, Donald 87
Allen, Dorothy 81
Allen, G.G. 81, 84, 87, 93, 98, 100, 112, 126, 136, 158, 163
Allen, J.S. 71, 85
Allen, James 60
Allen, L.B. 151
Allen, Miss 91
Allen, R.N. 68
Alwynse, John iv
Ambrose, Geo. 74
Ambrose, Geo. M. 74
Ames, Fern 89
Ames, I.M. 68
Ames, Inez 89

Andrew, H.N. 99, 105, 120
Andrew, Mrs. 141
Andrew, Oliver 120
Andrews, H.N. 9, 55, 98
Angermeyer, Mr. 15
Angus, J.J. 90
Appleton 1, 18, 35, 41, 58, 94
Argus, Harold 162
Armin, C.E. 82
Armour, W.J. 35
Armstrong, Allison 161
Armstrong, G.S. 85
Armstrong, John 83, 99, 149
Armstrong, Mary 81, 89
Armstrong, Miss 67
Arnauld, Max 150, 159, 160
Arvelt, Meta vi
Atkinson, Ft. 75
Atwood, Mrs. 65
Audubon, Iowa 76
Aurora, Ill. 50
Austin, A.S. 66
Austin, Lottie 66

**B**

Bachman 11
Bachman, C.R. 127
Bachman, Susie vi
Badger, O.S. 33
Bagley, L. 153
Baier, William 107
Baier, Wm. 69, 146, 167
Bair, Choir-master 29
Bair, Mr. 25
Baird, R.S. 152
Baker, Al 159
Baldwin, Fred 137
Baldwin, Mr. 104
Ballentine, Geo. W. 117
Bally, Mrs. 84
Baltes, Charles iv
Baltes, Myrtle vi
Baltimore, Md. 132
Banky, Arthur 78, 107
Banky, Mrs. 86, 94
Baraboo 1, 21, 31, 121, 132
Baradt, David 87
Barber, Benediah iii
Barber, Edward iv
Bardenwerper, H.A. 3
Bardenwerper, H.W. 4, 6, 50, 59, 137
Barfoot, Ernst iv
Barfooth, Dorothea 122
Barfooth, Ernest 122

Bark 12
Bark, Edgar 72, 81
Bark, F. 159
Bark, F.H. 62, 72, 81, 83
Bark, Ferd. 127
Bark, Ferdinand 3, 16, 81, 83, 111, 116, 123, 126, 130, 138, 160
Bark, Fred 41, 160
Bark, Fred H. 3, 6, 12, 16, 49, 138
Bark, Fred. 159
Bark, Fred. H. 127
Bark, Gertie 95
Bark, J.P. 123
Bark, Lillian 147
Bark, Lily 84
Bark, Mrs. 41
Bark, R.H. 166
Bark, Wm. 84, 92, 159
Barkhausen 103
Barneknow, Fred 140
Barnekow, Albert 151
Barnekow, Alice 66
Barnekow, Charles 165
Barnekow, Ernest 146, 167
Barnekow, F. 151
Barnekow, Frank 146, 167
Barnekow, Frank M. 66
Barnekow, Frederick 145, iv
Barnekow, Fritz 115
Barnekow, John 146, 149, 160, 167
Barnekow, M. 145
Barnekow, Otto C. 142
Barnes, A.E. 117
Barnes, Agelena 117
Barnes, Angelina C. 125, 130
Barnes, C.D. 117
Barnes, Charles D. 130
Barnes, Chas. 158
Barnes, D.B. 121, 122
Barnes, David 20
Barnes, Helen 19
Barnes, James iv
Barnes, Maud 37
Barnes, Maud H. 90
Barnes, Maude 59
Barnes, V.S. 114
Barnett, Dr. 37
Barrett, Eleanor 95
Barrett, Elinor 122
Barrett, G.W. 59, 124
Barrett, John D. iv
Barrett, Paul iv
Barry, Elizabeth 157
Bartel, George vi

Bartel, J.D. 28
Bartlet, Miss 69
Barton 43
Bates, Edith 159
Bates, Helen 72
Bates, William iv
Battle Creek, Mich. 78
Bauer, Edward A. 164
Bauer, Geo. P. 84
Bauer, M. 133
Bauer, P. 3
Bauers, H. 106
Baumbach 46, 52, 60
Baumbach, Alderman 12
Baumbach, Aldermen 98
Beale, C.H. 152
Beaman, Jacob 147
Beaver Dam 54, 93, 124, 153
Becker, A.G. 77
Becker, Adolph 110, 153
Becker, Julius 141
Becker, Lois vi
Becker, W.F. 110
Beecher, A.E. 115, 121
Beeter, C.A. 167
Beggs, Charles 58
Beggs, John I. 60
Beggs, Mr. 59
Beggs, Walter 58
Behling, F. 159
Behling, Fred 8, 25
Behling, R. 12
Behling, Robert 7, 31
Beichardt, G.F. 149
Bell, Supervisor 129
Belle Plain, Ia. 117
Beloit 34, 59, 82
Bendelow, Thos. 119
Benkendorf, Contractor 115
Bennet, William H. 166
Bennett, C.W. 94
Bennett, George 107, 146
Bennett, Harry 123
Benott, Atty. 110
Benoy, Cornelius v
Benoy, J. 107
Benoy, J.R. 158, 159, 168
Benoy, John 112
Benoy, John R. 91, v
Benoy, M.J. 91
Benoy, Niel 115
Benoy, Niely 107
Benson, H.H. 19, 40
Benson, Mrs. 2, 34

Benson, Rev. 2
Benton 23
Berg, J.A. 159
Bergholz, W. 37
Bergoman, Mr. 169
Bergoman, Mrs. 169
Berlin 14
Berlin, Wis. 50
Bernbach, Louisa 125
Berringer, Henry S. 153
Bessenger, Christion iv
Bestor, O.P. 69, 108
Beutler, Dr. 119
Beutler, W. 141
Beutler, W.F. 49, 106, 107
Beutler, Wm. F. 145
Bevier, Dr. 24
Bevier, Mrs. 40
Bickel, Miss 140
Bielfernicht, F. 122
Bielpernicht, F. 132
Bigsby, E. 121
Bigsby, Edgar 64
Bigsby, Kate 64
Bigsby, Mr. 158
Bilfernicht, F. 106
Birkett, E. 84
Bissell, Mrs. 45
Bjorquist, Mabel 10, 30
Blackburn, G.W. 41
Blackwell, Okla. 68, 105
Blackwell, Rev.Father 51
Blaeser, A.M. 136
Blaesser, A.M. 153
Blaesser, Esther 66
Blaesser, S. 117
Blair, E.Harding 22
Blair, Edward Hurding 12
Blake, Adele 68
Blake, E.B. 65
Blake, E.R. 85
Blake, James 69, 105
Blakesly, Mrs. 113
Blanchard, Albert iv
Blanchard, Hiram W. iii
Bleedorn, Miss 124
Bleifernicht, F. 114
Bliefernicht, F. 117
Blodgett, E. 42
Blodgett, E.L. 9, 28
Blodgett, Elbert 71, 108
Blodgett, Elmer 118
Blodgett, Isabel 64
Blodgett, Jere. 79

Bloedorn, Ethelyn 89
Blohm, John 33
Blohm, Mary 33
Bloomington, Ill. 118
Blum, Barney 37, 128, 135
Blum, John 166
Boddenhagen, F. 159
Boeder, Irma 69
Boetcher, Julia 140
Boetcher, Willig 140
Bogers, Harold 12
Bohler, Charles 3
Boldt, August 99
Bollenbach, Leslie A. 121
Bollenbach, Mrs. 143
Boller, Anra R. 106
Boone, Iowa 131
Boorse, Jesse 28
Boos, Imre 169
Booth, Alson 85
Booth, Sherman 46
Bort, A.N. 82
Boscobel, Wis. 91
Boseman, Mont. 28
Bossingham, J.T. 127
Boston 61, 82
Bostwick, Ella 73
Bostwick, H. 150
Bostwick, H.E. 73, 150, 158
Bowen, Ida 30
Bowen, John iii, 73
Bowling, P.F. 92
Boyden, Elizabeth 9, iv
Boyden, Miss 9
Bradford, Mass. 130
Bradley, Clerk 29
Bradley, Edith 78, 81
Bradley, H.B. 146
Bradley, H.F. 18
Bradley, H. 3, 6, 11, 12, 24, 27, 29,
    41, 76, 78, 79, 82, 91, 120, 124, 127,
    136, 138, 147, 160, 168
Bradley, Helen 78, 81
Bradley, Herbert P. 149
Bradley, Mr. 158
Bradley, Town Clerk 42
Bradley, W.C. 46
Brady, Anna J. 117
Brady, W. 102
Brantt, S.C. iii
Braun, Fred W. 4
Braunschweiger, Eug. 83
Brazee, Benson iii
Breblow, August 146

Breed  12, 38, 46, 98
Breed, A.O.T.  30, 98, iii
Breed, Alderman  24, 60
Breed, Aldermen  52
Breed, Allen  45
Breed, C.A.  82, 83
Breed, C.G.  30
Breed, Charles  104, 106
Breed, Charles A.  3, 5, 30, 98
Breed, Chas.  56
Breed, Chas.A.  12
Breed, Florence  30
Breed, G.A.  30
Breed, Margaret  98
Breed, Mrs.  56
Breed, Ruby  30
Breed, Ruby Louise  24
Breese, S.  77, 108
Brehm, M.E.  29
Breitkrentz, Otto  83
Brese, Annie  135
Brewer, D.R.  99, 157
Bribeckl?, Frank  106
Bridgeport, Conn.  58
Bridges, Leona  vi
Brier, George  102
Briggs, Mr.  25
Briggs, W.A.  36
Brobratz, W.  157
Brockway, Arthur  49, 102, 135, 143,
  146, 153, 165
Brockway, Arthur W.  93
Brockway, Gilbert  21, 24
Brockway, L.  14, 24, 34, 37, 51, 58,
  72, 83, 93, 100, 101, 103, 104,
  105, 110, 113, 123, 149, 160, 165
Brockway, Mildred  60, 69, 123
Brockway, Mrs.  133
Brodhead  41
Brodhead, Wis.  88, 90
Broegemann, Coroner  170
Broegman, Cororner  114
Broker, W.  77
Brookfield  29, 43
Brookins, Clark  iii
Brookins, SD  66
Brooklyn, NY.  22
Bros., Dearsley  70
Brothers, Sells  61
Brown, Agnes  63, 123
Brown, Alice  38
Brown, Arthur  78
Brown, Charles  iv
Brown, Charles L.  69

Brown Deer, Wis.  57
Brown, Elizabeth  69
Brown, George  139
Brown, H.M.  73
Brown, Julia  101
Brown, Julia M.  159
Brown, Mrs.  32
Brown, Nathan A.  69
Brown, R.M.  3, 67, 92, 97, 113,
  118, 143
Brown, Richard  26, 31, 32
Brown, Rudolph M.  69
Brown, Silas  69, iii
Brown, T.H.  131
Brown, Thomas H.  124
Browne, Helen  89
Browne, Katherine  89
Brownell, Edith  127
Brownell, J.C.  127
Brownwich, Mrs.  84
Brucehart, Della  88
Brumder, Geo.  99
Brunning, Norton  iv
Brunning, Randal  iv
Bruskowitz, Peter  25
Brussatt, Chas.  77
Bryan, J.  63
Bryan, Rosie  71
Bryne, Florence  64
Bryne, H.  57
Buch, F.  149
Buchman, H.  116
Buchman, Rudolph  160
Buck, Frank  17
Buck, Wm.  84
Buck, Worrel  115
Buckbee, J.L.  61
Buckingham, Mrs.  18
Buffalo  62, 67
Bullock, Wm.  168
Burdish, Nina  76
Burgmeyer, Simon  2
Burke, Jacob  48
Burkhart, Frank  127
Burnell, George W.  169
Burnside, C.V.  49, 80, 138, 156
Burnside, Mrs.  108, 113, 116, 124
Bush, Jeanette  91
Bush, John J.  61
Bushnell, Joseph  135
Bussewitz, C.F.  66, 92, 94,
  140, 163, 168
Bussewitz, C.P.  86
Bussewitz, E.M.  68, 101, 118, 145

Bussewitz, Ed 144, 153
Bussewitz, Edward 47
Bussewitz, F.C. 145
Bussewitz, Louis 118
Bussewitz, Max A. 92
Busz, Hulda 109
Butler 36
Butler, Chas. 49
Butler, Miss 30
Butler, Mrs. 30
Butters, Ernest 94
Butters, Eugene 51
Butters, May 131
Butterworth, Bessie 72, 84
Butterworth, E.B. 24
Butterworth, Elizabeth 96
Butterworth, F.A. 72, 102
Butterworth, Ned 72
Button, Louis 60

C

Cadillac, Mich. 77
Cadwell, Ethel 14, 33
Cadwell, Mrs. 14
Cadwell, R. 38
Cain, Robert 70
Cairncross, Claud 48
Cairncross, Claude 166
Cairncross, Dr. 63, 108, 118, 169
Cairncross, J.W. 83, 113, 116,
126, 127, 160
Cairncross, Mrs. 149
California 21, 24
Calumet, Mich. 55, 66, 128
Camden, NC 91
Cameron, D.E. 50
Cameron, Sam. 158
Campbell, Annie 111
Campbell, Miss 154
Canada 45
Canright, Blanche 78, 134
Canright, C.E. 105, 109
Canright, Calla 36, 64, 78
Canright, Claude E. 78
Canright, Eldon 78
Carde, Jos. 82
Carl, Emily 15
Carlton, A.L. 58, 63, 85, 122, 128
Carlton, Albion Leighton 130
Carlton, E.P. 128, 130
Carlton, May 1
Carlton, Will 130
Carmy, F.L. 117

Carpenter, M.P. 102
Carpenter, Paul D. 70, 77, 95, 106,
112, 119, 130, 152
Carpenter, W.P. 102
Carter, Bert 30
Carter, C.A. 159
Carter, C.S. 30
Carter, Clinton 64
Carter, E. 93
Carter, E. Clinton 117
Carter, E.B. 30
Carter, Elizabeth 80, 141
Carter, G.W. 30
Carter, Geo. 53
Carter, George 30
Carter, Jacob v
Carter, L. 93
Carter, L.E. 30
Carver, C.A. 24
Case, Bigelow iii
Case, Lucy 80
Cash 70
Casperson, M. 123
Casperson, Morton 158, 168
Catlin, Aaron iv
Cavalere, E.E. 114
Caway, Jannette 87
Cawker, E. Harrison 164
Cedar Lake 53
Ceell, Bir.Geo 87
Ceell, Thos. 87
Cervaart, Jacob 26
Chadbourne, Frank 45
Chafe, Robert 56
Chamberlain, A.E. 67
Chamberlain, Eva 27
Chamberlain, Mrs. 27
Chamberlin, Hattie 33
Chamberlin, Miss vi
Chandler, C.T. 18, 127, 151, 153, 166
Chandler, Phil 151
Chandler, S.A. 151
Charles City, Iowa 147
Chase, Charles iv
Chase, Chas. 46
Chatfield, A.M. 58
Chatfield, E.G. 14
Chatfield, Lorena 69
Chatfield, Mary 21
Chatfield, Minn. 97
Chatfield, Mrs. 21
Chatfield, Pearl 58
Chatfield, Rena 94
Chatfield, Sara 68

Chatfield, T.E. 73, 121
Cheany, Joseph 39
Cheever, W.H. 64, 139
Cheney, Mr. 11
Chilton, Wis. 25, 31, 77, 126
Chisholm, Miss 93
Christiansey, Sophia 159
Chubb, C.C. 168
Chubb, E.W. 48, 51
Chubb, O.S. 168
Churchill, Myron R. 44
Clansen, Elizabeth 71
Clansen, P.C. 61
Clapp, Luther iv
Clapp, Mary 43, 97, 126
Clapp, Mary Percilla 97
Clapp, W.A. 3, 46, 92
Clark, Andrew iv, vi
Clark, C.S. 58, 63, 73, 84,
87, 97, 141, 163
Clark, Elizabeth R. 130
Clark, Mrs. 139
Clark, W.H. 57
Clarke, Mrs. 108
Clarmont, New Hampshire 38
Clarus, Olle 76
Clausen, P.C. 80, 155, 156, 159, 160
Clausen, Winifred 80
Cleveland 75, 89, 100
Clibborn, Perey 92
Clifton, Ark. 56
Clinton, E.H. 64
Clinton Junction 65, 107
Clinton, Wis. 77
Cochrane, Myrtice 38, 100
Codding, Zoe 85
Coe, R.J. 57
Coe, W.S. 143
Coerder, Christian 164
Cogswell, Allen 40
Colby, H.D. 27, 33, 168
Cole, J.D. 49
Cole, W.D. 19
Coleman, Edgar W. 2
Collins, A.B. 87
Collins, E. 150
Collins, Mark 87
Colorado 2
Colorado Springs 14, 20
Colte, N. 159
Columbus, Ohio 41, 146
Columbus 52, 78, 86, 94
Colwell, E. 99
Colwell, Ethel 102

Colwell, Ethelyn 89, 124, 131
Colwell, Miss 124
Comstock, M.J. 28
Concord, Mass. 18
Conley, Elsie 12
Conley, Frank 137
Conley, Hettie 12
Conley, Hetty 30
Conley, Morris iv
Connell, F.Gregory 51
Connell, Gregg 85, 113
Connell, Gregory 158
Connell, Mrs. 133
Connery, John 94
Connilley, Arthur 143
Conrad, F.A. 7
Constantine, Mich. 129
Conway, Stanley 119
Cook, Abigail 164
Cook, E.W. 20
Cook, Gertrude 36, 45
Cook, Mrs. 32, 45
Cook, Neb. 94
Cook, Rev. 75
Cook, Rose A. 139
Cooke, Benjamin iv
Cooksville, Wis. 47
Cooley, D.A. 146
Cooley, Mrs. 147
Coon, John 109
Coon, John Roberts 111
Cooper, Katharine 96
Coorsen, Louis 162
Cope, Burt 145
Copeland, A.E. 128
Copeland, C.A. 101, 105, 107
Cordle, Lizzie 111
Cordy, Peter 157
Cornelius, E.C. 1, 9, 39, 62
Cornelius, George 43
Cornelius, Mr. 44
Cornelius, Mrs. 30
Cornelius, Prof. 40, 120
Cornwall, E.H. 105
Cory, J.F. 84
Cory, Jesse F. 55, 64, 139
Coughlin, Clerk 23
Coulter, S. 80
Coultes, Mr. 133
Coulthard, E. 72, 150
Coulthard, Edward 72, 83, 99,
152, 153, 159, 160
Coulthard, Mr. 156
Council Bluffs, Iowa 129

Coventry, VT. 33
Covington, Ky. 42
Cowan, S.O. 154
Cowan, Stanley 169
Cox, C.J. 25
Cox, Frank 60
Cox, Miss 157, 165
Cox, W.D. 166
Cox, William L. 60
Cox, Wm. L. 76
Crabtree, F.R. 10
Craig, Marion Jean 11
Craig, Mrs. 120
Crain, C.A. 64
Crain, C.E. 162
Crain, Charles 126
Crain, Gertrude 64
Cramer, Chas. 95
Crandall, Florence 87
Crandall, J.D. 87
Crane, Austin D. 66
Crane, Gertruce 49
Crane, Nettie 1, 9
Craven, J.W. 168
Crawford, John iii
Crawford, Rev. iv
Crawford, T.D. 20
Creek, Cedar 23
Crelley, C.J. 166
Cresco, Iowa 93
Creston, Ind. 26
Crilley, C.J. 145, 147
Croft, Contractor 120
Croft, Mr. 18
Croft, S.P. 15, 116, 147
Croft, Steph. 161
Croft, Stephen 45
Crombie, A.B. 140
Cronk, Francis 52
Cross, Arthur 128
Crowl, Ida 26
Crowley, Jas. 159
Cruickshank, W.A.C. 12
Cudelly, A.B. 52
Culver, W.L. 61
Cumberland, Md. 142
Cumberland Mills, ME 69
Cummerford, Howard 84
Cundal, W.R. 166
Cundall, Jessie 33, 93
Cundall, Roland 132
Cundall, W.R. 20, 33, 37, 41,
  62, 93, 132, 145
Cundall, Wm 146

Cuno, Chas. 31
Cupple, Charles iv
Curdall, Wm. R. 141
Curran, Robert iii
Currelley, A.B. 140
Currelley, Arthur 140
Currelley, Arthur B. 110
Currie 38
Currie, Adam 35, 40, 55, 83,
  121, 141, 150, 160
Currie, Allister 64
Currie, Ethel M. 84
Currie, Jessie 2, 30
Currie, Jessie V. 54
Currie, William 55
Curth, N.T. 86
Curtis 138
Curtis, C.A. 53, 81, 84, 96, 120
Curtis, C.E. 72, 87, 94, 100,
  136, 140, 146, 149, 160, 161
Curtis, Charles 109, 149, 159
Curtis, Charles E. 139, 157
Curtis, Chas. 83, 161
Curtis, Chas. E. 138
Curtis, Clara 47
Curtis, Don 125
Curtis, E.E. 120
Curtis, E.M. 51
Curtis, Elizabeth 40, 94, 131
Curtis, Frederick 143
Curtis, Guy 37
Curtis, L.M. 81
Curtis, Lucy 81
Curtis, Maud 23, 47, 132, 133, 139
Curtis, Maude 44, 59, 100,
  138, 140, 143, 146
Curtis, May 51
Curtis, Mr. 29
Curtis, S.K. 21
Curtis, Sarah 143
Curtis, Truman iv
Curtis., C.E. 93
Cushing, J.F. 24
Cushing, J.H. 50, 108, 118, 120, 156
Cutler, Dr. 85, 163
Cutler, H. 85
Cutler, J.D. 19
Cutler, J.S. 25, 26, 53, 55, 65, 83,
  103, 107, 132, 134, 136, 138, 146, 160
Cutler, Joseph 53
Cutler, L.S. 102
Cutler, Mary 102, 146
Cutler, Miss 85
Cutler, W.G. 26, 65

**D**

Daen, Mary 86
Dailey, Martin iv
Dalke, Chas. 61
Daly, Elizabeth 131
Dam, Beaver 24
Damon, C.W. 1, 68, 75, 77, 83,
   86, 99, 102, 121, 159, 162
Damon, Cyrus 20
Damon, Cyrus W. 154
Damon, Herbert iv
Damon, Lavinia 52
Damon, Lowell iv
Dane Co. 3
Danielson, Daisy Ruth 55
Danielson, Muriel 52
Darling, E.M. 73
Darling, Frances 42
Dartford, Wis. 47
Dascomb, H.W. 124
Davelaar 30
Davelaar, G.J. 49, 159, 160
Davelaar, Gilbert J. 150
Davelaar, J.G. 58
Davelaar, William 23
Davelaar, Wm. 65, 88
Davidson, Frank 154
Davidson, Margaret 154
Davies, Jeannette vi
Davis, B.F. 60
Davis, C.R. 49, 94, 149, 166
Davis, Charles A. 3
Davis, Charles R. 107
Davis, Chas. 48, 103, 162
Davis, Chas. R. 80
Davis, Frank 156
Davis, J.K. 144
Davis, J.S. 18
Davis, Katherine 153
Davis, L.J. 159
Davis, Mrs. 84
Davis, R. 94
Davis, Ralph 94
Davis, W. 30
Dawson, Alfred 30
Dawson, J. Bosworth 114
Day, Fiske Holbrook 60
Day, Mrs. 60
Dayton, Ohio 2
De Graff, M.J. 78, 81
De Leiuw, Marie 91
De Leiuw, Mrs. 91
de Nevlen, Mrs. 21
de Ranitz, S.T. 22

De Swart, Wm. 76
De Swarte, J.B. 54, 90, 95, 99, 136
De Swarte, John B. 83, 160
De Swarte, Lawrence 72
De Swarte, Thomas 72
De Swarte, Thos. 74
De Voe, Mr. 115
Dean, Jas.H. 50
Dearsley, J.W. 86
Dearsley, Walter 72
Decatur, Mich. 62, 104
Decker, S.J. 12
Decker, Samuel J. 3, 6
Deegaff, John 69
Deerfield 75
Delafield 2
Delafield, Wis. 71, 107
Delaney, M. 159
Delavan 38, 53, 131
Dellicker, J.H. 30
Delpsch, Bertha Florence 169
Delpsch, Charles 119
Delpsch, Chas. 169
Delpsch, Elizabeth 69
Delpsch, Florence 96
Delpsch, Ida 96
Delpsch, Laura 94, 169
Delpsch, Margaret 24, 94, 113, 169
Delpsch, R. 93, 119
Delpsch, Robert 169
Delsch, Margaret 118
Denning, Harriet iv
Denny 142
Denny, Alfred iv
Denny, Harriet iv
Denny, W.J. 115
Denton, Frank 85
Denver 20, 105, 138
Derbin, Margaret 36
Detroit 72, 103 139
Deuster, P.J. 8
Dewey, Dr. 163
Dewey, Miss 17
Dewey, Richard 72, 106, 131, 133,162
Dewey, Richard,Jr. 2
Dexter, D.H. 143
Dexter, Frank 143
Dexter, Mary J. 143
Dexter, Mira 87
Dexter, Miss 76
Dexter, Mrs. 141
Diamond, Thomas 29
Dick, P.G. 25
Dick, Phillip G. 23, 29, 32

Dickerson 23
Dickson, A.M. 79
Diedrich, Joseph 124
Diedrich, Peter 116
Dierke, William 111
Digman, Frank J. 36
Digman, Fred 82
Digman, H. 99
Digman, H.A. 99
Digman, Hubert 36, 82
Digman, Mrs. 36
Dillan, W.S. 104
Dillingham, A.W. 41
Dillingham, Harriet M. 82
Dillingham, Miss 91
Dillman 41
Dittmar, J.F. 46, 83, 99, 160, 163
Dittmar, John 17
Dittmar, John F. 4, 11, 83, 130
Dix, R.A. 14
Doble, Harry L. 78
Dodd, Gertrude 108, 110, 114,
153, 155
Dodd, Gertrude P. 89
Dodd, Miss 59
Dodge 109
Doenfield, Rev. 105
Doerfler, Christian 123
Doesburg, J.M. 110
Doherty, Daniel 54
Doherty, Lillian 23
Doig, Mrs 112
Domers, Fred 117
Donahue, Mrs. 107
Donahue, W.A. 65
Donahue, Wm. 93
Donnelly, Jeannette 154
Doty, Flora 161
Doty, Flora E. 93
Doty, Frank 161
Doty, Miss 3, 44
Doud, Gertrude 48
Douglas, A.S. 94
Douglas, C.K. 119
Douglas Heights 17
Douglas, J.K. 27, 144
Douglas, J.R. 46
Douglas, Z. 30
Dousman, G.P. 16, 29, 42, 78,
125, 145, 168
Dousman, Geo. P. 76
Dousman, George 131
Dousman, George B. iii
Dousman, K.C. 146

Downer, Ida 137
Drake, S.B. 150
Dreher, Rufus G. 129
Dreutzer, Annette 65, 125, 128, 134
Dreutzer, C.G. 47, 48, 55, 56,
65, 112, 123, 134
Dreutzer, C.S. 33
Dropp, Christoph 3
Dubuque, Iowa 83
Ducco, Mr. 164
Duenkel, Charles 7, 43
Duenkel, Christine 43
Duenkel, Henry 43
Duenkel, Herman 43
Duenkel, William 43
Duff, Katherine 39
Duff, R. 27
Duluth, Minn. 80
Dummer, John 39
Dunham, V.B. 125
Dunlop, Jno.M. 71
Dunlop, John 15, 22, 32, 45, 91, 165
Dunlop, John M. 5
Dunn, Mae 87
Durbin, F.H. 127
Durbin, Frank 45
Durbin, Margaret 48, 64
Durby, Miss 165
Dutcher, Mrs. 54
Duxborrow, Mrs. 94
Dysart, J.P. 15, 18, 91, 97
Dysart, Miss 151
Dysart, Mr. 117

E

Eagle 9, 45
Eagle, Wis. 55, 78
Earling, P.R. 85
Earls, Chas. 62
Earls, Mary 1, 38, 81
Earries 90
East Hamburg 67
East Hartford, Conn. 72
Eaton, Barney 49
Eaton, Lewis? H. 12
Eau Claire 59
Ebberthart, Mathilda 94
Ebberthart, Oscar 94
Eckel, C.F. 1, 11
Eckel, Stanley 11
Eckerd, Lawrence 167
Eckstein, C.F. 71, 127, 152, 155
Eckstein, Charles 127
Eddy, Cora E. 106

Eddy, Florence 10
Edgerton 124
Edgerton, Wis. 61, 146
Edgewood, Ill. 57
Edison, Neb. 32
Edwards, Cora 122
Eere, Lawrence 125
Eggleson, Thomas 54
Eggleston, R.A. 93
Ehrhard, G.A. 169
Ehrhardt, G. 106
Ehrhardt, G.A. 119, 144
Ehrhardt, Rev. 125
Ehrlicher, Matt J. 156
Ehrlicher, Matt. 62
Eldridge, E.C. 121
Elkhorn, Iowa 76
Elkhorn, Wis. 96
Ellis, Eveline 99
Ellis, Mrs. 43
Ellis, Ralph 62, 163
Ellis, Ruth 44, 66, 135, 156, 164
Ellsworth, C.F. iii
Elm Grove 39, 49
Elwell, Marie 37
Elyria, Ohio 75, 80
Emery, Miss 23
Encampment, Wyoming 45
Engelhardt, Nellie 159
Engelhardt, W.H. 83
Engelhart, Gertrude 64
Engelhart, Henry 56
Engelhart, Nellie 123
Engelhart, W.H. 123, 127
Engelhart, W.K. 160
Engle, Henry 112
Englehardt, W.H. 127
Englehart, Clara 88
Englehart, Nellie 63
Englehart, W.H. 19
Eppenberger, W. 70
Erickson, Gyda 163
Ericsson, Fred 59
Ernst, Martin 160
Ernst, Mrs. 160
Errickson, Misses 85
Espenett, Jeanette 26
Esslinger, W. 19
Etnyre, E.D. 99
Evans, E.C. 34
Evans, Lyman 153
Evans, Pearl 71
Evanston, Ill. 103, 122
Evansville 58

Evenstein, E. 52
Everett, C.J. 123
Everett, C.T. 49, 61, 66, 95, 97,
   103, 104, 108, 113, 120
Everett, Daisy 48, 68, 126, 135
Everett, Edith 154
Everett, Florence 48, 66, 68, 126, 139
Everett, Isabel 57, 61
Everett, Miss 139
Everett, Mr. 156
Everett, S.T. 67
Everhardt, Mary 164
Everhart, Mary 162

F

Fairbanks, J.C. 116
Fairbanks, J.I. 118, 140
Fairbanks, Mary 118
Fairchild, Edward T. 166
Fairweather, A.A. 105
Fairweather, N. 127
Falbe, Anton T. 26
Falk, Emma 135
Falkner, W.S. 94, 113
Farchman, John 69
Fargo, ND 34, 105
Faribault, Minn. 163
Faries, Dr. 67
Faries, Hannah P. 67
Faries, R.J. 67
Faries, Royal P. 67
Farmington, Wash. 88
Farnham, C.S. 17
Farnham, Charles 20, 86
Farnham, Charles R. 114
Farnham, Charles S. 114
Farnham, Katherine 16, 114, 165
Farnham, M. 99
Farnham, Miss 124
Farnham, Myrtle 48, 89, 93, 153
Farrell, Berkley iv
Farrer, R. 159
Farries, Albert 23
Farries, Anabel 54, 64, 169
Farries, B.B. 9
Farries, Belle 104, 105, 117, 119, 123
Farries, Byron 25
Farries, John 51, 105, 112
Farries, Mable Grace 51
Farries, Mrs. 28
Farries, Supervisor 25
Farries, William 24, 91, 101,
   108, 154
Farries, Wm. 27, 46, 50, 149, 160

Farris, William iv
Fauerbach, Emil 124
Faulkner, Mrs. 133
Faulkner, Russel 133
Faulkner, Russell 102, 149
Faulkner, W.S. 96, 120, 133, 134, 138, 150
Feerick, Henry W. 37
Fehl, Jacob 28
Fehling, O.A. 92
Ferdinand, Deputy Sheriff 23, 28
Ferdinand, Rudolph 9
Fergeson, E.N. 52
Ferguson, James 140
Ferguson, Sarah Smith 139, 140
Ferguson, T.J. 15, 49, 98, 137, 155
Ferris, Robt. 38
Fetterly 23
Fetterly, J.A. 131
Fexter, David iv
Filgge, Anna 102
Findley, Kenneth vi
Fingado, C. 21
Fingado, Charles iv
Fingado, Chas. 78
Fingado, Mr. iv
Fischer, Ernst T. 109
Fisener, Charles 69
Fisher, C.T. 16, 50, 91, 105, 110, 120
Fisher, Charles 7, 44, 134, 135
Fisher, Charles T. 149
Fisher, Chas. 16
Fisher, Chas. T. 160
Fisher, Chas.T. 49
Fisher, E.E. 77
Fisher, Ethel 64
Fisher, J.A. 77
Fisher, Josephine 54
Fisher, Lucy 96
Fisher, Mr. iv
Fisher, Nellie 49
Fisher, W.E. 7, 12, 61, 83, 116
Fisher, Wm. E. 110, 159
Fisk, Dr. 21, 89
Fisk, M.H. 129, 134, 137
Fisk, Mrs. 34
Fisk, Ray 21
Fisk, W.J. 20
Fitzgerald, J. 159
Flanner, Joseph 125
Flaven, Mary 51
Flemming, T.J. 19
Flizen, Mary 119

Florida 2
Flugado, Chas. 35
Foattler, Bessie 69
Foelske, H. 162
Foiler, May 26
Foley, Aldine 48
Foley, Elizabeth 103, 118
Foley, Frank 91
Foley, J.L. 83, 160, 163
Foley, James iv
Foley, James L. 104, 124, 166
Foley, Jas. E. 27
Foley, John 151, 163, iii
Foley, Mav 163
Foley, Max 8
Foley, May 87
Foley, Michael 8
Folkmar, Elnora C. 64
Fond du Lac17, 45, 53, 61, 66, 68, 71, 80, 94, 96, 100, 112, 133, 137, 149, 151, 168
Fond du Lac, Wis. 21, 41, 77, 93, 97
Fordham, James 97
Foreman, J.W. 17
Forepaugh, Adam 61
Forrer, Eliza. 109
Forsyth, Mont. 128
Foster, A.P. 72, 78, 88, 93, 138, 149, 151
Foster, Amos P. 169
Foster, Chas. 89
Fowle, Mrs. 107
Fowler, Albert iii
Fowler, Charles iv
Fowler, Daniel iii
Fowler, E.G. iii
Fowler, E.W. 33, 52, 160
Fowler, Elbert iv
Fowler, G.H. 30, 56, 78, 99
Fowler, George H. 98
Fowler, Myron 78
Fowler, V. 92
Fraham, Adolph 102
Frahm, Adolph 150
France, N.E. 57
Frank, B. Hemsing 55
Franklin 137
Franklin, C.P. 157
Franklin, Doris 155
Franklin, T.J. 155
Franz, Lizzie 109
Frawley, John F. 43
Frazier, Daniel 8
Frederick, Miss 94
Freshour, H.C. 58

Frey, Conrad 30
Freye, J.B. 107
Freysinger, Lucie 98
Frietche, Capt. 139
Frink, Edward 153
Frisbe, Ethel 91
Frisbee, Fred 151
Frisbie, H.E. 102
Fritz, F.A. 124
Fritz, Mr. 122
Fromman, Hugo 143
Frommann, Hugo 110
Frost, Pauline 106
Frye, Mrs. 94
Ft. Atkinson 57, 72, 74, 117
Fuchs, Harry 68
Fuller, A.B. 99, 112, 118
Fuller, E.B. 71, 118
Fuller, J. 155

G

Gable, John C. 141
Gaffney, Katherine 21
Gaffney, Nona 167
Galloway, John M. 55
Galloway, Sarah A. 55
Gamm, A.J. 14
Garrett, Ind. 63, 86
Garrison, G. 104
Garrison, George 148
Garvens 94, 103
Garvens, A.B. 36
Garvens, Charles 108
Garvens, Ed. 74, 83
Garvens, Flora 74
Garvens, G.W. 103
Garvens, H. 47
Garvens, Harold vi
Garvens, Henry 95
Garvens, Louis 108
Garvens, Mary 40
Garvens, Minnie 88
Garvens, Otto 31, 40
Garvens, W. 12
Garvens, Walter 24, 100
Gates, Edith 41
Gates, H. 16
Gates, Horatio 9, 11, 12,
   22, 69, 114, 125
Gates, Rector H. 29
Gates, Rev. 36
Gates, S. 82
Gaudern, E.E. 30
Gauger, William 73

Gaylord, W.K. 30
Gearhart, G.A. 152
Gensike, T. 110
Genske, Frank 92
Genske, Miss 34, 44
Gerggin, Peter 11
Geske, Richard 33
Gettelman 30
Gianella, R. 116
Gilbert, Elias iii
Gilbert, Ephriam iii
Gilbert, Evelyn 71, 80, 164
Gilbert, Fannie 65
Gilbert, Glen 43, 84
Gilbert, H.P. 50
Gilbert, H.Payson iii
Gilbert, Hezekiah iii
Gilbert, J.D. 42, 50, 134, 155
Gilbert, Jesse D. 132
Gilbert, Jessie 118
Gilbert, Mabel 80, 83, 126
Gilbert, Mary 43
Gilbert, Rachel 43
Gilbert, Richard 132, iii
Gilbert, Ruby 65
Gilbert Station, Iowa. 65
Gilbert, W.A. 20, 80
Gildas, W.I. 20
Gillett, Chas. 158
Gillyn, Miss 54, 57
Gilman, J.W. 96
Gilmette, Ethel 102
Gilson, Lizzie 11
Ginter, Jos. 128
Glasier, Edith 33, 88, 114
Glasier, G. 105
Glasier, Gilson 96, 99
Glasier, H.G. 2
Glasier, H.W. 4, 5, 12, 14, 17,
   35, 58, 61, 89
Glasier, Justice 42
Glasier, Mr. 91
Glen Park, Ill. 75
Glendene, Hattie 57
Gloed, Geo 148
Godfrey, Beth 38, 57, 68
Godfrey, Beth? 64
Godfrey, C.H. 126, 159
Godfrey, Charles 141
Godfrey, Charles H. 57, 95
Godfrey, Chas. 16, 21, 35,
   37, 92, 164
Godfrey, Dudley 163

Godfrey, E.R. 57, 66, 82, 83, 128, 132, 136, 137, 144, 155, 156, 159, 160, 163
Godfrey, Edwin R. 57
Godfrey, Harriet vi
Godfrey, Helen 37
Godfrey, James 1, 66, 128
Godfrey, James D. 57
Godfrey, Jas. D. 1
Godfrey, Margaret vi
Godfrey, Marion 43
Godfrey, Mayor 162
Godfrey, Paul 43
Godfrey, W.A. 12, 14, 58, 72, 75, 86, 112, 144, 163
Godfrey, Will 47, 124
Godfrey, William A. 57
Godfrey, Wm. 47
Goebel, Math. 98
Goebel, Matt 35, 157
Goebel, Matt. 83, 160
Gold 23
Goldsmith, Catherine 75
Goldthorp, C.E. 72, 87, 94, 101, 123, 133, 159, 161, 167
Goldthorp, Edgar A. 50
Goldthorp, Elma 107
Goldthorp, Mrs. 50, 103
Goldthorp, Rev. 54, 125, 140, 143
Goldthorpe, C.E. 60
Goldthrop, C.E. 86
Golley, Frank B. 162
Gombert, Frieda 137
Gombert, Victor L. 137
Goodall, Mr. 44
Goodall, W.H. 55, 110
Goodhue, Alle? 46
Goodhue, Lolita 62
Goodrich, C.P. 57
Goodrich, Chauncy 68
Goodrich, Grace 73
Goodrich, H.H. 30
Goodrich, Nancy J. 43
Goodrich, V.M. 109
Goodrich, W.V. 30
Goodwin, Bandmaster 38
Goodwin, Margaret 70
Gove, R.L. 11
Grafton, Mass. 52
Grand Forks, ND 115, 147
Grand Haven 65
Grand Rapids 40, 65, 66, 67, 97
Gransee, Constable H.W. 38
Gransee, H.W. 7, 12, 25

Grant, E.W. 161
Grant, Mrs. 125
Grant, N. 25
Granville 5
Grassie, Elizabeth 165
Grassie, M.E. 109
Grassie, Miss 90
Grassie, Mrs. 165
Grassie, Stella M. 109
Grassie, T.S. 90, 148
Graunke, Ottille Louise 82
Gray, F.S. 61, 73, 87, 96, 103, 111, 120, 127, 133, 134, 138, 148, 157, 163, 169
Gray, J. 100
Gray, Mr. 97
Gray, Mrs. 142
Gray, Rev. 75
Gray, Thos. S. 143
Grebel, Paul 33
Green Bay 50, 87, 148, 155
Green, Dr. 72
Green, J.J. 47
Green Lake County, Wis. 14
Greenfield 26, 40
Greengo, Claude 126
Greengo, Mrs. 77
Greenwood, Bessie 19
Greenwood, J.T. 2, 31, 34, 36, 158
Greenwood, John 37, 50, 51, 126
Greenwood, Miss vi
Greenwood, Ray 64, 131
Greenwood, Rosalie 162
Greenwood, Thomas 6, 162
Greenwood, Thos. 36
Gregg, A. 15
Gregg, A.S. 30, 40
Gregg, Adeline 75
Gregg, Arthur 126, 163
Gregg, Arthur S. 98
Gregg, Augustus 24, 30
Gregg, Austin 130
Gregg, Bell 88
Gregg, Belle 69
Gregg, Dolly 39
Gregg, E. 30
Gregg, Grace 88
Gregg, Gus 80, 122
Gregg, Gus. 165
Gregg, J.P. 87, 140
Gregg, Jefferson 73, 78, 90, 144, 148
Gregg, John P. 61, 100, 115, 136
Gregg, John Parker 108, 115, 138, 144, 155

Gregg, L.B. 30, 67, 75, 80, 139, 141
Gregg, Landlord 24
Gregg, Luther B. v
Gregg, Mrs. 80, v
Gregg, S. 30
Grider, A. 95
Grider, A.B. 143
Gridley 23
Gridley, ? 135
Gridley, A.R. 78, 155
Gridley, Albert R. 54
Gridley, Bert 23, 41
Gridley, L.L. 21, 53, 93, 102, 117, iii
Gridley, L.R. 3, 4, 14, 49, 54, 71,
    94, 99, 123, 149, 155, 159, 166
Gridley, L.V. 21, 165
Gridley, L.W. 155
Gridley, Lea L. 157
Gridley, Len 12, 105
Gridley, Lysander vi
Gridley, Lysander R. v
Gridley, O.L. 57
Griffith, Lewis J. 150
Griffith, Lou 107
Griffith, Matilda 150
Griffith, Paul 147
Griffith, R.B. 147
Griffith, Walter 117, 150
Griggs, S.F. 30
Grimming, Bildes 162
Gringam, Mable 98
Groot, Simon C. 43
Groskopf, E.C. 161
Gross, Arthur 124
Gross, Louis 159
Grosskopf, Dr. 119
Grosskopf, E.C. 29, 35, 41
Grosskopf, Jay 64
Grosskopf, Superintendent 166
Grover, T.F. 133
Grover, T.H. 150
Gruenwald, Director 22
Gruet, Mabel 134
Grundy, Miss 78
Grunewald, Albert 89
Gudden, Mrs. 131
Guentner, Julius 152, 155, 160
Guile, E.M. 49, 61, 85
Guile, Ella 84, 85
Gunderman, Clarence 125
Gunderman, Jacob 35, 141
Gunderson, Swain 159
Gunn 52, 60, 98, 157
Gunn, C.A. 83, 159

Gunn, Clarence 10
Gustafson, A.P. 95
Gutsch, Herman 87

H

Haase, Ella 164
Haase, Willie 119
Haash, E.C. 149
Hacker, A. 134
Hacker, Bertha 45
Hadfield, Mrs. 103
Hadley, Mrs. 16, 17
Hadley, W.H. 129
Hadley, W.J. 164
Haertel, Catherine 112
Haertel, Wm. 18, 35
Hahn, Robt 137
Hahn, Wm 137
Haisler, Mr. 145
Hales Corners 31
Hale's Corners 40
Hallett, H.D. 50, 99
Halsey, Judge 124
Halstead, Levi v
Halsted, L.C. iv
Halsted, Levi iv
Hamburg, Germany 74
Hamilton, A.P. 16
Hamilton, Bessie 164
Hamme 46, 52, 60, 98
Hamme, Ald.(alderman?) 79
Hamme, J. 10
Hamme, J.L. 132
Hamme, John 6, 10, 14, 67, 79, 82,
    83, 106, 149, 159, 160
Hamme, John L. 79
Hamme, Lydia 79
Hamme, Martha 79
Hammond, Loring 85
Hammond, T.M. 5, 41, 85, 98, 149
Hammond, Theodore M. 24
Hampton, Abner 92
Hancock, F.E. 67, 84
Hancock, Fred 113
Handley, Miss 95
Haney, C.A. 64
Haney, Madeline 38, 62, 64, 67,
    80, 100
Haney, Miss 131, 139
Haney, Mr. 64
Hanke, Gladys 164
Hanks, C.H. 82
Hanks, E.E. 96
Hanley, James 109

Hanley, Michael  109
Hanley, William  160
Hanley, Wm  150
Hansen, Albert  90
Hansen, Albert C.  114
Hansen, H. Theo.  86
Hansen, H. Theodore  115, 117
Hanson, A.C.  55, 62, 98, 105, 115, 155, 164
Hanson, Albert C.  108
Hanson, Chris.  167
Hanson, H. Theo.  72, 148
Hanson, Mr.  90
Harden, A.  75, 106, 124, 129, 144
Harden, Mr.  164, 168
Harden, W.M.  18, 45
Harden, Walter  83, 145, 160
Hardke, August  121
Hardtke, Ida  121
Hare, Mr.  114
Harlem, Ia.  120
Harman, E.  159
Harney, Edith  139
Harriettsville, Ohio  169
Harriman, F.J.  12
Harriman, Frank  64, 86, 89, 96, 97, 105, 137, 154, 160, 166
Harriman, Franklyn  46
Harriman, Hazel  62, 64, 84, 97
Harriman, J.F.  166
Harriman, Lou  33, 58, 64, 125, 141
Harriman, Miss  108
Harriman, Mr.  156
Harris, B.S.  110
Harris, G.  132
Harris, Juliet  48
Hart, Alice  48, 51
Hart, Allee  34
Hart, Charles  95, iii
Hart, Charles B.  95
Hart, Everett  102, 142
Hart, Everrett  89
Hart, J.G.  9
Hart, Jemima  122
Hart, Jesse  136, 147
Hart, Judson  iv
Hart, Judson G.  147
Hart, Lottie  84, 128, 157
Hart, Marga  77
Hart, Margaret  34, 67
Hart, Marjorie  71
Hart, Mary  56, 135
Hart, Mary E.  95
Hart, Miss  31

Hart, Oliver  iii
Hart, Oliver W.  147
Hart, T.B.  9
Hart, T.W.  9, 96, 136
Hart, Thomas B.  iii
Hart, Thomas Watson  147
Hart, W.A.  51, 61, 68, 96, 106
Hart, Wm.  30
Hart, Wm. A.  127
Harter, Mamie  156
Hartford, Wis.  45, 75, 91
Hartman, Lewis  iv
Hartung, Assemblyman  10
Hartung, Chairman  29
Hartung, Cora  124
Hartung, E.  146
Hartung, Fred  3, 91, 100, 112, 141
Hartung, Frederick  83
Hartung, Oscar  119
Hartung, Paul  155
Hartung?, Fred  49
Harturng, Fred  75
Harvey, Ehtel  104
Harvey, W.M.  16
Harwood, Oliver  162
Hasse, A.F.  90
Hasse, Carl  101
Hasse, Wm.  164
Hassinger, W.H.  159
Hatch, E.E.  166
Hatch, Everet E.  154
Hathaway, D.G.  36, 83, 91, 134, 135, 136
Hathaway, D.S.  142
Hathaway, Dr.  125
Hathaway, G.D.  10
Hathaway, Mrs.  126
Hathaway, Newton  91
Hathaway, Officer  29
Haubert, Anna  87
Haunne  157
Hausch  166
Hausch, Charlie  128
Hausch, John  162
Hawes, Geo.  11
Hawley, Alberta  68, 93
Hawley, D.G.  45, 100
Hawley, Frank  iii, iv
Hawley, L.E.  93
Hawley, L.W.  68
Hawley, Will  19
Hawley, Will.  155
Hawley, Wm.  3, 15
Hayden, M.S.  72

Hayes 30
Hayes, D.J. 65, 101, 110
Hayes, Edmond 120
Hayes, Ned 61
Hayes, Rich 100
Hayes, Richard 133, 136, 154, 165
Hays, D.H. 77
Hayward, Ralph 12, 38, 44
Heaford, C.W. 15
Heatford, C.W. 30
Heath, Frederick 67
Heath, M.G. 96, 137
Hebner, Anna vi
Hedtke, Auguste 112
Hedtke, G. 104
Hedtke, Gustav 89, 112
Hedtke, Gustave 106
Heideman, Charles 79
Heiden, F.M. 49, 81, 83, 160
Heiden, Fred 116
Heiden, Fred M. 92
Heiden, Friederica 92
Heiden, John 81, 92
Heigesen, Thomas 96
Heise, Adelbert 116
Helgesen, Mr. 29, 164
Helgesen, O. 82, 115, 123
Helgesen, Oscar 2, 55, 78, 119, 131
Helgesen, Thomas 131
Helgesen, Thos. 45
Helgesen, Tom 138
Helgesett, Elizabeth 78
Helgeson, Mr. 168
Hemphill, J.K. 131
Hempsing, B.F. 160
Hempsing, Elsie 60
Hempsing, H.P. 99, 127, 160
Hemsing, B.F. 50, 83
Hemsing, Elsie 69
Hemsing, H.P. 61, 63, 83, 104
Hemsing, Henry 46, 145
Hemsing, Henry P. 71
Hemsing, Mr. 46
Hemsing, William 55
Henke, August 118
Henke, Ella 75
Henke, Lizzie 75
Henke, Martin 75
Henke, Mildred vi
Henke, Rich 85
Henkel, Wm. 33
Hennessey, Richard J. 77, 79
Henniky, H.J. 104
Heritage, J. 108

Herriman, Frank 83
Hess, Bertha 37, 40
Hess, J.M. 2
Hess, J.W. 37
Hess, M.H. 115
Hess, Maurice 104
Hess, Morry 20
Hess, Mrs. 16
Hetkis, Mr. 87
Hibbard, Arthur 128
Hibbard, Jesse 148
Hicks, B. Herbert 22
Higging, Miss 23
Higgins, C.A. 162
Higgins, Gertrude 68
Higgins, Selma 68
Highley, J.W. 98, 120, 121
Hill, Dexter iv
Hills, A.M. 108
Hillsboro, Wis. 37
Hinckley, Miss 72
Hinckley, N.W. 122
Hines, Margaret 70
Hinn, Miss 60
Hirsh 70
Hoenecke, Adolph 95
Hoffmann, H. 110
Holden, C.H. 24, 63
Holliday, Elizabeth 101
Holliday, G. 125
Hollis, A.P. 1, 10, 18, 29,
    32, 37, 38, 41
Hollis, Mr. 42, 44
Hollis, Prof. 32
Holmes, Henry 106, 107
Holmes, S. 109
Holston, Mrs. 27
Holston, William iv
Holton, E.D. 8, 29
Hook 30
Hooker, Edith 64, 100, 126
Hooley, Edna 41, 44, 63,
    102, 125, 128
Hooley, Florence 81
Hooley, George 81
Hooley, J.H. 81
Hooley, J.L. 4, 63, 98, 162, 166
Hopeman, Elam iv
Hopkins, W.E. 53
Hoppe, Herman 118
Hoppin, Anna L. 52
Hoppin, Richard iv
Horicon 44
Horicon, Wis. 54

Horle, Joseph 107
Horle, Mr. 29
Horning, Bessie 18, 67, 100, 146, 151
Horning, Lawerance 38
Horning, M. 20, 96, 100, 133, 151, 165
Horning, Mary 18, 120, 122, 132
Horning, Mrs. 1, 28, 124
Horning, Olive 43
Hornings, M. 153
Hosford, Mrs. 166
Hosmer, Irwin W. 86
Hotchkiss, M. 76
Hotchkiss, Mabel 60
Hoth, Ernst 104, 106
Howard, L.T. iii
Howard, William iv
Howell, Mich. 163
Howie, D.W. 99, 162
Hoyt 38
Hoyt, Catherine 112
Hoyt, Demerit 41, 47, 51, 94, 96
Hoyt, E.D. 12, 31, 113, 120, 165
Hoyt, Emerson D. 4, 82, 83, 154, 156, iv
Hoyt, Hannah iv
Hoyt, Henry H. iii
Hoyt, M. 154
Hoyt, Mayor 12, 35, 46, 52, 60, 75, 80, 98
Hoyt, Miriam 31, 86, 107, 131, 133, 136
Hoyt, Miss 48, 51
Hoyt, S.D. 17, 38, 61, 68, 144, 153
Hoyt, Thomas D. iii
Hoyt, W.H. 3
Hubbard, A.P. 148
Hubbard, A.T. 134, 137
Hubbard, Mr. 124
Hubbel, Levi iii
Hubbell, Charles iv
Hubbell, Samuel iv
Huder, Dorathy 98
Hudson, A.H. 40
Hudson, Mich. 68
Hughes, C. 57
Hughes, Harry 27
Hughs, Albert 146
Hulbert, D.W. 24
Hulbert, Judson 24
Hulbert, Mary 66
Hulburt, D.W. 51, 54, 59, 82, 108, 113, 123
Hulburt, Isabel 154

Hulburt, Isabelle 138
Hulburt, Judson 76, 123
Hulburt, Mary 117, 138, 154
Hulburt, Mary E. 58
Hull, England 168
Humphrey, W.F. 84, 103, 151
Humphreys, F. 98
Hunt, Eliza 132
Hunt, G.W. 85, 119, 136
Hunt, Geo. 50, 148
Hunt, George 51
Hunter, D.L. 7, 12, 14
Hunter, H.B. 2, 80, 87, 88, 128, vi
Hunter, Henry B. 131, 154, 166
Hunter, Joyce 41, 45
Hunter, Mrs. 14, 37, 41
Huntoon, Jean 138
Hurlburt, D.W. 104
Hurlburt, J. 12
Hurlburt, Mary E. 100
Hurlbut, E. 127
Hurlbut, Fern 1, 150
Hurlbut, Harry E. 87
Hurlbut, L. 27
Hurlbut, Oscar 29
Huson, Mrs. 74
Hutchinson, Dan 33
Hutchinson, Daniel iv
Hyde, Edwin 60, 133, 161, 163
Hyde, J.W. 136

I

Illiment, John 123
Ingreham, E.S. 76
Iowa 1, 15, 76
Ives, Misses 86
Ives, Morse 58, 99, 112, 144

J

Jacks, Robert iv
Jackson, D.W. 17
Jackson, Janet vi
Jacksonport, Wis. 27
Jacobs, C.H. 34
Jacobs, H.H. 166
Jacobson, Hans 143
Jacobus, C.C. 21, 25, 31, 37, 65, 74, 83, 102, 149, 155, 160, 162, 166
Jacobus, Charles 21, 112, 138
Jacobus, Charles C. 154
Jacobus, Chas. 151
Jacobus, D.C. vi

190

Jacobus, Garry 21
Jacobus, V. 21
Jacques, W. 132
Jager, Herman 95
Jager, Jacob 104
James, Charles iii
James, Geo. A. 83, 91
James, Mary 28
James, W.A. 153
Jamestown, North Dakota 56
Janesville 14, 19, 28, 31, 37, 41, 46, 54, 63, 64, 77, 78, 90, 124, 155
Jeffrey, G.R. 159
Jeffrey, Geo. R. 160
Jeffrey, George 7, 12
Jeffrey, George R. 149
Jenkins, M.L. 167
Jens, A.E. 167
Jerome, Moses iv
Johann F. Schell 70
John, Dr. 41
Johnson, ? 154
Johnson, Archie 40, 156, vi
Johnson, Archie C. 111
Johnson, Art 104
Johnson, E. Payson 76
Johnson, Edith 65
Johnson, Eliza 63
Johnson, George 113
Johnson, George H.D. 116
Johnson, George J. 111
Johnson, Gertrude 75
Johnson, J.B. 37, 40, 151
Johnson, J.H. 42
Johnson, J.R. 61
Johnson, Jacob 64, 112
Johnson, Jacob Berkstresser 111
Johnson, Jake 25
Johnson, Jean vi
Johnson, Joseph 11
Johnson, Judge 109
Johnson, M. 122
Johnson, Miss 40
Johnson, Mrs. 163
Johnson, Newton iv
Johnson, S.D. 65
Johnson, W.W. 76
Johnstone, Lois vi
Jones 46, 60, 98
Jones, D.M. 20, 158, 159
Jones, D.P. 3, 12, 14, 83, 123
Jones, David P. 6
Jones, I. 84
Jones, J. 138

Jones, Mary 84
Jones, T.J. 64
Jones, Winifred 53, 102
Jones, Winifred E. 30, 89
Judson, C.E. 128
Judson, Charles E. 128, 164
Judson, Chas. 165
Judson, J. Watts 118
Judson, J.B. 71, 118, 124
Judson, John B. 127
Jullet, Wm. 118
Jung, Louis 169
Justice, Miss 104

K

Kalfahs, A. 136
Kalfahs, F.W. 6
Kalfahs, Frank 136
Kallis, Michael 10
Kallths, Emilla 150
Kaltenborn, Mrs. 88
Kaltenborn, Walter 71
Kansas 89
Kansas City, MO 73
Karel, John C. 79
Kavanaugh, W. 161
Kealies, August H. 141
Kearney, E.J. 153
Kearney, Mr. 120, 128
Kearns, James 132
Keats, F.M. 64, 71, 93, 120
Keats, Frank 166
Keats, Jane 64, 65
Keats, Ned 39, 131, 132
Keefe, Peter iv
Keek? 30
Keeler, Jerry 40
Keeler, Joe 37
Keeler, Joseph 83, 88, 132
Keeter, Joseph 135
Keisen, Walter 134
Kellog, A.F. 12
Kellogg, A.F. 4, 78, 83, 99, 105, 106, 159, 160
Kellogg, Alonzo F. 4, 154
Kellogg, Mary Belle 33
Kellogg, Rev. 139
Kelly, Bryan 16
Kelly, Ellen 16
Kelly, Garret 16
Kelly, James 16
Kelly, John 16
Kelly, Miss 49
Kelly, Mr. 1

Kemper, Mr. 29
Kempser, Mr. 164
Kendrick, Wm. J. 125
Kenister, Lucy 109
Kennedy 60, 98
Kennedy, I.W. 90, 159
Kennedy, Ira 34
Kennedy, J. 168
Kennedy, J.W. 82
Kennedy, Marie 91
Kennedy, Mr. 156
Kenosha 2, 40, 59
Kenyon, F.L. 2
Kenyon, Steward 14
Keokuk, Iowa 69
Kerber, John 39
Kerber, William 121
Kerin, John 146
Kerr, A.E. 46
Kershaw, Alice 57, 105, 108
Kershaw, Alice Mabel 108, 114
Kershaw, Geo. 103
Kershaw, George 64, 112, 114,
    118, 136, 148
Kershaw, J.A. 55, 114
Kershaw, J.H. 105
Kershaw, Joseph A. 108
Kershaw, Miss 37
Keuter, F.S. 106
Keyeser, Wis. 128, 130
Kieckhafer, Charles 110
Kieckhefer, Charles 116
Kieckhefer, F.A.W. 111
Kieckhefer, Superintendent 119
Kieler, Margaret 87
Kiemert, Herman 164
Kihman, Katy 133
Kihnow, Katie 143
Kilbourn City 77
Kilbourn, Wis. 96
Kimball, Mrs. 93
King, Chas. 161
King, Louisa 140
Kinney, Helen 64, 67
Kirschner, Lillie 44
Kissinger, Sam. 57
Klatke, Bettie 109
Klatke, Betty 123
Klein, Josie 1
Klein, Rev. 56
Kleinman, William iv
Kluth, John 60
Knapp, Henry 120
Kneeland 12

Kneeland, Carrie A. 73
Kneeland, Ella 112
Kneeland, Fred 126
Kneeland, Messrs. 75
Kneeland, Miss. 73
Kneeland, N.L. 5, 12, 45, 73, 126,
    141, 144, 163, 164, 165
Kneeland, Norman L. 3
Kneeland, Otis 126
Kneeland, Ralph 1, 99
Knolle, G.G. 95
Knowles, J.M. 116
Knowles, Mrs. 16
Knowlton, E.A. 116
Knox, Maud 64
Knoxville, Ill. 59, 96
Koch, Fred 140
Kocher, Fred 115, 121
Kochsick, Wm 102
Koegel, Alma 112
Koenig, A. 18
Koenig, Arthur 72, 122, 161
Koenig, Fred 18
Koenig, Hans 133
Koenig, Walter 18, 72, 105
Koenig, Walter L. 67
Koenitzer, Christian 141
Koepp, Herman 150, 160
Koeppel, G.Y. 159
Koeppen, August 135
Koerner, George 24, 41
Koerner, John 14, 28, 31
Koerner, Margeret 27
Koerner, Mrs. 28
Koerner., John 24
Koessler, Chas. 97
Kolba, Gertrude 143
Koney, Henry B. 12
Koon, Justus iv
Koon, Samuel iv
Kopp, Caroline 82
Kossow, Louisa 79
Krafcheck, Cynthia 169
Krafcheck, Jos. 169
Krafezyk, Joseph 109
Krantz, Albert H. 119
Kratz, Rosa 98
Krauss, Adam 102
Kreger, Louis 135
Krehl, August 18, 40
Kreutzberg, Anton 119
Kringel, August 33
Kringel, August F.W. 166
Kringel, Superintendent 119

Kroesing 108
Kroesing, Charles 126
Kroesing, Chas. 99
Kroesing, M. 49
Kroesing, Matilde 139
Kroesing, Meta 77, 138
Kroesing, O. 127
Kroesing, Oscar 139
Kroessing, Matilda 168
Kroessing, Oscar 168
Kropp, C. 12, 166
Kropp, Ch. 86
Kropp, Christoph 5
Kruger, Otto 143
Krysch, Ida 132
Kuchynski, A.C. 71, 127
Kuechle, G.E.G. 110
Kuehltan, George 140
Kunth, Rev. 105
Kurth, Henry 35
Kurtz, G.A. 3, 4, 38, 82, 83,
141, 154, 160
Kutzner, J.W. 56

L

La Crosse 53, 56, 64, 148
La Homadien, Miss 103
La Mont, Fred 50
La Valle, Wis. 105
LaFollette, L.M. 133
Laird, Robert 114
Lake Beulah 40
Lake Mills 57, 128
Lamb, Ben 47
Lamb, Ellis 131
Lamb, W.H. 28, 131
Lambrecht, F.W. 14
Lamont, Fred 110
Landold, Louise 48
Landoldt, Lou 58
Landolt, A. 62, 65, 85, 88, 104, 127
Landolt, Albert 85
Landolt, Blanch 140
Landolt, Blanche 19, 64, 73, 87, 108,
114, 120, 132, 134, 138, 148, 155
Landolt, Captain 104
Landolt, Edward 19
Landolt, Esther 23, 120
Landolt, Loleta 23, 38, 62, 64,
74, 99, 137
Landolt, Loreta 155
Landolt, Lou 99, 100
Landolt, Louise 1, 19, 40, 64, 68, 87,
102, 108, 114, 128, 146, 154, 155

Landolt, Louise J. 121
Landolt, Louise U. 157
Landolt, Mr. 65
Landolt, Postmaster 20, 22, 93
Landolt, W. 157
Landolt, W.H. 19, 23, 29, 48, 50, 64,
65, 74, 78, 88, 110, 144, 157, 160
Landolt, Wm. 156
Langdon, E. 159
Lange, Celia 69
Lange, Oscar 69
Laning, Charles 123
Lansing, Mich. 60
Larson, Anna 75
Larson, Minnie 87
Lass, Lilie 95
Launer, M.E. 145
Laurie, James 154
Laurner, M.E. 110
Lawrence, Kansas 97
Lawrence, Margarette E. 138
Layton, John 21
Leadville 51, 113, 118, 158
Lee, H.R. 98
Lee, O.F. 86, 103, 149
Leegson, Ida 77
Lefeber 12, 52, 60, 70, 157
Lefeber, Abe 63, 84, 168
Lefeber, Abram 103, 133, 138,
149, 153
Lefeber, Aldermen 46
Lefeber, Amanda 36, 54
Lefeber, Cornelius 89
Lefeber, Edwin 84
Lefeber, Ernest 96
Lefeber, Florence 60, 135, 136
Lefeber, J.C. 83, 130, 160
Lefeber, James 83, 96, 102, 103,
126, 133, 135, 137, 151, 160
Lefeber, Jas. 36, 65, 82, 159
Lefeber, Jos. 63, 105
Lefeber, Joseph 50, 54, 77, 130,
138, 153, 158, 165
Lefeber, Mabel 69, 93, 96, 131, 134
Lefeber, Mable 60
Lefeber, Mrs. 63
Lefeber, Olive 89, 123, 135, 157
Lefeber, Sylvia 36, 104, 120
Lehman, A.W. 151
Lehman, Kate 37
Lehman, Van 128
Lehmann, A.W. 115
Lehmann, Harriet 103
Lehmann, Miss 102

Lehmann, Will 46
Leicester, Mass. 142
Leighton, J.M. 1
Leisk, Capt. 27, 141
Leisk, Captain 169
Leisk, H. 53, 55, 92, 141
Leisk, Henry 2, 123, 125, 127
Leiske 108
Leister, H.E. 83, 95, 116, 160
Leister, Sam 143, 158
Leland, Nathaniel iii
Leland, Phineas iv
Lemits, Frank 159
Lench, Henry 133
Lennox, NY 147
Lentz, Adolph 69, 70, 99, 101
Lentz, Emil 101
Lentz, Frank 69
Lentz, Fred 69
Lentz, Gustave 35
Lentz, Ida 69, 88
Leonard, Geo. F. 86
Leonard, George Francis 97
Leonard, J.E. 22
Leonard, James E. 11
Leonard, Mrs. 89
Leonard, S.S. 11, 42
Leutzow, Albert 78
Leutzow, C. 115
Leutzow, Charles 49, 149
Leutzow, Chas. 70
Leutzow, Lou 69
Lewis, Assistant Postmaster 55
Lewis, D.A. 1, 21, 121
Lewis, D.B. 62, 128
Lewis, Dwight 81
Lewis, Dwight B. 22
Lewis, E.M. 35, 71, 77, 110,
  144, 153, 159
Lewis, Helen 33
Lewis, James B. 153
Lewis, Mabel 34, 72, 74, 80
Lewis, Mable 71
Lewis, Mr. 134
Lewis, P.G. 63
Lewis, Postmaster 80
Lewis, S.S. 21, 41, 62, 72, 74,
  80, 121, 132
Lewis, Wm. 34
Lewiston, Mich. 75, 126
Lewiston, Mont. 130
Lewiston, Montana 63
Liebig, Mrs. 66
Lillibridge, Ella 89, 90, 125, 140

Lillibridge, I.C. 49, 76, 101,
  131, 135, 151, 153
Lillibridge, Ira 16
Lillibridge, Miss 18, 151
Lillibridge, Mrs. 84, 106
Lillibridge, Roy 71
Lincoln County, SD 121
Lincoln, Mrs. 139
Lincoln, W. 97
Lincoln, W.B. 112, 133, 140,
  161, 163, 164
Lincoln, Wm. B. 138
Lindow, Mr. 162
Lindower, Max 164
Lindsay, E.W. 115
Lingelbach, George 16
Lingelbach, Mrs. 35
Link, Albert 103
Link, Carrie 103
Lipscomb, W. 109
Lisbon, Waukesha county 142
Little, C.A. 19
Little, Hannah A. 77
Little, Mrs. 157
Livey, C.S.G. 12
Lizette, Maude 113
Lizette, Miss 116
Lockmann, Mrs. 168
Loerx, Gerhart 119
Loery, H.A. 104
Loew, E.J. 60, 92, 159
London, Canada 84, 102
Lonfellow, Perry W. 51
Long, Lois 98
Longfellow, Faith 64, 114
Longfellow, Mrs. 89
Longfellow, P.W. 51, 54, 59, 74, 79,
  88, 91, 96, 104, 108, 111, 113, 124, 134,
  142, 152, 156, 160, 166
Longfellow, Rev. 140, 147
Longstreet, William R. iii
Loomis, C.W. 36, 109
Loomis, Charles 130, 134
Loomis, Chas. 43
Loomis, Clarence 75
Loomis, H. 148
Loomis, H.S. 158
Loomis, Lizzie 148
Los Angeles, Cal. 148
Losburg, H 159
Loveland, F.E. 12, 82, 83, 84, 113,
  120, 149, 159, 160
Loveland, Frank 17
Loveland, Frank E. 3, 4

Loveland, Laura  12, 43, 84
Loveland, Lena  43, 89, 143
Loveland, Superintendent  118
Lovelard, Laura  135
Lowe, Victor  121
Lowell, Wis.  61
Lowther, Mr.  25
Lucas, A.M.  153
Lucus, A.M.  93
Ludington, Alice  49
Ludington, Fred  49
Ludington, Frederick  56
Ludington, H.  116, 131
Ludington, Harrison  88, 131, iii
Ludington, Harry  56
Ludington, Mich.  18
Ludington, Sylvester  88
Ludwig, Elizabeth  104
Ludwig, Judge  109
Luehring, Otto  25
Luening  166
Luening, Mr.  80
Luetzou, Erving  vi
Luetzow  38
Luetzow, A.  127
Luetzow, Albert  20
Luetzow, Charles  83, 109, 127, 154, 160
Luetzow, Chas.  127
Luetzow, Elizabeth  20
Luke, Joseph  11
Lumb  23, 29
Lumb, W.H.  40
Lund, Everett  vi
Lund, George  157
Lutzen, Ed  157
Lydston, F.A.  11, 15
Lydston, Prof.  22
Lyman, Mrs.  59
Lynds, Fred G.  129
Lynes, Jas  137
Lyon, Evangelist  113, 124
Lyon, M.H.  127
Lyon, Mr.  133
Lyon, Rev.  123
Lyons, David  60
Lyons, Julia  60
Lyons, Moses  iv

M

Madsen, Tina  125
Maher, William  129
Mahnke, Willie  137
Mahnke, Wm.  109, 123

Maloy, Blanche  109
Mancelonn, Mich.  88
Manchester, Iowa  84
Manitowoc  66
Manlius, Onondaga Co., NY  98
Mann, Judge  109
Mann, Ray  117, 150
Mannegold, L.  147
Manning, W.R.  iv
Manon, Miss  23
Manuegold, Louis  22
Marggraff  79
Marggraff, Edward  67
Margraff, Edward  77
Margraff, Herman  67
Margraff, William  77
Marinette, Wis.  44
Marken, Emma  98
Marling, Miss  10
Marling, W.G.  10
Marquardt, J.J.  123, 149
Marquardt, John  135, 169
Marquardt, Marshal  15
Marquette, Mich.  149
Marrinette, Wis.  103
Marshall, Alice  139
Marston, Robert  156
Marston, Thomas  96
Martin  52
Martin, Albert A.  169
Martin, Gertrude  80
Martin, J.O.  9
Martin, J.W.  80
Martin, Minnie  112
Marvin, Mary E.  126
Maryland  27
Masch, Chas  102
Mason, J.T.  167
Mason, T.  159
Masschusetts  62
Mastinbrook, Minard  82
Matheson, E.C.  166
Matheson, M.  111
Mathias, R.J.  83
Mathison, Chas.  17
Matias, Daziel  146
Matteson, C.E.  57
Matthews, S.S.  3
Matthias, Justice  59
Matthias, R.J.  7, 10, 12, 27, 149, 160
Matzahn, Lizzie  53
Maxon, Ada  130, 133, 151
Maxon, Elizabeth  107
Maxon, W.D.  121

Maxon, Will 65, 163
Maxon, Wm. 53, 92
Mayer, Frank 24, 128
Mayhew, Mr. 145
Maynard, Hosea L. iii
Maynard, Lowell iv
McAdams, James 158
McBeath, H.F. 64
McCabe, Bishop 56
McCarthy, Geo. C. 32
McChesney, E.S. 19
McClintock, Charles 122
McClintock, Justice 8, 10
McClintock, W.H. 23, 25
McClintock, William 8
McConnell, Edward M. 68
McCormack, Nellie 88, 127
McCormack, S. 127, 151
McCormack, Smith 27, 94, 102,
  121, 130, 131, 149
McCormick, Smith 161
McCulloch, John 158
McDermott, Miss 32, 99
McDonald, Hughie 135
McDonald, Ida 150
McDonald, Mame 157
McElroy, L.A. 97
McFadden, Donald 165
McGill, Arthur 162
McGrath, Ellen 16
McHugh, James 135
McKay, Chas. 17
McKowan, Miss 44
McKowen, W.R. 127, 137
McLean, Alice 19, 23
McLean, C.S. 104
McLean, Lillie 47
McLean, Miss 22
McMillan, St. Clare 118
McMynn, Robert F. 110
McNab, J.L. 144
McNab, Joe 110
McNab, John 168
McNab, Joseph 24, 168
McNair, M.M. 88
McNair, W.G. 13
McNary, Rev. 39
McPheeters, Claudia 117
McPheeters, Miss 59
McPherson, W.L. 153
McRavey, F.W. 78
Meacham, Mrs. 81
Meadville, Pa. 101, 103, 104
Meahl, Fred 66

Medina 15
Meinder?, M. 135
Melcher, C. 107
Mellvaine, W.D. 33
Mellvaine, Wm. 52
Melrose, Minn. 56
Memphis, Tenn. 62
Menasha 1, 90
Menasha, Wis. 34, 90
Menesh, Misses 27
Menish, Duncan 38
Menish, F. 17
Menish, Flora 59, 78
Menish, Florence 39
Menish, Grace 17, 39
Menish, Neil 53
Menninger 52, 60, 98
Menninger, Ald. 135
Menninger, W. 113
Menninger, William 145, 154
Menninger, Wm 149
Menninger, Wm. 63, 68, 74, 79, 82,
  83, 96, 144, 153, 159, 160,
  163, 168
Menomonee Falls 57
Menten, Mary 97
Menton, Mary 107
Merica, Charles O. 108
Merica, Chas. O. 106
Merica, F.M. 83, 86, 97,
  105, 160, 168
Merica, Francis M. 89, 135
Merica, Mrs. 101, 116, 124, 131
Meriett?, Mrs. 63
Merrick, Louis 14
Merrick, Mr. 5
Merrill 23
Merrill, S. iv
Merrill, Wis. 71
Merritt, L. 30
Merton 64
Messre, Henry 150
Meyer, Alice E. 130
Meyer, B.H. 128
Meyer, E.W.A. 170
Meyer, H. 30
Meyer, Henry 69
Meyer, Julius 98
Meyer, N. 167
Meyers, Helen 80
Meyers, J.O. 113, 144
Michigan 19
Milier, Susan 157
Millar, Nettie 125

Millard, C.J. 128
Millard, F.C. 66
Miller, Ed 162
Miller, Herman 117
Miller, Margo vi
Miller, Mr. 100
Miller, Mrs. 150, 153, 169
Miller, Nettie 162
Miller, Susan 164
Milton 3
Milton Junction 48
Milwaukee 3
Miner, L.A. 11
Mineral Point, Wis. 129
Minneapolis 16, 17, 21, 106, 124, 137, 163
Minnehan, Gusie 74
Minnehan, Susie 74
Minninger, Wm. 73
Minor, Dr. 67
Minot, N.D. 54
Minton, Louise 19
Mitchell, Corinne 1, 41
Mitchell, Mrs. 111
Mittelstadt, Jno. 161
Mittelstaedt, Adeline 64
Mittelstaedt, Clara 64
Moan 157
Moan, A.J. 102, 141, 149, 159
Moan, Allen 128
Moan, Allen J. 131, 154
Moan, Harriet E. 74
Moan, Hattie 48, 83
Moan, Mr. 162
Moersch, Annetta 63
Moersch, Lou 63
Moersch, Rosa 63
Moll, A. 115
Molltar, Alma 66
Monroe 1, 151
Monroe, Wis. 62, 87
Montana 132
Montello, Wis. 45, 50
Montgomery, Ala. 99
Monty, Miss 23
Moore, B.H. 105
Moore, C.K. 38
Moore, Charles 12
Moore, Chas. 44
Moore, Edward 135
Moore, Elsie 61, 150
Moore, Fannie 151
Moore, Florence 64
Moore, H.L. 50, 78, 151

Moore, Jennie Estelle 142
Moore, M.T. 56
Moore, Stella 139
Moore, W.H. 99, 139
Moore, William 108, iv
Moore, Wm. 56, 89
Moore, Wm. H. 142
Moorehouse, Mrs. 32
More, E.A. 97
More, H.L. 56
Morehouse, C.E. 113
Morehouse, Linden 81
Morehouse, Lizzie 81
Morehouse, Miss 81, 139, 156
Morgan, David iii
Morgan, Frank iii
Morion, Howard vi
Moritz, F.G. 78
Morley, E.B. 4, 12
Morley, Edward R. 4
Morley, F.B. 19
Morris, Ann 88, 149, 164
Morris, C. 164
Morris, Charles T. 124
Morris, Chauncey 149
Morris, Chauncy 74, 75, 88
Morris, Elizabeth 124
Morris, Mr. 104
Morrison, Rolland 149
Morse, H.P. 50, 80, 97
Morse, Mr. 128, 152
Morse, W.B. 70, 90
Morton, C.G. 156
Morton, Cathryn vi
Morton, F.L. 149
Morton, Fred 35, 62, 68, 108
Morton, Fred. L. 159
Morton, Frederick L. 36
Morton, G.E. 106, 164
Morton, H. 141
Morton, H.G. 35, 126, 149
Morton, Harry G. 57
Morton, J.L. 32, 36, 61, 62, 68, 72, 74, 82, 124, 126, 141
Moss, Ethel 159
Moss, John 82, 159
Mower, A.B. 21
Mower, Augustus 46, iv
Mower, Caroline 37
Mower, Carrie 94
Mower, Charles iv
Mower, George iv
Mower, H.E. 74, 86, 91, 94, 95, 96
Mower, Lida 64

Mower, Margaret  68, 80, 92
Mower, Theresa  90
Mower, Timothy  iii
Mower, Warner  46
Mowry, Duane  86
Moxcoy, Mary E.  104
Mt. Sterling, Ill.  160
Mueller, Ed  159
Mueller, L.J.  28
Muenster, J.H.  68
Mukwonago  23
Muller, John  38
Munger, Nelson  89
Munns, Annie  163
Munroe, Alexander  iii
Munroe, John  iii
Murphy  23, 30
Murphy, G.C.  47, 156
Murphy, G.W.  40
Murphy, M.J.  148
Murphy, Miss  14
Murphy, Mrs.  16
Murphy, T.C.  17
Muscoda, Wis.  158
Muth, Philip  iv
Myer, Mr.  165
Myers, A.B.  25, 85
Myers, Clara  93
Myers, Helen  32, 43, 97
Myers, J.O.  20, 22, 29, 32, 60,
  72, 83, 95, 99, 104, 160
Myers, Mary  33, 58, 62, 73
Myers, Mrs.  108
Myers, Percy  12
Myers, Perey  24, 58, 135

N

Nader, Max  157
Nangle, Fanning  iv
Nash, E.A.  11
Nash, Fred C.  165
Nash, Hattie  17, 55, 56
Nash, J.  16
Nash, J.M.  9, 17, 112
Nash, John M.  57
Nash, Mattie  112
Nashville, Tenn.  131
Nauerts, Mrs.  146
Nauertz, Peter  165, 167
Neary, Mattie  44
Nedean, Fred  159
Neef, Wm  162
Neelen, Judge  118, 147
Neetrel, Leonard  157

Neib, Jacob W.  141
Nelson, E.G.  123
Nelson, Lloyd  109
Nelson, Mrs.  117
Nelson, Stella  138, 146
Neosho  37, 46, 128
Netherent, Commissioners  25
Netherent, John  149
Netherent, Mary Belle  154
Netherent, Mr.  25
Netherent, W.R.  83, 104 144,
  154, 160
Netherent, William  71
Netherent, Wm. R.  149
Netherent, Wm.R.  25, 52
Nettleton  70
Nettleton, C.A.  100
Nettleton, C.E.  85
Nettleton, Carroll  98
Nettleton, E.C.  25, 35, 107, 120,
  127, 135, 138, 144
Nettleton, Mertie  115
Nettleton, Mrs.  46
Nettleton, Myrtle  20, 46, 48, 55, 98
Neubauer, Louise  77
New Orleans, La  41
New Salem, Mass.  9
New Ulm, Minn.  47
New York City  67
New York  15
Newstab, N.E.  156
Nichols, Mrs.  139
Nichols, Verna  124
Nickel, L.  13, 123
Nickel, Louis  115, 118
Nickel, Peter  118
Nickerson, H.W.  52
Nickerson, Harold  59, 141
Nickerson, Mrs.  113, 144
Niedecken, H.  99
Niese, Lena  151
Nieuemarn, H.  99
Noble, N.H.  18
Nobles, William  iii
Nolte, H.  63
Nolte, H.A.  161
Nolz, Nic.  116
Noonan, Katie  92
Norfolk, Nebraska  28
North Dakota  143
North Lake  145, 163
North, Miss  42
Norton, C.G.  96, 103, 148, 156
Norton, C.H.  46

Norton, Miss 30
Norton, Thomas 118
Norton, Tom 64
Notbohm, W.L. 85, 123, 159, 160
Notbohm, W.S. 83
Noyes, C. 128
Noyes, John iv
Noyse, Mr. 97

**O**

Oak Park 33, 49, 61, 65, 74, 78
Oakfield, Wis. 42
Oakland, Cal. 50, 61
Oakwood, Wis. 44
Oberlin, Ohio 68, 97
O'Brien, Patrick D. 132
O'Connell, P. 20
O'Connor, Jewel 112
Oconomowoc 31
O'Cornell, Patrick 159
Oelwein, Iowa 158
Oenow, Lilli 98
Oertel, M.E. 107, 133
Ogden, Utah 101
Ohio 19
Olds, Mrs. 66
Oliphant, Mr. 103
Oliphant, Rev. 163
Ollvet, Mich. 76
Olson, Amanda 112
Omaha, Neb. 87
Omro, Wis. 87
O'Neil, C.H. 110
Ontonagon, Mich. 64, 101
Opsal, Elling 121
Ordway, Blanchard Ross 9
Ordway, F.J. 23
Ordway, Frank 9
O'Regan, M. 21, 159
Oregon, Wis. 21, 37, 151
Orendorf, Alfred iii
Orr, Emma 81
Orr, Mary 81
Orvis, Fred 65
Osborn, Tobias iii
Oshkosh 2, 21, 27, 44, 50, 68
Osten, Paul 87
Oswale, Mr. 145
Oswego, NY 127
Ottowa, Wis. 2
Ottumwa, Iowa 65
Owens, A.H. 77, 153

**P**

Packard, O.L. 99
Packer, M.A. 48
Paine, O.W. 125
Painter, R. iii
Palm, Angela 98
Palmer, Wm. 96
Palmyra 1
Papie, Carrie 107
Pares, Ada 43, 53
Pares, E.B. 13, 112
Pares, Edward 55, 59, 118
Pares, Mrs. 137
Park Ridge, Ill. 38
Parker, B.F. 119
Parker, C.L. 162
Parker, Mr. 39
Parkinson, John 90
Parkinson, Maud 87
Parkinson, Maude 99
Pasadena, Cal. 82, 91
Patter, Harry 125
Patton, W.J. 124
Paulsen, A. 110
Pavey, Edward 148
Pavey, Lester 53
Pavy, Ed 12, 90, 97
Pavy, Edward 135
Pavy, F.A. 10
Pavy, Lester 94, 153, 168
Payne, A.C. 50
Payne, C.A. 123, 166
Payne, Charles A. 121
Payne, Chas. A. 106
Peake, Frank 80
Pearce, Maud 89, 153
Pease, L.S. 45, 50, 75, 134, 163, 166
Pease, Lila 157
Pease, Lynn S. 169
Pease, Spencer 43
Peck, A.M. 84
Peck, Anna 122
Pederick, Cyrds 69
Pedrick, C. 88
Pedrick, Cyrus 37, 148
Pegler, Margerite 76
Pelton, H.L. 62
Pelton, J.L. 108
Pelton, John iv
Pelton, Lillie 159
Pelton, Lily 119
Pereles, Judge 109
Perey 23
Perkins, Miss 21

Perkins, Robert Sandford 64
Perkins, W.A. 13, 158
Perkins, Walter 151
Perkins, Walton 103
Perry 73
Perry, C.B. 27, 54, 99, 123, 127, 133, 165
Perry, Charles B. 3, 4
Perry, Charles G. v
Perry, Charles R. v
Perry, Chas. B. 83, 88, 90, 159
Perry, Mr. 156
Perry, Rev. 55
Peschman, Frank L. 133
Peters, John 133
Peters, Laura 150
Peters, Miss 131
Peterson, K. 123
Peterson, Mr. 40
Petri, E.M. 126
Pettibone, C.A. 101
Pewaukee 3, 57, 124
Phelps, F.O. 156
Phelps, Frank 108
Philadelphia 126
Philipp, D.F. 45, 75, 93, 134
Philipp, D.W. 107
Philipps, D.F. 149
Philips, Sadie 24
Phillip, D. 72
Phillipps, D.F. 121
Phillips, Alice 10
Phillips, Allan 101
Phillips, Alvin 64
Phillips, Bessie 74
Phillips, D.F. 81
Phillips, G.G. 10
Phillips, Henry 137
Phillips, J.E. 62
Phillips, Jean 154
Phillips, John 101
Phillips, Norma 72
Phillips, Sadie 44, 64
Phillips, Winnefred 12
Phillips, Winnie 64
Picker 12, 157
Picker, F 62
Picker, Fred 83, 162, 166
Picker, Fred. 53
Picker, William 155
Picker, Wm. 159
Pierce, Ella 18
Pierce, J.E. 76, 107, 129, 136, 140, 145, 148

Pierce, Jack 126, 148
Pierce, Oscar 134, 136
Pigeon, F.A. 104
Pilgrim, D.T. 5, 14, 15, 41, 49, 99, 126
Pilgrim, Daniel T. 5
Pilgrim, Elmer 123
Pilgrim, Lou 136
Pilgrim, Lou J. 123
Pilgrim, Miss 31
Pilgrim, P.D. 98
Pine River, Wis. 102, 103
Piper, Irving 45
Pitcher, H.J. 9
Platteville 57, 58
Pleasants, Elnora B. 54
Plymouth, Wis. 63, 74
Poeck, Viola 72
Polarek, Stanly 169
Polkow, Johann 133
Pomeroy, Ohio 74
Pond, O.B. 141
Pontine, Mich. 73
Poppleton, W.E. 99
Port Washington 1, 11, 23, 68
Portage 81
Porter, A.K. 112
Porter, Arthur 65
Porter, C.A. 6
Porter, C.G. 4, 14, 65, 83, 98, 145, 160
Porter, Chester 145
Portland, Me. 88
Portz, Andrew 75
Portz, Irma 75
Postel, A.F. 57
Potter, Alice 12
Potter, Henry iv
Potter, John 65
Potter, L.B. iii
Potter, L.F. 120
Potter, M.B. 78, 120
Potter, Mabel 38, 43, 131, 134
Potter, Miss 39
Potter, Mr. 29
Potter, T.M. 96
Potter, Theresa 50
Potter, W.J. 4, 6, 22, 45
Powell, Prof. 44
Powell, William 119
Powers, Mich. 61
Prentice 34
Prentice, G.W. 87, 127
Prentice, Hally E. 87

Prentice, Hattie 44
Prentice, Mr. 69
Prest, G.H. 45
Prest, Geo. 73
Prest, George 146, 158
Prest, Herbert E. 152
Preston, F.D. 30
Prhudis, Fred 160
Princeton, Wis. 131
Pritchard, Jos 95
Pritchard, Marion 89
Pritchard, Miss 136
Propp, H.A. 3, 50, 64, 99
Propp, Margaret A. 64
Protzmann, Chas. 104
Prouditt, Wm. 105
Prudisch, Fred 60, 149, 160, 162
Prudish, Fred 83
Prust, H. 149
Putham, Mrs. 66
Putnam, K.N. 51
Putnam, Kirk 108, 156
Putnam, Kirke 163
Putney, J.C. iii

Q

Quebec, Canada 96
Queechy, Vt. 17
Quentall, Miss 129
Quimby, Mable 98
Quin, Norman 50
Quintal, Miss 76

R

Raby, Lizzie 115
Rachow, Henry 115
Racine 3, 53, 71
Radcliff, Bertha 115
Rader, Pastor 2
Rader, Rev. 67, 111
Rader, William 122
Rader, Wm. 30
Rading, J. 167
Rading, Rev. 146
Radtke, Chas. 102
Radzinski, Edward 35
Raesser, C.S. 32
Randolph, Gail Mirian 13
Raschka, James Gregg v
Rausch, Justice 19
Ravenswood, Ill. 68, 85
Raymer, John 42
Razorina, Rosa 98

Red Wing, Minn. 136
Reed, Altie 119
Reed, Reuel C. 137
Reedsburg, Wis. 48
Regan, J.J. 156
Regan, J.P. 16
Regan, John M. 75, 83
Regan, Thos. 32
Regan, Tom 21
Regan, Wm. 32
Reichardt 166
Reichardt, G.E. 83
Reichardt, G.F. 85, 160, 162, 165
Reichardt, Gottlieb F. 154
Reichardt, Rosa 74
Reichert, Wm. 159
Reid, J.H. 159
Reilly, Daniel iv
Reilly, Thomas iv
Reimer, Paula 69
Reinertsen, Engineer 43
Reiter, John M. 83
Relpsch, R. 154
Reuiie?, Wm. 64
Reuter, G. 99
Reuter, Isabel 82
Reuter, John 150, 160
Reyher, Grace 97
Reyher, Miss 135
Reyher, Mrs. 97
Reynels, Mable 82
Reynolds, Dolly 140
Reynolds, Thos. 27
Rhinehart, Lud 23
Rhinelander, Wis. 4, 63
Rhodes, Ellis 101
Rhodes, Helen 87, 88, 90
Rhodes, L. 49, 65, 84
Rhodes, Louisa 54, 88
Rhodes, Louise 90
Rhodes, Mrs. 88, 103
Rice, A. 66
Rice, A.G. 103
Rice, Agnes 84, 103, 149
Rice, Arba 41, 149
Rice, Arba M. 66
Rice, Charles 86
Rice, H. 45
Rice, Harriet 155
Rice, Harriett 108
Rice, Harriett E. 87, 90
Rice, Helen 53
Rice Lake 28
Rice, Miss 59

Rice, Thomas J. iii
Rice, Thos. 16
Rice, W.B. 50, 58, 65, 74,
  94, 100, 103, 151, 159
Rice, Walter 56
Richardson, E.E. 55
Richardson, Rev. 138
Richert, Christoph 77
Rickert, Christoph 79
Riddle, T.M. vi
Riddle, Thomas vi
Riddle, Thomas M. iii
Rider, H.J. 82
Riebe, A. 127
Rieck, A. 157
Riedeburg 23
Riel, A. 141
Riley, Matthew 8
Rinehardt, Frank 164
Ringle, Marathon Co., Wis. 139
Ringrose, Chas. 94
Ringrose, Florence 3, 36, 50, 59
Ringrose, G.W. 15, 84, 94, 107, 123
Ringrose, George W. 3, 41
Ringrose, Mrs. 48
Ringrose, S.D. 99
Ripon 18, 53
Ripon, Wis. 37
Ritchie, Frances 100
Ritchie, John 94, 136
Rix, Carl 83
Rix, Lulu 87, 110
Robbins, A.S. 99
Robbins, Edward W. 162
Roberts 23
Roberts, C.E. 77, 107
Roberts, J. Emory 117
Roberts, M.L. 93
Robertson, C. 45
Robertson, O.W. 116
Robertson, W.R. 133
Robinson, John J. 18
Rochester, NY 150
Rock Co., Wis. 5
Rock Island, Ill. 98
Rockel, Mrs. 162
Rockford, Ill. 61, 96
Roddis, A.A. 132
Roddis, Agnes 34, 37, 39, 44, 79
Roddis, Mrs. 54, 99
Rodehl, Emma 102
Rodger, Miss 154
Rodger's Park, Chicago 163
Roehl, Joe 22

Roepke, Eric vi
Rogers 12, 23
Rogers, Alex 28, 105
Rogers, Alex. 115, 131
Rogers, C.J. 36, 90, 115
Rogers, C.K. 2, 12
Rogers, Charlotte 53, 164
Rogers, E.A. 100
Rogers, Earl 112
Rogers, Fay 36, 64
Rogers, Frank 4, 12
Rogers, G.C. 59
Rogers, G.H. 62, 162
Rogers, Geo. 64
Rogers, Geo. H. 100
Rogers, George 30, 131, 148
Rogers, Harold 34, 43, 44,
  90, 105, 148
Rogers, Isabel 147
Rogers, J.P. 31, 34, 36
Rogers, James 112
Rogers, Jerry 130
Rogers, L.C. 12, 16, 53
Rogers, Lois 1
Rogers, Louis 17
Rogers, Marion 43
Rogers, Mr. 31
Rogers, Mrs. 53
Rogers, O. 73
Rogers, R.W. 31, 34
Rogge, Fred 159
Romadka, John 124
Rome 124
Rome, Wis. 102
Rood, J.F. 140
Rood, Mae 53
Rood, Miss 58, 59
Root Creek, Milwaukee Co., Wis. 147
Rork, A.A. 35
Rose, ? 156
Rose, Elgar iv
Rose, H.E. 105, 108, 116,
  131, 156, 157
Rose, Henry 131, 156, iv
Rose, Lee 161
Rose, Wm. S. 88
Rosenthal, Bea 68
Rosenthal, Cora 66
Rosenthal, Gertrude 59, 66
Rosenthal, Hilda 80
Rosenthal, John 137
Rosenthal, Max 3, 4, 42, 66,
  137, 141, 149
Ross, Hiram J. iii

Ross, Nellie 102, 121, 161
Rother, Fred 40
Rotterdam, Holland 91
Rowe, G.E. 67
Ruanie, Arthur L. 159
Rudolph, H. 21
Rudolph, Moritz 98
Ruggles, C.H. 53
Ruggles, Gen. 113
Ruggles, Mrs. 139
Rundle, Joseph 123
Rusk, Josephine 162
Russel, J.B. 83
Russell, J.B. 64, 97, 100, 110, 168
Russell, L.J. 11
Rust, J.P. 101
Rust, Mrs. 104
Rust, T.D. 103
Ryan, Mr. 58
Ryder-Myers, Lucy 19

S

S--, Regina vi
Sabin, Ellen C. 57
Sabin, H.A. 66
Sabin, Mary 122
Sabine, Mary 66
Sabins, F.A. 58
Sackett, Edwin iv
Sackett, Squire iii
Sage, Chas. 131
Sage, Janette 151
Sage, Jeanette 53
Sage, Jeanette L. 89
Sage, Laura 151
Sage, Mary 53
Saginaw, Mich. 66
Salt Lake City, Utah 53
Sampson, J. 150
Sanborn, Miss 53
Sanborn, S.W. 168
Sanderson, Alice 76
Sanderson, Allee 10
Sanderson, Billy 2
Sanderson, France 121, 129, 148
Sanderson, Frane 59
Sanderson, Franee 2, 27, 30
Sanderson, Franey 41
Sanderson, Mrs. 139
Sanderson, Will 16, 42, 145
Sanderson, William 11, 148
Sanderson, Wm. 27, 64
Sanford, G. 140, 151

Sanford, G.W. 50, 65, 69, 74, 91,
    92, 121, 132, 159
Sanford, George W. 119, 129
Sangston, Mrs. 160
Santa Cruz, Cal. 155
Santley, E.D. 32
Sarnow, Chris 25
Sassanske, Otto 98
Sasse, Otto 43
Sausen, Joe 116
Saylesville 36, 117
Schafer, Harry 79
Scharver, Jacob 148
Scheffler, Chas. 98
Scheibe, Gustav 33
Scheibe, Martha 33
Schell, Wilhelm 70
Schenck, C.G.B. 162
Schenk, Allan 107
Schenk, C.G.B. 105
Schenk, G.C.B. 107
Scherer, Hattie 148
Schern, Walter 146
Schiltz, E. 157
Schinitz, E.A. 17
Schleantek, Franz 76
Schlehlein, Michael 8
Schleifer, Bertha 142
Schleifer, Miss 139
Schlenger, M. 93
Schlichter, Ida 146
Schmeling, Louis 111
Schmelling, Miss 13
Schmidt, F.J. 3
Schmidt, Frank 84
Schmidt, Jacob 37
Schmidt, Michael 95, 116
Schmidt, Peter 116
Schmidt, W. 52
Schmidt, Wm. F. 87
Schmitz, E.A. 16, 55, 123,
    156, 160, 166
Schneck 25
Schneck, C.F. 87, 105
Schneck, Clarence 163
Schneck, F.W. 9, 20, 31, 50, 59,
    63, 90, 95, 141, 158, 165, 168
Schneck, Geo. 39
Schneck, George 34, 38, 89,
    116, 135, 144, 163
Schneck, R.W. 105
Schneckaal, F.W. 62
Schneider, Archie 21, 24
Schneider, John 22, 26, 31, 36, 43

Schneider, M  102
Schneider, Rev.  24, 32
Scholl, Nina  38
Scholler, John P.  77
Scholtka, Julius  153
Schoonmaker, H.  81
Schoonmaker, H.G.  5, 15
Schoonmaker, Mr.  18
Schreiber, Minnie  153
Schroeder, G.W.  157
Schroeder, George  65
Schrubbe, F.  32
Schubel, Hugo  72, 81
Schubel, Theresa  45
Schubel, Walter  81
Schuek, Alma  117
Schultz, Clara  133
Schultz, F.  25
Schultz, Fred  73
Schultz, H.F.  110
Schultz, H.L.  42
Schultz, Henry F.  39
Schultz, Johanna  122
Schultz, Louis  73
Schultz, Mrs.  132
Schulz, Fred  159
Schuster, Henry  167
Schwada, John  145
Schwaiger  70, 71
Schwaiger, E.H.  13, 27, 53, 99, 150
Schwaiger, J.A.  85, 107, 118
Schwaiger, Jos.  136, 160
Schwaiger, Joseph  49, 83
Schwandt, Otto  118
Scotland  35
Scott, Clara  132
Scott, Florence  vi
Scott, T.H.  40, 91
Scott, Tom  vi
Scranton, Pa.  87
Scribner, Vernon  141
Scully, D.J.  155
Scully, Wm.  159
Seaforth, Minn.  64, 161
Seamans, Emily  96, 125
Seamans, Stephen H.  36
Seattle, Wash.  85
Secromb, John  129
Secromb, Mary A.  129
Secrombe, Harriet  151
Seed, Nathan  102
Seefeld  29
Seefeld, H.F.  3
Seflute, George  146

Seidel, Mr.  145
Seigfried  29
Seisser, Clara  146
Seivers, John  50
Sell, George  87
Sercomb, Cussius  74
Sercomb, J.W.  58
Sercomb, John W.  100
Sercombe, H.S.  30
Servis, Chas  148
Servis, Mrs.  28
Seuberth, Edward  170
Seuberth, Hazel  170
Seuberth, Lillie  170
Seuberth, Lyda  170
Seuberth, Mr.  170
Seuberth, Roy  170
Seuberth, Victor  170
Severance, C.G.  45
Sewell, Gussie  72
Seymore, Florence  10
Seymour, Chas.  1
Seymour, Florence  27
Seymour, Frank  133
Seymour, Mrs.  17
Shannon, Ill.  165
Shaw, C.H.  40, 113
Shaw, Chas.  148
Shaw, J.D.  127
Shaw, James  3
Shaw, Lula  1
Shaw, Lulu  135
Shaw, Mrs.  16
Shearer, O.L.  157
Sheboygan  9, 66, 124
Sheboygan Falls  33, 68
Sheldon, Dr.  29
Shenk, George  152
Shepard, Irwin  101
Shepard, R.  63
Sheppard, Luman  76
Sherf, Herman  125
Sherfy, Alice  135
Sheriff  30
Sherin, F.M.  91
Sherman, J.D.  30
Sherwin, R.C.  30
Sherwin, Richard C.  98
Shields, Ada  94
Shields, Ella  94
Shields, Mrs.  163
Shinner, Roy  114
Shrubbe, F.  31
Siefert, J.W.  109

Siegart, H. 144
Siegert, Benjamin iv
Siegert, Herman 157
Siegfried, Aug. M. 75, 91
Siegfried, August M. 3, 83
Siegler, A.F. 64, 75
Siegler, Clara 28
Siegler, F. 28, 37
Siegler, Lena 161
Siegler, R. 64
Sieglow, August 41
Sieloff, A.E. 99
Silver City 7
Silverstone 70
Simmons, Gertrude 59
Sims, E.A. 39
Sinclair, G.S. 133, 134
Sioux Falls, Dakota 102
Sisson, Lillian 132, 146
Skillman, George 138
Skinner, ..bel 159
Skinner, Isabel E. 115
Skinner, Isabelle 106
Skinner, Miss 139
Smith 23
Smith, A.I. 83, 128, 151, 160
Smith, A.L. 118, 146, 152
Smith, A.W. 50, 54, 83, 154, 160
Smith, Alfred 75
Smith, Alice 12, 39, 61, 135, 147
Smith, Ann 37
Smith, Bessie 58
Smith, Charles 157
Smith, Charlotte Parry 131
Smith, Della 69
Smith, E. 121
Smith, Ella 58, 100, 150
Smith, Frank 154
Smith, Fred 163
Smith, G.E. 54, 62, 99,
  118, 152, 154
Smith, Geo. 131
Smith, George 120
Smith, Granger 48
Smith, H.E. 139
Smith, I.B. 77, 126
Smith, J.M. 99
Smith, Janet 54, 67, 90, 154, 169
Smith, Janet M. 89
Smith, Jeannette 154
Smith, L.B. 108
Smith, Marian 132, 146
Smith, Millard vi
Smith, Miss 3, 39, 44, 72

Smith, Mr. 97
Smith, Nettie 71, 80
Smith, Thomas 37
Smith, W. 12
Smith, W.A. 96
Smith, Walter 135
Smith, Wm. C. 106
Snyder, Clara 20
Soe, Dr. 76
Soe, Jens 76
Soendsch, C. 106
Soendsen, C. 106
Somers, Peter J. 54
Sommer, Chris. 159
Sommers, Matt 69
Sooysmith, Charles 168
South Bend, Ind. 21
South Dakota 48, 97
South Haven, Mich. 80
South Milwaukee 55
South St. Paul, Minn. 48
Spalding, Anne vi
Sparling, Mrs. 120
Sparling, Wm 46
Sparta 17, 114, 129
Spears, Mr. iv
Speigel, Adolph 19
Speigelberg, Miss 44
Spooner, Mrs. 50, 148
Sporleder, Alma W. James vi
Sporleder, August 13, 162
Sporleder, F.H. 99
Sporleder, Fred 13
Sporleder, Miss 116
Sporleder, Rex 159
Sporleder, Richard 48
Sporleder, Ruth 139, 156
Springsted, Mabel 40
Spuhrieder, Emma 123
Squires, Sidney 2, 28
St. Gallen, Switzerland 37
St. Joseph, Mo. 86
St. Louis 64, 66, 126
St. Paul 17, 103, 119, 133, 136,
  154
Stacey, Alice 144
Stacy, J.C. 125
Stacy, Mrs. 158
Stafford, Charles 115
Stafford, Chas. 110, 166
Stafford, George 35
Stafford, W.H. 82
Stafford, Wm. 77
Star Lake, Wis. 31

Stark, William 116
Staube, A.H. 115
Stearn, Myrtle 85
Stein, William 26
Steinea, Steve 125
Steinhagen, G. 15, 22, 70
Sterling, Miss 101
Steusloff, H.M. 17
Stevens, Charles 81
Stevens, E.C. 50
Stevens, Fayette 75
Stevens, Lutie E. 124
Stevens Point, Wis. 71
Stevens, Ray 56
Stewart, C. 18
Stewart, F.L. 132
Stewart, Flora 130
Stewart, Laura 38
Stewart, Mary B. 82
Stewart, Miss 91
Stewart, Supervisor 19
Stickney 38
Stickney, Charles 51, 83, 107,
    109, 118, 126, 160, vi
Stickney, Chas. 31, 33, 50, 158, 165
Stickney, Fannie 126
Stickney, Helen 12, 85, 92, 133
Stickney, Isabel 9, 45
Stickney, Isabelle 17, 51
Stickney, J.S. 15, 37, vi
Stickney, Maud 87
Stickney, Miss 44
Stickney, Mr. 46, 79, 99, iv
Stiles, Mr. 39
Stiles, Superintendent 34
Stiles, W.F. 57
Stiltz, Henry 66
Stockdale, Mr 163
Stocks, Robert 2
Stokdyk, F. 122
Stone, H.O. 63
Stone, Henry O. 118
Story, A.L. 6, 15, 29, 93, 152, 159
Story, Albert L. 83, 149, 160
Story, Treasurer 56
Story, William F. 152
Story, Willis E. 152
Stoughton 71, 75
Stout, Gretchen 71
Stout, Lucile 69, 80, 122
Stout, Lucille 67
Stover, J.H. 26
Streeter, E.S. 135
Stringham, Mrs. 17

Strong, M.W. 15
Strong, Miss 17
Stroud, A.E. 8
Stumpf, E.O. 134
Sturgeon Bay 65
Sturges, F.S. 151
Sullivan, R.E. 33
Sun Prairie 65, 100, 140
Superior 124
Surges, C. 159
Sussex 66
Sutherland, J.W. 30
Sutherland, Judge 6
Sutherland, Miss 1
Sutherland, N. 34
Sutherland, Rev. 18, 29
Sutton, Bernice 48
Sutton, Eugene 48
Swan, A.H. 162
Swan, Alvin iii
Swan, Dave 39
Swan, David 12, 34, 38, 39, 165
Swan, David M. 85
Swan, E.A. 91
Swan, Earling 117
Swan, Eleanor 43
Swan, Emery 172
Swan, Hattie 38
Swan, N.J. 22
Swan, Nathaniel iii
Swan, O.J. 91, 126
Swan, Orlin J. 159
Swan, S.J. 39
Swan, Seth iii
Swann, Earling 118
Swann, Elinor 73
Swann, Frank E. 15
Swann, N.J. 32
Swann, Nathaniel J. 162
Swett, Chas. 47
Sylvester, G.A. 123
Sylvester, Mr. 31

T

Taek, Martin 135
Taff, W.H. 7, 12, 19
Talford, William iv
Tanner, E.V. 37
Tarrant, Warren D. 46
Taylor, Albert 21, 26, 31,
    32, 99, 100, 168
Taylor, C. 53, 68, 116
Taylor, Dr. 54
Taylor, Edith 26

Taylor, Frank 56
Taylor, H.V. 92, 154
Taylor, Howard 36
Taylor, John 16, 127, 166
Taylor, John H. 91, 155
Taylor, Mamie 74
Taylor, Mart 79
Taylor, May 93
Taylor, Stanton 68, 131
Taylor, W.G. 36, 40, 47, 96
Taylor, W.S. 34
Teal, Miss 135
Teal, Ora E. 93
Teeths, Nick 140
Tegtmeyer, Fred 162
Temple, Edward 126
Temple, H.S. 34, 80, 126, 132, 135, 146
Temple, Helen 132, 146
Temple, Miss 34
Tennant 108
Tennant, Agnes 123
Tennant, Agnes S. 96, 103, 152
Tennant, Miss 105
Tennant, R. 42, 127
Tennant, Rich 89, 97
Tennant, Rich. 86
Tennant, Richard 105, 116, 143, 144
Tennants, Agnes 138
Tennessen, Jacob 160
Tesch, C.H. 34, 38, 43
Thain, A.R. 47, 90, 99, 109, 119, 130, 168
Thain, Dr. 52, 81, 104, 121
Thain, Eva 80
Thain, Miss 73
Thain, Mrs. 61, 84
Thain, Rev. 147
Theis, Wallis 169
Thickens, J.W. 94
Thiele, Dietrich 116
Thierfeldt, A. 62
Thomas 46
Thomas, Arthur 12, 39
Thomas, B.J. 35
Thomas, Grant 121
Thomas, J.B. 83, 95, 109, 121
Thomas, J.E. 49
Thomas, J.R. 56
Thomas, John 133, vi
Thomas, Mabel 12
Thomas, Mrs. 84
Thompkins, Gilbert 118
Thompson, Albert 115

Thompson, George 140
Thompson, J.P. 74
Thompson, Mary 73
Thompson, Miss 80, 96, 134, 158
Thompson, Robert 143, 152
Thorburn, Adam 54
Thorburn, Mary E. 54
Thorp, Louis 123
Thrall, Ida May 132
Tibbits, S.M. 127
Tichenor, Alice 152
Tipple 30
Tipple, H.S. 9, 31, 40
Tipple, "Kid" 23
Tipple, R. 23
Tisdale, E. 134
Tisdale, L.C. 58, 129, 134, 164
Tisdale, Mrs. 16, 17, 56, 141
Titsworth, Alice vi
Titsworth, Judson vi
Titus, W.H. 98
Toledo, Ohio 40
Tomah 131
Tompkins, J. 156
Tompkins, J.A.R. 99
Tompkins, Mr. 31
Toohey, John 69
Tory, H. 115
Tragard, Helen Grace 47
Tragard, Kenneth 47
Tragard, Loraine Armin 47
Tragard, Lorraine 21
Tragard, Rudolph 47
Tralil, Alice 148
Trausfeldt, Christina 60
Traver, F.A. 106
Traverse City, Mich. 116
Travis, E.A. 148
Travis, Leslie 154
Trempeleau 46, 48, 120
Trever, Mr 101
Trost, Joseph 120, 137
Trottner, Michael 104
Troy Center 13, 20, 27, 46
True, John M. 86
Truesdale, Wis. 115
Truss, Mr. 145
Tschergi, William 158
Tuck, Wm. 93
Tuder, Pastor 13
Tullar, Je... 162
Tulley, M. 154
Tully, Maude 132
Tully, Mr. 132

Tully, Mrs. 134
Tupper, Claude 41
Tupper, Claude A. 50
Tupper, L.V. 41
Turneaure, Prof. 19
Turner, Charlotta A. 77
Turner, E.S. 11, 17
Turner, L.M. 3, 30
Turner, Mary Ann 77
Turner, Mr. 44
Turner, Wm. 30
Turney, Kate 40
Turnsey, Leonora 137
Turynski, Annie 112
Tuttle, J.H. 62, 104
Twinem, Cross 126
Tyler, C.E. 108

U

Uhl., Emma 13
Uhl., Leonard 13
Ulrich, O. 127
Underwood, E.D. 46, iii, iv
Underwood, E.W. 142
Underwood, Enoch D. 142
Underwood, F.D. 142
Underwood, Fred D. 142
Underwood, George D. iv
Underwood, Harriet D. 142
Underwood, Lucy R. 70
Underwood, W.J. 5, 21, 47, 142
Underwood, William O. iii

V

Van Alstine, Chas. 30
Van Antwerp, Mary 117
van Baumbach, Lill 134
Van Buren, C. 159
Van De Kamp, Frank 121
Van Ellis, A. 95
Van Uxem, A. 114
Van Uxem, John 114
Van Vechten 144
Van Vechten, E.F. 34
Van Vechten, J.T. 20, 27, 106,
115, 121, 128
Van Vechten, Lizzie 159
Van Vechten, Miss 37
Van Vechton, J.T. 46
Van Vecten, J.T. 103, 151
Van Vecton, J.T. 102
Vandalia, Mich. 67
Vandercook, F. 107

Vaughan, R.M. 64, 90, 91
Vaughn, R.M. 46
Vaughn, R.W. 27
Vernett 23
Viall, Charlotte 89
Viall, Grace 89
Viall, R.A. 89
Vining, V. 115
Vining, V.V. 74, 82, 146
Voetz, Fred 99
Voigt, F.C. 12
Voigt, F.C. Charles 7
Vollrath, F.W. 32
Voltz, Herman 128
Volz, Simon 86
Volz, Sophie 85
von Baubach, Wm. 3
von Baumbach, Lili 87
von Baumbach, Lill 61, 84, 92
von Baumbach, Lilli 145
von Baumbach, Lillian 16, 27, 34
von Baumbach, Lillie 19
von Baumbach, Miss 34
von Baumbach, President 75
von Baumbach, William 5, 82, 154
von Baumbach, Wm. 12, 37, 71, 88,
149, 153

W

Wade, C.G. 52, 72, 112
Wadsworth, C. 116
Wadsworth, Mr. 10
Waetjen, Geo. L. 167
Wagner, A. John 71
Wagner, A.J. 106
Wagner, E.J. 117
Wagner, Edward 148
Wagner, Frances 63
Wagner, John 38
Wagner, Juilana 148
Wahl, C. 159
Wahl, Frederick 38
Wahl, Frederick B. 39
Waite, Brevit 31
Wakefield, Geo. M. 117
Wakefield, Vernon T. 116
Waklie, Florence 36
Waldie, Florance 77
Waldie, J.H. 40, 91, 101
Waldie, Jesse 64, 140
Waldie, Jessie 77
Waldo, Nellie 68
Waldo, Sheboygan Co., Wis. 51
Wales, Gideon iii

208

Wales, Mary 56, 117
Walker, Archibald O. 87
Walker, Clara 95
Walker, Henry 51
Walker, Isabel R. 55
Walker, Miss 3, 39, 44
Walker, R.S. 2, 13, 20, 32, 69
Walker, Robert 46
Wallace, Irene 101
Wallace, Margaret 27, 38
Wallace, Marguerita 17
Walter, Arthur 147
Walter, Thomas 159
Walters, Chas. 85
Walters, O. 127
Walworth, Wis. 150
Ward, Capt. 158
Ward, J.O. 53, 90
Warner, Adelaide 148
Warner, Alice 159
Warner, Mr. 104
Warner, Nellie 12
Warren, C.A. 65
Warren, C.G. 115, 140, 153
Warren, Carrie 26, 28, 66, 72,
    88, 154, 161, 163
Warren, Carrie G. 79, 122, 162
Warren, Charles 124
Warren, Commissioner 48
Warren, Harriet F. 162
Warren, J.A. 47, 97, 108, 130
Warren, J.B. 159
Warren, J.D. 3, 17, 33, 52, 82,
    83, 89, 99, 109, 113, 129, 131,
    156, 160, 166, iv
Warren, J.M. 46
Warren, John 69, iv
Warren, Jonathan iii
Warren, Jonathan M. 52
Warren, Jonathon v
Warren, Joseph iii
Warren, Joseph A. 79, 162, iv
Warren, L.A. 122, iii
Warren, Lois 88
Warren, Luther 33
Warren, Luther A. 52
Warren, Mr. 66, 156
Warren, Paul 26, 39, 68, 105
Warsaw, Ind. 106
Wasburn, S.A. 96
Wasmansdorf, Mae 63
Wasmansdorf, Mary L. 130
Waterford 18
Waterloo, Iowa 89

Watertown, Wis. 82
Watner, Grace 73
Watner, H. 19, 56, 102
Watner, Henry 17, 50, 68, 73, 82,
    99, 100, 135, 145, 146
Watner, Mrs. 32
Watner, Roy Rherman 82
Waton, Stanley 100
Watson, Charles D. iv
Watson, Dwight 24
Watson, Dwight C. 155
Watson, George Moore 51
Watson, M.E. 24
Watson, Mabel 107, 109, 111
Watson, Stanley 107, 121, 151
Watson, Willis 51, 97, 111
Wau-wau-tae-sie, Chief iii
Waucoma, Iowa 165
Waukegan, Ill. 153
Waukesh 11
Waukesha 1, 9, 17, 20, 46,
    56, 74, 77, 79, 82, 147
Waupaca 22, 73, 89
Waupun 37, 88
Wausau 36, 87
Way, J.V. 70
Webber, Frank 115
Weber, A.F. 145
Weber, Arthur 47
Webo, Carroll 93
Weid, Rena 140
Weifenback, Walter 69
Weisel, Fred 153
Welch, Grace 89
Welch, Mrs. 136
Wellauer 116
Wellinghurst, Mr. 161
Wells, C.R. 80
Wells, Catherine 130
Wells, Daniel 25
Wells, Edward 154
Wells, Florence 85, 123
Wells, G. 30
Wells, G.E. 90
Wells, Geo. E. 85
Wells, George 5, 130, 132, 154
Wells, George E. 161
Wells, Harry 85
Wells, Nellie 45
Welms, Herman 122
Welsher, H.W. 150
Welsher, Herbert 150
Welsher, William 150
Wenborn, Harry 117

Wendel 10
Wendel, Dr. 81, 169
Wendel, W.C. 25, 56, 77
Wendt, Ewald 54
Wentworth, SD 113
Wenzel, Martha 75
Wepfer, Geo. 127
Werner, E.C. 108
Werner, Earnest 125
Werner, Ernst 99
Werner, Mr. 100
Werner, Mrs. 125
Wescott, Roy 146, 147
Weslher, Frank 150
Wespetal, A. 156
Wesson, Frank iv
Wesson, John iv
Wesson, Nathan iv, vi
Wesson, Warren iv
Wesson, William iv
Wesson, William F. 98
Wesson, Wm. 56, 104
Wesson, Wm. F. 30
West Bend 73, 87, 105
West Concord, Minn. 63
West, Kate 84
West Salem, Wis. 75
Westby, Wis. 59
Westover, C.S. 30
Westover, F.H. iv
Wharton, Ione 84
Wheaton, Mrs. 94
Wheeler 11, 29, 73
Wheeler, A.H. 15
Wheeler, Catherine 66
Wheeler, Cornelia 11
Wheeler, H.G. 147
Wheeler, J.M. 89
Wheeler, J.W. 33
Wheeler, John M. 40, 52
Wheeler, L.C. 59, 66, 74,
  84, 127, 137
Wheeler, L.G. 18, 49, 59, 69, 79,
  83, 115, 137, 144, 148, 160, 165
Wheeler, Laurence 74
Wheeler, Leverett C. 70
Wheeler, Lyman 47, iii
Wheeler, Lyman G. 10, 25, 156, v
Wheeler, Rollin iv
Wheeler, Roy 101
Wheeler, Sanford iii
Wheelock, Benjamin F. iii
Wherry, George 119
White, Bessie 40

White, Fred 112
White, J.M. 16
White, Levi 123
White, M.J. 2, 16, 133
White, Matti 135
White, Moses 62
White, Moses J. 110, 147
White, Mr. 29
White, Mrs. 79
White, Reg. 62
White, Reginald 79
White, W.E. 27
Whitefish Bay 58, 66
Whitewater 44, 62, 93, 168
Whitnall, C.B. 103
Whitney, Clarence 28
Whittaker, W.B. 94
Wichita, Kas. 67, 161
Wickers, Tess 162
Wickersham, L.B. 110, 113
Wienhold, Lucille vi
Wiese, L. 101
Wietschak, M. 141
Wilcox, Estella 87
Wilcox, Frances 77
Wilcox, Geo. 166
Wilcox, Mr. 123
Wilcox, Mrs. 45
Wilde, Mrs. 104
Wilder, Daisy 80
Wilder, Miss 88
Wilder, R. 30
Wildish, J.E. 19
Wilke, Fred 115
Wilkinson, Mrs. 59
Willets, Miss 10
Willets, Mr. 10
Williams, Allen 50, 68, 91, 116, 150
Williams Bay, Walworth Co., Wis. 71
Williams, Charlotte 39
Williams, Fora vi
Williams, Helen 154
Williams, J.P. 150, 160
Williams, Joseph 98
Williams, L.C. 30
Williams, Lulu vi
Williams, O.A. 66
Williams, O.T. 116
Willis, A.J. 143
Wilmette, Ill. 112
Wilmot, Minnie 109
Wilson, B.F. 31
Wilson, C.E. 107, 168
Wilson, Catherine 142

Wilson, Gertrude 113
Wilson, Mrs. 20
Wilson, O.E. 66
Wilson, O.F. 113, 141
Wilson, O.T. 156
Wilson, W.K. 9
Winding 23, 30
Winding, George 25
Winding, Ilma 69
Winifred, SD 150
Winkenwerder, C. 99, 146
Winona, Minn. 68, 101, 131
Winters, Edna 88
Winters, Ida 51
Winters, John 131
Wisconsin Dells 60
Wise 156
Witcher, Chas 148
Witte, Geo. 157
Witte, George 70, 106
Witte, R.A. 143
Witte, R.C. 73
Wodertz, William 74
Wolf, Clarence 156
Wolf, Leonard J. 142
Wolf, Mrs. 111
Woller, F. 149
Woller, F.E. 60, 83
Woller, Frank 164
Woocester, Miss 48
Wood 30
Wood, A.J. 77, 88
Wood, F.W. 36
Wood, H.O. 64, 80, 101,
  107, 150, 158
Wood, Jessie 12, 50
Wood, Joseph 97, 101, 124, 128
Wood, Katharine 158
Wood, Katherine 102
Wood, Katherine M. 89
Wood, Miss 124
Wood, Mr. 29
Wood, Sterling 58, 64, 114, 140, 148
Wood, Walter 20, 64, 148
Woodmansee, E.P. 1
Woodmansee, J.F. 1, 10
Woodmansee, Mrs. 27
Woodmansee, Warren 119
Woodmansee, Wm. 39
Woodmansee, Wm.R. 14
Woodside, John 23
Woodworth, Wis. 34
Worm, Charles 14
Worm, William v

Wright, E.P. 148
Wright, E.T. 145
Wright, Eugene 1, 23, 131
Wright, Eugene Turner 57
Wright, George H. 116
Wright, Inez 56, 131
Wright, Laurine 2, 27, 56
Wright, Loraine 156
Wright, Louis, 100
Wright, Mrs. 108
Wright, "Pokey" 23
Wright, Rev. 36
Wright, S. 23
Wright, S.E. 106
Wright, "Squib" 30
Wright, Thomas 1
Wright, Thomas Gore 13
Wright, Thos. 11
Wright, W.H. 1, 13, 27, 45, 100
Wright, Walter 92, 155
Wright, Walter H. 124
Wuerst, Frances A. 139
Wurderle, L. 135
Wyman, C. 164
Wyman, Charlotte 128
Wyman, W.C. 148
Wyoming, Ill. 85

Y

Yank, Gerty 148
Yanke, F. 2
Yehle, Contractor 78
Yehle, F. 128
York, New 9
Youmans, H.M. 124
Young, Art 42
Young, Grace 54
Young, John 125, 132, 136, 161
Young, M.L. 112, 117
Young, Mr. 53
Youngclaus, Margaret 58
Ypsilanti, Mich. 9, 17

Z

Zahn, Wm. 47
Zarse, H.F. 24
Zarse, Mr. 35
Zehen, H. 137
Zeldell, Lille 102
Zickuhr, Chas. 32
Zieglmann, Lydia 133
Ziekuhr, Chas. 28
Zillmer, E.E. 162

Zillmer, Otto  39
Zillmer, Otto A.  139
Zillmer, Otto Augustus  142
Zilmer, Otto  103
Zimmer, William  79
Zimmerman, H.W.  74
Zimmerman, John  130
Zimmerman, John T.  137
Zimmerman, T.E.  74, 89, 120, 159
Zimmerman, Wm.  36
Zimmermann, G.E.  98
Zimmermann, Geo.  95
Zimmermann, J.C.  99
Zimmermann, T.E.  3
Zimmermann, T.T.  18
Zimmermann, Theodore E.  3
Zinn, Bruno  164
Zion City  122
Zoll, P.P.  115
Zunker, Emma  69

www.ingramcontent.com/pod-product-compliance
Lightning Source LLC
Chambersburg PA
CBHW070909270326
41927CB00011B/2498